Becoming Intercultural

Becoming Intercultural:
Inside and Outside the Classroom

Edited by

Yau Tsai and Stephanie Houghton

CAMBRIDGE
SCHOLARS
P U B L I S H I N G

Becoming Intercultural: Inside and Outside the Classroom,
Edited by Yau Tsai and Stephanie Houghton

This book first published 2010. The present binding first published 2013.

Cambridge Scholars Publishing

12 Back Chapman Street, Newcastle upon Tyne, NE6 2XX, UK

British Library Cataloguing in Publication Data
A catalogue record for this book is available from the British Library

ISBN (10): 1-4438-4873-5, ISBN (13): 978-1-4438-4873-2

TABLE OF CONTENTS

FOREWORD

KAREN RISAGER

This book presents a wealth of insights into processes of experiencing interculturality – *becoming intercultural* – mostly, but not only, among international students in higher education, who are learning and using a language that is not their first language, for example during studies abroad. The focus is both on students' language and intercultural learning in the institutional setting at the university, and on students' everyday life with the foreign language and the foreign cultural contexts outside the classroom.

One of the strengths of the book is its occupation with the intricacies of the concept of *interculturality*, as can be seen in the whole of Part I. The abstract concept of interculturality is used here as an umbrella term for a range of theoretical perspectives and traditions covering also terms such as intercultural education, intercultural communication, and intercultural competence. The first chapter traces the relationship between the two first-mentioned traditions, showing their different origins and traditional applications to two quite different fields of practice: the concept of intercultural education tending to relate to general and academic education, mainly addressed at children, young people, and university students, and the concept of intercultural communication tending to relate to training and preparation for professional work abroad, mainly addressed at adults already having a job. The second chapter focuses on the complexities of the concept of intercultural competence, and the third takes a closer look at the general term interculturality, emphasizing that interculturality should be seen as a discursive construction. The authors show how interculturality is constructed and deconstructed in the course of a research project on secondary school teachers, and their chapter adds to the many voices today that advocate for a view of culture (and perhaps indirectly interculturality) that abandons reifications and essentialisations and stress the work of discourse in our categorisations and understandings of the infinite complexity of world life. The fourth chapter addresses the issue of interculturality in national education policies in a range of different countries all around the world. Thus the whole of Part I may be said to build bridges between sometimes very different paradigms of theoretical and practical thinking in the field of interculturality – an example of interparadigmatic dialogue.

Cultural complexity is almost everywhere, even in villages far away from urban centres. People, food, textiles, mobile phones and radios, commercials, ideas and discourses may have originated in distant places, and together they form local cultural complexity. If interculturality is a way of talking about and relating to cultural complexity, it is ultimately relevant for everybody. Whether you are a psychiatrist or a soldier, whether you are from a majority or a minority, whether you are black or white, whether you are old or young, whether you are rich or poor, whether you are left wing or right wing, whether you live in a centre or a periphery, you are living in a culturally complex world that implicitly or explicitly demands of you that you are, or become, *intercultural*. And the way you become intercultural, may be related to your position in the power structure of society and of the world.

This book makes a choice among all these possibilities: it focuses on (mostly higher education) students in the process of learning and using a foreign language for their further studies. It thus takes its point of departure in a category of young people who tend to be quite mobile, relatively well-educated, and probably coming from families that are comparatively well-off. The students want to get an academic degree, and they are willing to learn a foreign language if this is needed, and to go abroad if this is needed. The book can show how learning to be intercultural may proceed among people who are internationally oriented and motivated, and who will probably be members of the future elite. This is a relevant and interesting point of departure for a field of study that is potentially very much larger and encompasses all social groups and all kinds of institutions and organisations. The book illustrates that even with the group of international students, the development of interculturality is neither automatic nor easy.

In many cases, learning to be intercultural may not involve other languages than your first language. If you are (ethnically) English, you can learn through contact with people from various parts of the world, using only English. But this book emphasizes the importance of languages for the understanding of the world and for offering opportunities of taking new perspectives. The world is multilingual, and student populations at international universities are multilingual. Life at universities can potentially further students' interculturality – depending on how the university organises cultural and linguistic diversity.

Part II focuses on the question of becoming intercultural outside the classroom. It explores how people do, or do not, become intercultural in a natural untutored way in everyday situations. Chapter 5 considers the possible effects of intercultural learning upon interculturality and second/foreign language acquisition when studying abroad, and chapter 6 discusses the intercultural experience as expressed through metaphor in international students studying abroad to highlight the psychological tension that can characterise intercultural competence. While it may often be assumed that the development of foreign language competence automatically results in the development of intercultural competence, chapter 7 presents an empirical study that shows that this is not always the case. The need for systematic approaches towards intercultural learning will thus become apparent in this part of the book.

Part III deals with how people become intercultural as a consequence of being the language learner under the direction of a teacher. Chapter 8 focuses on the concept of criticality as an element of intercultural competence, and chapter 9 explores self-reflection in response to intercultural experience that may involve (re)construction and (re)negotiation of identity. Chapter 10 shows how learners can learn to take control of their own self-development through intercultural language education. Thus three examples of classroom research will be presented in Part III of the book that illustrate different ways in which intercultural learning may take place in a foreign or second language learning classroom.

A concluding point in the book is that we should try to conceptualise a new component of intercultural competence: knowing how to become. Chapter 10 refers to Michael Byram's model of intercultural communicative competence (1997) that encompasses five components (or in French, *savoirs*): knowledge (*savoirs*), skills of interpreting and relating (*savoir comprendre*), skills of discovery and interaction (*savoir apprendre/faire*), attitudes (*savoir être*), and critical cultural awareness/political education (*savoir s'engager*). Beside these components, chapter 10 suggests the introduction of a sixth one: knowing how to become (*savoir se transformer*). This component could be about the ability to make conscious decisions concerning value change within your own self. And value change is in this chapter exemplified by a change in the direction of a greater concern for human rights and democracy.

The book throws a bridge from Europe to East Asia. It is a result of research conducted in the international network CULTNET, which originated in Britain and now has members from almost all of Europe and from a number of countries elsewhere, not least in East Asia. The book unites scholars from multilingual and multicultural Europe with scholars from multilingual and multicultural East Asia and neighbouring countries such as New Zealand. At the same time the book unites a vision of interculturality in global society with a practice of interculturality in research. It will be a valuable inspiration for people who are in search of ways of studying cultural complexity and its significance for people's lives.

PREFACE

As people around the world move into the new era of the twenty-first century, they will have increasing opportunities to communicate and interact with others using foreign languages. Whilst this will naturally generate wide-ranging intercultural experience, people may not be alert to it in everyday life and teachers may not know how to address the issues that arise. Thus, the main purpose of this book is to introduce the concept of interculturality, to examine how it can emerge in an unplanned way and to consider ways in which it can be more systematically addressed particularly through immersion in the target culture or through foreign language education.

Most of the contributors to this book are members of CULTNET, an international network of researchers interested in combining and researching foreign language education and intercultural communication in different ways. The CULTNET group, initially set up by Emeritus Professor Michael Byram, has met annually in England in recent years for the purposes of research development. To accommodate members who had relocated to Asia and who wanted to maintain professional and personal links with other members, the first ASIAN CULNET seminar was held at Daito Bunka University in Tokyo, Japan in 2008, which is where the ideas for this book were first conceived.

We warmly acknowledge the contributions of researchers to this book who include Mari Ayano (Seijoh University, Japan), Michael Byram (Durham University, England), Josep Cots (University of Lleida, Catalonia, Spain), Yumiko Furumura (Kyushu University, Japan), Manuela Guilherme (Universidade de Coimbra, Portugal), Yannan Guo (University of Nottingham, England), Prue Holmes (Durham University, England), Stephanie Houghton (University of Kitakyushu, Japan), Enric Llurda (University of Lleida, Catalonia, Spain), Gillian O'Neill (University of Waikato, New Zealand), Lynne Parmenter (Waseda University, Japan), Yau Tsai (Fooyin University, Taiwan) and Etsuko Yamada (Kanda Gaigo University, Japan). The development of this book reflects the shared interest and vision of contributors of what it means to become intercultural, and the role that education and intercultural experience can play in enhancing the process in systematic ways. It is hoped that this book will help readers understand interculturality and its development, as well as the related effects of intercultural experience.

We would like to express our deepest gratitude to our mentor, Emeritus Professor Michael Byram, not only for setting up CULTNET but also for guiding us both through our doctoral studies with calm clarity of vision, and for connecting us to other researchers in ways that have enriched us personally and professionally. We also want to thank the editorial staff at Cambridge Scholars Publishing for their professionalism and support.

—Yau Tsai and Stephanie Houghton
31 May 2010

PART I:

THE DEFINITION OF BEING INTERCULTURAL

CHAPTER ONE

INTERCULTURAL EDUCATION AND INTERCULTURAL COMMUNICATION: TRACING THE RELATIONSHIP

MICHAEL BYRAM AND MANUELA GUILHERME

Concepts and Dichotomies

There are a number of tensions and dichotomies in research and teaching/training in our field of study, not least in the question of what label we give to the field. Phrases include *intercultural communication studies, cross-cultural communication, intercultural language education, cross-cultural business communication* and so on. This is not the place to suggest the definitive label since the field is continually developing as contextual factors change. What we propose here is to focus on historical and contemporary events in the evolution of the field, and in passing, perhaps throw a little more light on labels, origins and relationships among different components of it. For it is the purpose of the present volume to take an eclectic view and explore *intercultural learning*, wherever it takes place.

The dichotomies in the field which are most interesting, and most difficult to overcome, include that between the academy and the workplace. This is at two levels. First there is the dichotomy of *theory* and *practice* which haunts any field of applied studies, be it science and technology or the study of education on the one hand or, on the other, the practice of teaching or managing schools and universities and their curricula. It is interesting to note how the tension between linguistics and its applications has been resolved by the appearance of applied linguistics as a discipline in its own right. Whether this could happen in our field remains to be seen, but in the meantime there are those who research and teach cultures, and others who teach and train people to engage with and live in other cultures. The ensuing tension is evident both among those who work in education systems and those who are engaged in workplace training. In the former case, the tension might be between the *study of* other cultures and the development of intercultural competence through teaching and learning in the foreign language classroom. In the second case, it might be between academic study of psychology in different cultures, and the use of knowledge about psychological characteristics of people from other countries in business negotiation training.

The contrast between the academy and the workplace can take a second form. Teachers in education systems, whether at school level or later, have difficulty in understanding trainers in business and industry, and vice versa. There are a number of reasons. They include the different conditions of teaching and training – longer and shorter period of time, contractual conditions, age groups of learners – but also characteristically different views on the place of language learning. This is partly a matter of disciplinary origins: in education systems, the teachers in question are usually linguists with high competence in one or more foreign languages, whereas workplace trainers seem to be more often psychologists or anthropologists. It is also a question of theoretical perspective and practical application. Many linguists will argue that language and culture are inseparable, but psychologists will not. Language teachers work in education systems where learners have and need much time, over several years, for language learning, whereas trainers have seldom more than a few days or weeks to complete their task.

More recently, research on language education and linguistics has progressively focused on intercultural communication and some of these scholars have found the purpose and context of their teaching and research in the workplace. They have also gradually introduced a critical perspective into meaning and power negotiation as well as becoming more concerned about social responsibility matters as related to linguistic and discursive aspects of intercultural communication. Furthermore, a few communication studies departments worldwide, mainly in America and northern Europe, have also focused some of their research on intercultural communication topics and their researchers have been collaborating with private companies, governmental and non-governmental entities and carrying out professional development workshops for them. Amongst the first communication experts to focus their research on Intercultural Communication in the United States was Gudykunst who devoted his life to research on interpersonal communication, namely on anxiety/uncertainty issues (culminating in posthumous Gudykunst 2005), together with

Wiseman who wrote on intercultural communication competence and theory (1995), followed by Ting-Toomey who developed a theory of face-negotiation, with Kurogi (1998), on mindful communication (1999) and on conflict negotiation, with Oetzel (2001; 2006), all of them originally based at California State University, Fullerton, at the Department of Human Communication Studies. Also noteworthy is Kim, an author who, again in the field of communication studies, has given a strong contribution with her theories on interethnic communication (1986) and cross-cultural adaptation (2001). The above mentioned studies brought new energy to the field since, starting from Hofstede's national and regional taxonomy that provided a rather static and stereotyping but widely accepted vision of intercultural communication, they adopted and developed various perspectives from different angles on any communication that is intercultural. More recently, some international and intercultural programmes and departments have also appeared in Europe, notably German and Scandinavian universities (Soederberg and Vara 2003), although most of these are mainly connected to Management, Political Science and Cultural Studies.

There has also been a very evident movement in research in the field, evolving from the concept of being international to the one of being intercultural and thence concentrating more closely on interethnic communication, between different intra-national communities and between individuals in groups, viewed mostly from within a process of globalisation. Institutes, Centres and doctoral programmes on Intercultural Communication, using this terminology, are proliferating all over the world in Departments of Communication, and very recently within Faculties of Humanities and Social Sciences, as well as Departments of International Relations, Schools of Modern Languages and occasionally in Schools of Education. However, Departments of Intercultural Communication, with this name or combining communication and cultural studies, are almost inexistent in higher education institutions, except for the Department of Intercultural Communication and Management and the Department of International Communication and Cultural Studies (with the recently created CBS Center for Negotiation), emerging from the former Faculty of Languages, Culture and Communication at the Copenhagen Business School, as well as the College of Intercultural Communication, at undergraduate level, at Rikkyo University, Tokyo.

These organisational and research developments have occurred in parallel with discussion about the definition(s) of intercultural competence(es). This term, originally called communication or communicative competence, depending on its origins in communication or linguistics theory, has been grounded on both of these concepts and benefited from the discussion of the controversial notion of *competence*. Coined relatively recently, *intercultural competence* has been the object of various attempts at theorisation, from different disciplines or research fields, from different regions of the world and nations, from different professional or organizational contexts. The expression *intercultural competence* seems to entail quite paradoxical meanings within it. The concept of competence is often used to seize the dynamics of something fluid and unpredictable implied by an intercultural *relation* and *communication* with notions of skills, abilities and capacities, and then to describe and evaluate them. On the other hand, the word *intercultural* expresses the impact of the unexpected, the surprising, the potential rather than the pre-structured, the foreseen or the expectable. The paradoxical composition of this expression has motivated various approaches emphasising the one or the other, depending on situation and circumstances or, more recently, its focus has been widened with attempts to combine its functional, technical, cognitive, critical, civic and ethical dimensions. It has thus become increasingly ambitious and challenging.

The term *competence* was brought into education through vocational education, where the emphasis on skills and behaviours, rather than content knowledge, was prioritised. However, it has acquired a broader scope, in particular in international guidelines for school and professional education, coming to include "a combination of knowledge, skills, attitudes, values and behaviours" (Council of Europe 2005). This has followed the trend set by other projects, for example the PISA – Programme for International Student Assessment (OECD) and the DeSeCo Project – Definition and Selection of Key Competences (OECD), which singles out the "ability to interact in heterogeneous groups" as one of its three key competences. The DeSeCo Project aimed mainly to define and select "individually based key competences in a lifelong learning perspective" (Rychen and Salganik 2003, 2). While identifying such "key competences", this project also included a "criticism of an overemphasis on knowledge in general education and specialization in vocational education" (Salganik and Stephens 2003, 19). Furthermore, it underlines the need to respect and appreciate the "values, beliefs, cultures, and histories of others", within a sub-category it identifies as "the ability to relate well to others", which focuses on personal relationships, and reports that the need to acknowledge and value diversity had also been mentioned in the project's country reports (Rychen 2003, 87). In sum, the idea of competence has become ever broader, expanding into the understanding that "the evolution of competence frameworks has the potential to pose questions about the purpose of knowledge and how it contributes to the good of society and the individual" (Fleming 2007, 54).

Similarly, the idea of intercultural competence continues to develop in different directions, either in more abstract or in more specific terms and, if in the latter, attempts to respond to different needs in different contexts and at different stages. On the one hand, some general but brief definitions of intercultural competence, such as "the ability to interact effectively with people from cultures that we recognise as being different from our own" (Guilherme 2000, 297) and "the appropriate and effective management of interaction between people who, to some degree or another, represent different or divergent affective, cognitive, and behavioural orientations to the world" (Spitzberg and Changnon 2009, 7) tend to bring some broader consensus to the field. Spitzberg and Changnon proceed with the descriptions of various contemporary models which they aggregate in a taxonomy of "compositional", "co-orientational", "developmental", "adaptational" and "causal path" models. On the other hand, other descriptions tend to focus on specific context demands or to build some competence lists "that are just that, a lengthy listing of the many competences that are part of intercultural effectiveness" (Pusch 2009, 67). Nevertheless, some would argue, such lists may "provide an excellent starting point for assessing the appropriate characteristics for the specific situation, even though, of course, "no list fits all cultures, all contexts, all conditions" (Bennett 2009, 122). Furthermore, more recently, there are some voices supporting different world-visions that generate other views of intercultural communication. These may be based, for example, on "different dimensions of self" that make it "quite legitimate and "real" in many Asian societies to interact at the level of role and face" (Parmenter2003, 128ff). Another claim made by authors that "have looked to the communitarian theories and practices of indigenous social movements in Latin America" is that "to be truly effective, intercultural communication should move beyond the limits of individualistic and interpersonal concerns" (Portillo and Sinnigen 2009: 260).

Attempts to overcome dichotomies and tensions take place from time to time, through combined conferences or publications (e.g. Feng, Byram and Fleming 2009). Another approach is to attempt to understand different standpoints according to their historical origins, but hitherto there has been a separation of methods here too.

Approaches to History

Since the field of study is still relatively young, it is not surprising that historical accounts are few. With respect to education systems (let us call this *intercultural education*), the situation has improved tremendously with the publication of two authoritative volumes by Risager (2006 and 2007), based on a single volume Danish original (2003). The situation in workplace-based research and training (let us call this *intercultural communication*) is less developed and limited to a number of articles, usually associated with SIETAR and its publications[1].

It is interesting to compare one of these, by Hart (1996), with Risager (2007). Hart traces the beginnings of intercultural communication to the 1950s and the work of Edward Hall and others at the American Foreign Service Institute. Risager places the beginnings of intercultural education or "culture pedagogy" in her phrase, in the 1880s, when foreign language teaching began to take its place in schools and universities alongside classical languages. Hart's historiographic method is to draw on Kuhn's notion of paradigm change in scientific disciplines. Risager refers to the discourse analytical approach, tracing changes in scientific discourse over time, and the use of periodisation by decades, although she says the latter is a matter of convenience and does not imply that each decade is a "turning point". To some extent, Hart too uses the decade as a tool for organising an overview, although without consciously referring to this. Perhaps, ultimately, the analysis by discourse and the analysis by paradigm shift are complementary but the work to bring them together in both intercultural education and intercultural communication remains to be done. What we can attempt here is only to look at some examples, and compare and contrast where possible.

In 1918, in Britain, a now forgotten report commissioned during the First World War was published with the title "Modern Studies". This was known as the Leathes Report after the chairman of the Committee on the Position of Modern Languages in the Educational System of Great Britain. The suggestion that "modern languages" should become modern studies, and change from the focus on literature and philology to include study of

---

[1] A different perspective is offered by anthropologist Dahlén (1997).

the economic, political and social systems of countries was motivated by
the conclusion that language studies had not been helpful in either peace
or war:

> The war has made this people conscious of its ignorance of foreign
> countries and their peoples (...) The masses and the classes alike were
> ignorant to the point of public danger. Ignorance of the mental attitude and
> aspirations of the German people may not have been the cause of the war;
> it certainly prevented due preparation and hampered our efforts after the
> war had begun; it still darkens our counsels. Similar ignorance of France,
> greater ignorance of Italy, abysmal ignorance of Russia, have impeded the
> effective prosecution of the war, and will impede friendly and co-operative
> action after the war is over. (...) In this field Modern Studies are not a mere
> source of profit, not only a means of obtaining knowledge, nor an
> instrument of culture; they are a national necessity (Leathes Report 1918,
> 32)

The report was however shelved and forgotten, despite attention drawn
to it at the time in the USA, where a similar debate was taking place about
language studies (Olmsted 1921).

A parallel with the beginnings of intercultural communication after the
Second World War is striking. Hart (1996) reminds us that the USA was
the only major economy left intact, and began to offer assistance to rebuild
Europe with the Marshall Plan. This was relatively successful but similar
attempts to aid non-western developing countries were less so because:

> Unfortunately, many of their attempts at communication across these
> cultural boundaries were superficial and sometimes dominated by economic
> theories of development that cast some doubt upon cross-cultural theories
> of social change (Dodd 1995, quoted in Hart 1996, 7)

The result of this, as Hart (1996) says was a new development at the
Foreign Service Institute and this was, as subsequent history tells us, more
effective than the recommendations of the Leathes Report. Those in
charge of programmes were not specialists in language pedagogy, but
rather anthropologists and specialists in non-verbal communication. Hart
quotes Leeds-Hurwitz to summarise this:

> [I]ntercultural communication [study] grew out of the need to apply
> abstract anthropological concepts to the practical world of foreign service
> diplomats [at FSI] (Leeds-Hurwitz 1990, quoted in Hart 1996, 7).

At the same time, and as a result of the civil rights and human rights movements and consequently the reinforcement of ethnic pride, research on multicultural education as well as a variety of multicultural education programmes experienced a boom in North America. Bilingual education was already a tradition in the United States since the 19th century and, although at that time it was not considered a political issue, it became a controversial one during the 20th century. During the first half of the century along with the 2nd World War, its almost total extinction due to the need for a stronger image of the young United States nation abroad and to the bad image of the German language that was dominant in bilingual programmes nearly erased bilingual education from the education scene in the United States. In mid-century, after the civil-rights movement, bilingual education programmes came to the fore and raised the question of their purpose, whether assimilation or pluralism (Padilla and Benavides 1992; Walsh 1991). This discussion stood side by side with the development of multicultural education research and programmes having in mind the non-European minorities who had most suffered discrimination and, for that very reason, had kept their linguistic and cultural communities more intact and were, at the same time, the fastest growing groups in the United States, both by birth rate and by immigrant flow, such as the African-American, Latinos and Asians (Banks 1975, 2009; Sleeter 1991). Bilingual and multicultural programmes growth in the United States, as well as later in Europe, have evidenced an increased awareness and recognition of diversity and, therefore, of discrimination, xenophobia and even racism in their societies.

However, it is also important to note the difference between the multicultural and intercultural paradigms that determine the understanding of the essence and nature of such educational programmes and research related to cultural diversity and intercultural communication. Multicultural and intercultural visions of difference are not only defined in different sociological terms, the static and the dialogic, but they have also invaded various cultural, social and political systems and are based on historical roots. We may trace their origins according to a north-south dichotomy (Santos 2007a, 2007b). Historically, the contacts between European sailors and settlers overseas, between the 15th and the 19th centuries, followed different paradigms originating in the cultural systems of colonisers and colonised. By and large, the colonisers interaction types prevailed since they were the most powerful, although the colonised social structures also determined the linguistic and cultural impact of colonisation, e.g. between Africa and Asia. However, European countries had their differences and particularities in their ways of approaching and dominating the colonised peoples, and there were two general and diverging, north versus south, tendencies in the ways Europe colonised the world. They are obvious not only in the social and political remains in the new post-colonial countries, e.g. North and South America, but also in the philosophical, political and sociological reception of their immigrants in Europe. This was evident in the findings of the INTERACT project whose European participant member-states (Portugal and Spain, Denmark and the United Kingdom) examined European and national political and policy documents and interviewed teachers and policy-makers and could support this hypothesis (www.ces.uc.pt/interact). Nevertheless, the multicultural and intercultural conceptions of cultural difference now coexist in most official documents and scientific research on ethnic, cultural and linguistic diversity. While the term *multicultural* was predominant from the 1950s to the 1980s in the Anglophone world, the idea of *being intercultural* has been expanding from the south to the north, both from southern Europe and from the southern hemisphere of the globe, and is now predominant both in official documents and in scientific research to describe cross-cultural exchange.

After this period, this time as a consequence of terrorism, rather than classical warfare and colonisation – the Twin Towers attack in September 2001 – another kind of reaction was stimulated. This time, as Kramsch tells us, new policies to develop language teaching were introduced in a highly focused way: not to engage large numbers of Americans with the role of the USA in the world, as had happened after the Sputnik surprise, but "to create a cadre of language professionals that, with advanced knowledge of the language and the culture, are able to collect and interpret intelligence necessary for US national security" (2005, 556). This time the task was conferred on the Department of Defense, rather than Education, and appears to be developing effectively.

Yet another example is that of Germany in the 1930s, again in response to the effects of war. This is the example often cited to show how foreign language education can become nationalistic, like all other aspects of education. For example in a text for practising reading skills, where an Englishman is supposedly cited, it is clear that German students of English should be reinforced in their national identity and pride:

> We in Great Britain are now intensely jealous about Germany (…) because in the last hundred years, while we have fed on platitudes and vanity, they have had the energy and humility to develop a splendid system of national

education, to toil on science, art and literature, (....) to clamber above us in
the scale of civilisation (Lehrbuch der englischen Sprache, 1927).

In the period of Nazi domination, foreign language teaching was
misappropriated to reinforce Germanness and denigrate the cultures of
others. This explicitly political misuse of education was an extreme
example, but it reminds us that any representation of other cultures will
carry conscious or unconscious messages about the relationship of *our*
culture to *theirs*. As Kedourie says, nationalist theory has a clear purpose:

> in nationalist theory (…) the purpose of education is not to transmit
> knowledge, traditional wisdom (…) its purpose rather is wholly political,
> to bend the will of the young to the will of the nation. Schools are
> instruments of state policy, like the army, the police, and the exchequer
> (Kedourie 1966, 84 – our emphasis).

It is important therefore that teachers and learners should become
aware of and able to analyse the relationship between *us* and *them*, as
exemplified in the following two cases of materials development.

ICOPROMO – Intercultural Competence for Professional Mobility (European Commission - Leonardo da Vinci Programme)

This 3-year European project (2003-2006) was developed under the
auspices of the European Commission, funded by the Leonardo da Vinci
Programme (www.ces.uc.pt/icopromo), and involved four academic teams
based at the Centre for Social Studies, University of Coimbra (Portugal,
coordinator), the Department of English, University of Jáen (Spain), the
Language Institute, Johannes Kepler University (Austria) and the Ashcroft
International Business School, Anglia Ruskin University (United
Kingdom). The latter replaced the University of Göttingen during the last
half of the project.

The originality of this project was that it brought together multinational
teams from different organisations with diverging approaches to
intercultural competence both in theory and in practice. On the one hand,
one of the four teams mentioned above (Portugal) is part of a Research
Centre in the Social Sciences, although its members had specialised in
language education and sociolinguistics, while another team (Spain)
comes from a Department of English Philology and specialises in teacher

education. On the other hand, the other two teams (Austria and the United Kingdom) develop their work in language education and intercultural communication in Business Schools. In addition, the project included an active Advisory Group whose members came from different professional settings such as a multinational company (Siemens-VAI, Austria) and two professional training organisations, one for managers in northern European countries (International Management Education, Finland) and the other, at a national level, for local government workers (CEFA, Portugal). Furthermore, previous to the material production stage, the project participants carried out individual interviews with both national and foreign professionals from business companies and governmental and non-governmental organisations with experience in working in multicultural and multilingual teams. The materials produced were then carefully evaluated and assessed by the Advisory Group and where necessary re-written, before being tested with a variety of volunteers in free workshops. The participants in the testing workshops were undergraduate and graduate students majoring in Business, Tourism, Modern Languages, Education, researchers in Intercultural Communication and Education, local workers and trainers working with immigrants. All the process described above generated a complex, sometimes tense, but enriching discussion and collaboration between such a variety of experts and experienced professionals.

During an introductory stage, which lasted for the first year of the project, the four international teams attempted to define intercultural competence by analysing existing models, first proposing their team models and then agreeing on a common project model as shown below. During this period, they also carried out an international needs assessment field study, as mentioned above. The common project model, shown below, involved eight thematic axes – Biography, Ethnography, Diversity Management, Emotional Management, Intercultural Communication, Intercultural Interaction, Intercultural Responsibility and Working in Multicultural Teams. Based on these themes, the teams produced almost one hundred activities aimed at developing intercultural competence in pre-service and in-service professionals for the purpose of work in multicultural teams/groups. These activities were to be implemented with the help of groups of pre-service and in-service professionals, ranging from un-experienced to experienced and even expert target groups. The project design aimed to step beyond individually-based competencies and to focus on the communication and interaction dynamics between team-based individuals. In addition, it intended to explore the grounds between citizenship education and professional development, that is, what is more often distinguished as, respectively, education and training (Feng, Byram and Fleming 2009).

The ICOPROMO project also targeted mobility as a key concept defined, both in real and symbolic terms, and as the process of entering new ethnic cultures, either abroad or at home, directly or indirectly, in person or through technology. It aimed to contribute to the process of building up a Europe of knowledge, set out by the European Council in Lisbon in 2000, which establish that Europe should become "the most dynamic and competitive knowledge-based economy in the world" by 2010 but one whose knowledge is heterogeneous, interactive and promotes the validation of different intra- and international representations in the public arena.

Societies are undergoing a transformation, moving towards new forms of politics, social life and economic organisation. Such transformations include tendencies towards increased globalisation and internationalisation, alongside the development of network structures. This process translates into a switch from a static-functional orientation of organisations and institutions toward a more dynamic, procedural orientation. Employees must increasingly cope with inter*cultural* (not necessarily only inter*national*) encounters in their professional contexts. They therefore have to establish *active* communication with their colleagues, especially since virtually all organisations have gradually been promoting horizontal work structures which generate even stronger dynamics between diverse groups, often based in different locations.

The eight thematic axes ranged in their level of generality, and in some cases drew on existing fields of research, e.g. emotional management, while others brought new aspects to the fore, (e.g. "intercultural responsibility"), a new term coined in the project. These eight thematic areas made up the main axes which were deemed most relevant for the development of intercultural competence in the workplace:

- biography
- emotional management
- diversity management
- intercultural interaction
- communicative interaction
- ethnography

- intercultural responsibility
- working in MCTs

The project drew on personal experience and management, such as biographical reflection and emotional mindfulness. It also involved basic ethnographic observation and a meticulous analysis of intercultural interaction. It looked at communication strategies and dared to venture into power and ethical issues. Every thematic area covered all of the aspects mentioned above to greater or lesser extent, despite their focus on one aspect in particular. The project worked on a broader idea of competence and produced a work-in-progress concept of competence that aimed to develop a critical cultural awareness of their own shifting identities, of the communication and interactions taking place as well as of the reciprocal responsibility in developing a professional, if not personal, relationship among the members of multicultural groups/teams.

In sum, the ICOPROMO project intended to promote a dialogue and establish links between research on intercultural communication competence in different academic and national contexts, that is, a research centre, modern language departments in the Humanities and in Business Schools and training centres. The material developers researched theoretical models with different approaches to intercultural competence and produced their own models, which they discussed in order to agree on a common framework. It also sought information from a wide range of professionals from different types of organisations and in the various participant countries. Finally, it had their products tested and evaluated with a varied number of workshop participants. This means that the purpose of this project was to combine different theories of intercultural competence, to respond to different needs and to offer a wide variety of materials showing different perspectives and approaches (Guilherme et al., 2010). Some materials revealed a concern with citizenship and social issues while others discussed more personal themes, and yet others worked on more functional skills. This was the main aim of this project, to find common ground between intercultural communication theories and methodologies developed both in education, namely within foreign language education and citizenship education, and those provided by Management and Communication studies.

The Autobiography of Intercultural Encounters
(Council of Europe – Language Division)

The Autobiography of Intercultural Encounters (AIE) is an online document which guides users through an analysis of any intercultural encounter they consider significant for them. It consists of a series of questions in nine different groupings. The questions focus first on description – asking who was involved and where – passing through questions about the user's own reactions to the encounter and those of the others involved, and ending in questions about how the encounter has affected the user, and what changes or actions the user might engage in in the future.

There is a version for children and one for adolescents and older people. It is accompanied by notes for facilitators – be they teachers, social workers or others – who might introduce the AIE to people with whom they work. It can be used in a variety of ways, with suggestions included in the facilitators' notes. Various potential uses both in education systems, in *intercultural education*, and in the workplace, in *intercultural communication*, and the AIE is therefore an instrument which might bridge the gap between the two strands of our field.

The interest of the AIE here is in its historical origins and evolution as a response to socio-political factors. It is an instrument of the Council of Europe produced within the section dealing with language policy and education but drawing on expertise from sections responsible for education for democratic citizenship and education about religions. This constellation of expertise is itself an indication of socio-political factors in contemporary Europe to which the Council of Europe as a whole is responding, symbolised most potently in its producing a White Paper on *intercultural dialogue*. The AIE is however also the outcome of a process reaching back over several decades. That process will be described here briefly as an example of how the field of intercultural education and communication has developed.

We saw earlier how one of the stimulants for intercultural communication training at the American Foreign Service Institute was the need, from the 1950s, for US Americans to be able to *go out* to work successfully in other countries. At about the same time, in Western Europe, it was the phenomenon of people *coming in* to seek work as economic migrants which began to present problems. Germany, France

and other Western European industrialised countries encouraged men –
and initially only men, who left their families behind – from poorer
countries to come to help develop post-war industrial change. If the
workers came from former colonies, as was the case in the UK, then they
were likely to have some competence in the host country language, even
though it was soon realised that this was not unproblematic. In the case of
workers from other countries – Turkish workers in Germany, Portuguese
workers in France, Italian workers in Belgium, for example – linguistic
competence in the host language could not be assumed. Such workers
would often have received minimal education, not including foreign
language learning. They needed the linguistic means to live and work in a
new environment, and they needed to acquire them quickly. Council of
Europe experts addressed this question from the 1960s. They analysed
needs; they defined the necessary language to fulfil those needs – the
"functions" and "notions" for specific "speech acts" – and they produced
"objectives", i.e. descriptions of the necessary language, the minimal or
"threshold" level workers and others would need to acquire to function
satisfactorily in a new social environment. They also suggested ways of
teaching and learning which connected immediately and obviously with
everyday communication, and which therefore had strong "face validity".
(For a detailed account, see Trim 2007).

    All of this dealt above all with language users' linguistic competence,
their ability to carry out speech acts, but it was also recognised that
competence in the language itself has to be combined with knowing how
to use the language appropriately, drawing both on socio-linguistic
knowledge and socio-cultural knowledge, i.e. knowing how to use the
appropriate language for a given situation but also knowing about the
cultural context in which the situation is embedded (van Ek 1986). The
starting point had been in language because the experts involved were
language specialists working mainly in education, in contrast to the origins
of intercultural communication in the work of anthropologists and
psychologists. It was now time, in the 1990s, to turn attention to
sociocultural competence but the experts involved were still linguists,
albeit with an interest and experience in ethnography.

    The socio-political changes which took place in this period are
reflected in the titles of the Council of Europe language projects. In the
period 1978 to 1981, the project was called "Modern Languages:
improving and intensifying language learning as factors making for
European understanding and mobility". By the 1990s, after the changes in

Central and Eastern Europe of 1989, the project from 1990 to 1997 was called "Language Learning for European Citizenship". A vision of Europe not just as an economic entity but as a polity where over 800 million citizens might live, was beginning to evolve on many levels. In language teaching terms, such a polity would need greater cooperation among education systems, formal and informal, and greater transparency in working methods and mutual recognition of qualifications. This led to the *Common European Framework of Reference* (CEFR) in which competences of all kinds necessary for social interaction were described, including cultural competences as well is linguistic competence.

The most successful and influential aspect of the CEFR was the description of levels of linguistic competence. An attempt to provide similar descriptions of levels of sociocultural (or intercultural) competence was abandoned. There are simply descriptions of pluricultural (sometimes referred to as "intercultural") competence, based on work commissioned of Byram and Zarate (for more details, see Byram 2009). The question of further work on intercultural competence and in particular any attempt at describing levels of competence was left unresolved at the publication of the CEFR in 2001.

It was unresolved but not forgotten, and the wish of the administrators and experts of the Council of Europe to address the question again was taken up several years later as the significance of intercultural competence in language education became more widely recognised. This impulse was much reinforced by socio-political events of many kinds in Europe, but particularly those related to – or claimed by – groups identifying themselves as representatives of religions, ethnicities, or nations. At European levels, the need for *social inclusion* to overcome or reconcile the demands of marginal groups became a key phrase for various policies, including education policies. The notions of *understanding, co-operation and mobility* had evolved into *European citizenship* and this was to be expressly democratic and inclusive, facilitated by *intercultural dialogue*. The European Union declared 2008 as the year of intercultural dialogue, and the Council of Europe published its *White Paper on Intercultural Dialogue* (Council of Europe 2008), with the sub-title "Living Together as Equals in Dignity".

The AIE was under construction from 2004, initially as an extension to the European Language Portfolio (Council of Europe n.d.), but soon as a document which can be used independently. The link with language learning was gradually dissolved partly because some language teachers reacted by saying that this would demand too much and take attention away from language competence, partly because of the recognition that all teachers – and eventually any facilitator in formal or informal education – could take responsibility, and thirdly because of the need within the Council of Europe as an institution to operationalise the White Paper discourse on social inclusion and dialogue in ways which went beyond the focus on (foreign) language learning.

The AIE is, in short, a product of processes both internal to an institution and evident in societal change. It began within work on language education and, for a time, was seen as a potential instrument for *intercultural education*. As socio-political circumstances changed, the focus shifted to include issues which might be recognised by those involved in *intercultural communication*, but also went further than their concerns with people engaging with other countries and their populations, to include intercultural interaction in any social circumstance, within or among societies or countries. The extension of the circle of expertise also demonstrates this to include experts in education for citizenship, in education about religions and in cross-cultural psychology. The AIE is a product of academic and intergovernmental response to changing social and political times.

Conclusion

The dichotomies and tensions we introduced at the beginning of this chapter are disciplinary, historical, theoretical and practical. Our field of study is evolving quickly, as we have shown in our survey of literature, teaching locations, historiography and our two cases studies of contemporary projects. As Mughan (2009) points out, cross-fertilisation from business and management to foreign language education involves risk-taking by language teachers. Other interactions of an interdisciplinary nature are equally demanding. They require that we see ourselves as others see us, and respond accordingly from our own identities and understandings of our disciplines and purposes. But is that not in itself a description of being intercultural – and therefore the necessary foundation for success?

Bibliography

Banks, J. A. 1975. *Teaching strategies for ethnic studies.* Boston: Allyn & Bacon.
—. (ed.) 2009. Multicultural education: Dimensions and paradigms. *The Routledge International Companion to Multicultural Education*, 9-32. New York: Routledge.
Bennett, J. 2009. Cultivating intercultural competence: A process perspective. In *The SAGE Handbook of Intercultural Competence*, ed. D. K. Deardoff, 121-140. Sage: Thousand Oaks, Ca..
Byram, M. 2009. Intercultural competence in foreign languages. In *The SAGE Handbook of Intercultural Competence*, ed. D. K. Deardoff, 321-332. Sage: Thousand Oaks, Ca.
Byram, M., M. Barrett, J. Ipgrave, R. Jackson and M. Mendez Garcia. 2009. *Autobiography of intercultural encounters.* Strasbourg: Council of Europe. http://www.coe.int/t/dg4/autobiography/default_EN.asp?
Council of Europe 2001. *Common European Framework of Reference for Languages. http://www.coe.int/t/dg4/linguistic/CADRE_EN.asp*
Council of Europe (n.d.) *European Language Portfolio.* http://www.coe.int/t/dg4/linguistic/Portfolio_EN.asp
—. 2005. *The competency workbook. Mobility and competence project* (2001-2004). https://wcd.coe.int/com.instranet.InstraServlet?Command=com.instranet.CmdBlobGet&DocId=1155136&SecMode=1&Admin=0&Usage=2&InstranetImage=124228
—. 2008. *White Paper on Intercultural Dialogue.* http://www.coe.int/t/dg4/intercultural/Source/White%20Paper%20final%20EN%20020508.pdf
Dahlén, T. 1997, *Among the Interculturalists - An emergent profession and its packaging of knowledge.* Stockholm: Stockholm Studies in Social Anthropology
Feng, A., Byram, M. and Fleming, M. 2009 *Becoming interculturally competent through education and training.* Clevedon, England: Multilingual Matters
Fleming, M. 2007. The use and misuse of competence statements with particular reference to the teaching of literature. *Towards a Common European Framework of Reference for Language(s) of school education.* Proceedings of an international conference organised by the Council of Europe and the Jagiellonian University in Kraków, Poland, April 27-29, 2006.

Gudykunst, W. B. (ed.) 2005. *Theorizing about intercultural communication.* Thousand Oaks.

Guilherme, M. 2000. Intercultural competence. In *Routledge Encyclopedia of Language Teaching and Learning,* ed. M. Byram, 297-300. London: Routledge.

Guilherme, M., Glaser, E. & Méndez-García, M. C. (eds.) (2010) *The intercultural dynamics of multicultural working.* Clevedon, England: Multilingual Matters.

Hart, W. B. 1996. A Brief History of Intercultural Communication: A Paradigmatic Approach. Paper presented at the Speech Communication Association Conference, November, 1996 in San Diego, USA.

Kedourie. E. 1993. *Nationalism.* Oxford: Blackwell.

Kim, Y. Y. (ed.) 1986. *Interethnic communication: Current research.* Newbury Park, Ca.: Sage.

—. 2001. *Becoming intercultural: An integrative theory of communication and cross-cultural adaptation.* Thousand Oaks: Sage.

Kramsch, C. 2005. Post 9/11: Foreign languages between knowledge and power. *Applied Linguistics* 26, 4: 545-567.

Leathes Report (Committee on the Position of Modern Languages in the Educational System of Great Britain). 1918. *Modern Studies: Being the Report of the Committee.* London: H.M.S.O.

Mughan, T. 2009. Business and management theories and models of intercultural competence: implications for foreign language learning. In *Interkulturelle Kompetenz und fremdsprachliches Lernen. Modelle, Empirie, Evaluation. Intercultural Competence and Foreign Language Learning. Models, Empiricism, Assessment*, eds. A. Hu and M. Byram, 31-47. Tübingen: Gunter Narr Verlag.

Olmsted, E.W. 1921. A justification of modern languages in our schools. *The Modern Language Journal* 6, 1: 1-11.

Oetzel, J.G. and S. Ting-Toomey (eds.) 2006. *The SAGE Handbook of Conflict Communication.* Sage: Thousand Oaks, CA.

Padilla, R. V. and A. H. Benavides. 1992. *Critical perspectives on bilingual education research.* Tempe, Arizona: Bilingual Press.

Parmenter, L. 2003. Describing and defining intercultural communicative competence – international perspectives. In *Intercultural competence*, ed. M. Byram, 119-147. Strasbourg: Council of Europe.

Medina-López-Portillo, A. and J.H. Sinnigen. 2009. Interculturality versus intercultural competentes in Latin America. In *The SAGE Handbook of Intercultural Competence*, ed. D. K. Deardoff, 249-263. L. A.: Sage.

Pusch, M. D. 2009. The interculturally competent global leader. In *The SAGE Handbook of Intercultural Competence*, ed. D. K. Deardoff, 66-84. L. A.: Sage.

Risager, K. 2006, *Language and culture. Global flows and local complexity.* Clevedon: Multilingual Matters.

—. 2007, *Language and culture pedagogy. From a national to a transnational paradigm.* Clevedon: Multilingual Matters.

Rychen, D. S. 2003. Key competencies. In *Key competencies for a successful life and well-functioning society,* eds. D. S. Rychen and L. H. Salganik, 63-107. Toronto, Ont.: Hogrefe & Huber Pub.

Rychen, D. S. and L.H. Salganik. 2003. Introduction to *Key competencies for a successful life and well-functioning society,* by D. S. Rychen and L. H. Salganik, 1-12. Toronto, Ont.: Hogrefe & Huber Pub.

Salganik, L. H. and M. Stephens. 2003. Competence priorities in policy and practice. In *Key competencies for a successful life and well-functioning society,* eds. D. S. Rychen and L. H. Salganik, 13-40. Toronto, Ont.: Hogrefe and Huber Pub.

Santos, B. S. (ed.) 2007a. *Another knowledge is possible: Beyond northern epistemologies.* London: Verso.

—. 2007b. Beyond abyssal thinking: From global lines to ecologies of knowledges. *Review* XXX, no. 1: 45-89.

Sleeter, C. E. (ed.) 1991. *Empowerment through multicultural education.* Albany: State University of New York.

Søderberg. A. M. and E. Vaara (eds.) 2003. *Merging across borders: People, cultures and politics.* Copenhagen: Copenhagen Business School Press.

Spitzberg, B. H. and G. Changnon. 2009. Conceptualizing intercultural competence. In *The SAGE Handbook of Intercultural Competence*, ed. D. K. Deardoff, 2-52. L. A.: Sage.

Ting-Toomey, S. 1999. *Communicating across cultures.* London: The Guilford Press.

Ting-Toomey, S. and A. Kurogi. 1998. Facework competence in intercultural conflict: an updated face-negotiation theory. *International Journal of Intercultural Relations* 22: 2,187-225.

Ting-Toomey, S. and J.G. Oetzel. 2001. *Managing intercultural conflict effectively.* Sage: Thousand Oaks, CA.

Trim, J.L.M. 2007. *Modern languages in the Council of Europe*, 1954-1997. http://www.coe.int/t/dg4/linguistic/Publications_EN.asp

Walsh, C. E. 1991. *Pedagogy and the struggle for voice.* New York; Bergin and Garvey.

Wiseman, R. L. (ed.) 1995. Intercultural communication theory. *International and Intercultural Communication Annual,* 19. Thousand Oaks, CA.: Sage.

van Ek, J. 1986. *Objectives for foreign language learning. Volume 1: Scope.* Strasbourg: Council of Europe. http://www.coe.int/t/dg4/linguistic/Publications_EN.asp#P470_25692

CHAPTER TWO

THE CONCEPT AND DEVELOPMENT
OF INTERCULTURAL COMPETENCE

YANNAN GUO

Introduction

The term intercultural competence (IC for short) has been used increasingly in academic and non-academic discussions over the last three decades. There is, however, a lack of consensus about the precise meaning of the term, partly due to the fact that it has been used in a wide range of contexts, including educational, political, business, social, and health services, each of which has its own perspective and approach. The other side of the coin, however, is that different terminologies have been used for ideas or concepts that appear to be similar in nature or closely related, as we shall see.

Although the social phenomena being addressed in these varied social contexts are intrinsically the same, the objectives and foci of the studies or discussions are different. For instance, educational institutions would place more emphasis on issues such as personal growth, empowerment, social responsibilities, and ultimately, on the healthy development of future society, while large international corporations would more likely focus on successful business operations, often overseas. Similarly, what concerns politicians and policy makers differs yet again from educators and business managers whose attention would be oriented more towards social policies regarding social cohesion and social stability. In addition to that, there is a lack of clarity so far in regard to the conceptualisation of the competence that is deemed necessary for successful intercultural interactions or communication. This has been, understandably, an obstacle for researchers and practitioners to share information and resources, and thus hinders further development of this field.

However, in spite of diverse interest and a lack of agreement on the precise meaning of the terminology used between researchers and scholars, intercultural studies, including theoretical studies and practical applications, have developed rapidly. As far as intercultural education is concerned, progress has been made both in terms of social impact and theoretical/pedagogic studies. That is, apart from the advancement of knowledge about intercultural phenomena and intercultural education, there has also been a lot of progress at various levels in terms of teaching, training and curriculum setting for IC development. However, there are still questions that are not yet fully answered, especially with regard to assessment standards and methods of IC development.

This chapter will focus on the concept of IC and its development. It consists of two parts. The first one will try to answer the question of what IC is about. It covers issues such as the basic nature and the main fabric of IC and why it is difficult to get consensus on a definition for this social ability. The second part will provide a brief review of IC development and intercultural education, focusing mainly on the expansion of the conceptual framework of IC development. It will introduce some recent discussions on the objectives of and the main components of intercultural education/training. The discussion will start with an overview of the confused state of terminology use, which will not only contribute to an understanding of the richness of the IC concept, but will also give a taste of the wide scope and complexity of intercultural studies and the vast effort made to understand intercultural experience. This will be followed by a discussion of some key issues in understanding IC.

The Concept of Intercultural Competence

What is intercultural competence? To discuss this we need to have some idea about the basic nature of intercultural interaction. According to Bennett (1993, 1998), our natural responses to cultural differences tend to be negative, such as fear, distrust, and the attempt of eliminating them. The source of the negative psychological reaction is closely associated with the experience of a changing cultural environment. The lack of shared language, behavioural patterns, and value standards, makes the communication of meaning, understandably, much more difficult in an intercultural context than in a monocultural one in which people act on shared assumptions. It is therefore risky for those involved in terms of losing control of situations and/or being treated unfairly. Ways of dealing with difference thus lies at the heart of intercultural interaction. There is a need to overcome shortage of information on the one hand and to cope with psychological discomfort on the other hand. It will become evident through the following discussion that intercultural interaction is a complex process involving many factors, and that the term intercultural competence is by no means a concept whose meaning is straightforward and static. Instead, it is a concept that has been evolving along with our understanding of the process and consequences of intercultural interactions. To appreciate the fluidity and complexity of the concept, it will be useful for us to start our discussion with an overview of some different terminologies used in the field of intercultural research, which will be followed by a discussion of the different aspects of IC.

Terminology–Muddled Field

A recent survey by Deardorff (2006) shows little consensus on terminology among intercultural researchers and scholars as far as intercultural experience is concerned. She came to the conclusion that not only different terminology has been used to conceptualise the experience of intercultural encounters, the same term, namely, intercultural competence, is also found to bear meanings that do not mean entirely the same thing for different researchers and scholars.

On the one hand, this reflects the broad range and complex nature of intercultural studies, as mentioned at the start of the chapter, and on the other hand, it is an indication of a lack of adequate collaboration between different disciplines or research interests, as well as being a sign of the relatively short history of the development of intercultural studies, the origin of which can be traced back to the early research efforts in cross-cultural psychology and cross-cultural behavioural studies in the later 1960s to the early 1970s (Brislin and Lonner 1972; Dinges 1983). As pointed out by Van de Vijver and Breugelmans (2008, 114), intercultural competency remains a "construct beset by problems of definition, a relative paucity of measuring instruments, and methodological pitfalls".

In his review of intercultural communication studies or intercultural studies, Wiseman (2002) identified a number of terms being used as synonyms for the concept of being competent in intercultural communication or intercultural interaction, such as intercultural understanding, personal growth/adjustment, cross-cultural adaptation, intercultural sensitivity, cross-cultural effectiveness, and intercultural communication competence. The term intercultural competence is thus just one of a few used to describe largely the same meaning, though it is perhaps more general in nature. The variation in terminology, as Wiseman (2002) points out, is basically a reflection of differences in research focus and in theoretical orientation. That is to say, there are no fundamental differences between them in terms of the nature of the object being studied and of what is perceived as necessary competence in handling intercultural interactions. Therefore, they may be seen as being complimentary to each other.

In reviewing the development of the theories and models of IC developed between 1960s and 1980s, Dinges (1983) compared and examined some different approaches taken to analyse intercultural experience and to formulate the concept of IC. In his summary entitled "Intercultural Competence", no clearly articulated definition of IC is offered. Instead, he offers a discussion of a number of different models or paradigms that had been developed to identify the qualities for successful intercultural interaction, such as multicultural identity and social skills. These models or paradigms reflect various perspectives and different approaches. Some take cognitive and psychological awareness or adaptability as a way to evaluate IC, paying attention to how individuals overcome cognitive and psychological difficulties caused by cultural differences; others are more interested in identifying behavioural patterns between cultures for the purpose of facilitating work efficiency and adjustment in cross-cultural contexts; and yet others look more closely into the impact of cultural differences on identities and relationships.

From these early efforts of conceptualising IC, we can see that the issue of intercultural competence was explored from various theoretical perspectives including *social behaviourism and culture learning, life transition, overseasmanship* and *trans-cultural maturity and competence*. What matters to our discussion here is two-fold. First, some key factors of intercultural interaction were identified, such as relationship management, communication styles, stress tolerance and information processing. Secondly, instead of a clearly formulated definition, the prototype of IC was a set of different paradigms and models, as noted by Dinges (1983, 176): "This is an ill-defined area. Concepts of intercultural competence are often vague and at best implicit in discursive analyses of overseas experience and long lists of desirable sojourner traits, or are embedded in the goals of various cross-cultural training methods".

This example illustrates the point that IC is a very elusive and all-embracing concept. It was not satisfactorily formulated at the time when Dinges made his survey, and it seems that the situation has not improved significantly even now in the sense that there is still little agreement on the definition of IC across disciplines. It is even suggested by Simensen that the term has become an educational cliché and no one seems to know precisely what it means (Lund 2008).

On the other hand, intercultural studies have moved forward rapidly. The importance of promoting IC has been widely recognised, and IC training/education programmes have been included in business agendas of all sorts of organisations recently. But more importantly, intercultural education has been evolving continuously and swiftly, and as we shall see later, current discussions on being intercultural have further extended to include some important issues of human rights, such as social justice and equality. The widening of the scope of intercultural education may complicate the definition of IC even more.

As we can see, intercultural study is not a precise science and the meaning of the different terminologies is neither clear-cut nor mutually exclusive. The term IC has often been used as a general term to refer to the ability of handling problems induced by intercultural contact. As suggested by Dinges (1983), IC has been treated, in some contexts, as an overarching concept, under which different approaches are implicitly applied and different disciplinary assumptions are assumed. It is sometimes used to refer in a vague and all-embracing manner to non-specifically qualified competence that is assumed to work in an intercultural context.

The discussion on terminology has provided a picture of the complexity of IC. In the following section, we will look into what IC consists of and how the different factors influence each other.

The Triadic Model of and Criteria for Intercultural Competence

What is culture? This question has been asked again and again and numerous answers have been offered from various perspectives. For Edward Hall (1976), who believes that a society is organised through shared experience of its members, culture is information, and thus is communication. He asserts: "any culture is primarily a system for creating, sending, storing, and processing information" (Hall 1998, 53). Interaction between cultures, from this perspective, is communication between different man-made systems, or meaning systems. This view has great impact on intercultural studies. Based on this notion of culture, interaction between cultures is often referred to as intercultural communication, and the competence for successfully carrying it out therefore as intercultural communication competence or intercultural communicative competence (Byram 1997; Gudykunst 1998; Kim 2001). These two terms are sometimes used interchangeably with IC, but in some cases, communicative competence is used with an implication of explicit emphasis on linguistic competence, or perhaps more accurately, having the linguistic aspect being addressed more explicitly in the process of the competence development (Byram 1997; Johnson 2003).

What makes it challenging to communicate between systems is that every system is unique not only in terms of communicating meaning, but also in terms of setting boundaries to separate its members from those of others (Bochner 1982; Ting-Toomey 1999). Communication across cultures therefore means that one has to be able to overcome both cognitive and emotional barriers so as to function effectively in an intercultural context. Cognitively, it is necessary for people to be able to recognise and deal with new rules of social interaction or different social conventions, and psychologically, it requires the attitudes to face up uncertainty and anxiety induced by unfamiliar circumstances and challenges to self identities (Argyle 1982; Gudykunst 1998; Stephan and Stephan 2002).

Spitzberg and Cupach (1984) stated that to be interculturally competent, one needs to produce behaviours that are both appropriate to the context and effective in terms of fulfilling the intended objectives of the interactants. Based on their studies on intercultural behaviours, they proposed a triadic model of intercultural competence, in which they presented three elements that are thought to be fundamental to successful communication: *motivation, knowledge,* and *skills,* also known as *affective, cognitive,* and *operational* capabilities (Kim 2001). This model has been well adopted and has had great impact on competence studies (Wiseman 2002).

Being appropriate and effective requires knowledge as well as motivation and skills to manage the challenges posed by intercultural interactions (i.e. uncertainty and anxiety as well as knowledge deficiency). First of all, the context of intercultural interaction is very different from intra-cultural interaction, so the knowledge people have acquired in their home cultural context is not enough for them to deal with a new context. This is made even more difficult by the fact that appropriateness is subjective depending on how the interactants interpret it. Without shared meaning, this is obviously problematic. On the other hand, effectiveness depends as much on people's perceptions of the situation and their goals of interaction, as on their abilities to respond appropriately and their willingness to cooperate with each other. The criteria set by Spitzberg and Cupach (1984) thus indicate that meaning is dynamically created during the process of communication rather than being static, and that it is the interactants themselves who make judgments on appropriateness and effectiveness (e.g., whether their goals are achieved). To have a better understanding of how the three elements – motivation, knowledge and skills, function to enable interactions with others, it is useful to take a close look at the process of production and perception of meaning.

Perception–the Interface of Convention, Relationship, and Action

According to Gudykunst (1998), meaning production is based on three sources: *habits*, *intentions*, and *emotions*. Habits are referred to as the behavioural patterns individuals follow without conscious decisions being made about what to do. "When we are communicating habitually, we are following scripts" (Gudykunst 1998, 10). These *scripts* are the structure of knowledge in terms of social behaviour (Van Dijk 1990) that individuals have accumulated through socialisation. What is significant of this habitual behaviour is that "the cultural scripts we enact provide us with shared interpretations of our behaviours" (Gudykunst 1998, 11). It is the shared meaning that enables us to make sense of others' behaviours and to expect to be understood by others. One of the barriers to effective intercultural communication is the absence of shared interpretation of meaning.

However, we would be mistaken to think that our behaviour and perceptions of meaning are directed by scripts alone. As suggested above, meaning production is a dynamic process in which interactants keep on construing and monitoring their interactions with each other with reference to their notion of appropriateness and effectiveness. McCann and Higgins (1990) pointed out that the fast development of social cognition studies since 1970s has provided us with the key to understanding the process of meaning-production. That is, in contrast to the traditional approach which does not consider interactant perceptions of on-going meaning production, which subsequently affect their decisions about how to behave, the social cognition approach does recognise the profound impact of personal constructs – knowledge of self and others (McCann and Higgins 1990) – on the way interactants perceive the progress and outcomes of their interactions with each other, and thus on the subsequent behavioural production.

What is at the core of this approach is the assumption that the process of meaning production is guided by our self-conception, i.e., "our views of ourselves" (Ting-Toomey 1999, 76), through which we make distinctions between ourselves and others, and that enables us to order our perceptual framework in relation with the outside world, that is, to make sense of the events that happens to us and around us. It means, even if people have few problems with *scripts*, they may still choose not to follow them because they lack motivation. In fact, the way people act or react to the situation they are in is, to a large degree, determined by their motivation or intention – the second operational factor of meaning production.

Obviously, motivation is a large topic involving many factors, purpose of communication, for instance. So, behaviour could be the outcomes of various factors or combination of factors. By identifying intention as a source of meaning production, this approach draws our attention to the fact that meaning is derived not only from scripts, but also from one's expectations, i.e., evaluation of the on-going situation in terms of whether intended goals are or could be achieved.

In explaining how individuals perceive themselves in relation to others, Tajfel (1981, 254) made two assumptions: 1) individuals differentiate self and others in their social interactions (through social categorisation and social comparison); 2) individuals always strive to achieve a satisfactory concept or image of themselves. These assumptions underpin social identity theory as a whole, which opened the door to questions related to how and why people are influenced in their decisions on what message/s to convey, and how and when they act or react in their interactions with others. With the knowledge that perception is affected by self-identities, it becomes evident that if individuals feel that their expectations of self-conception and purposes of communication are not met, they are likely to be negatively motivated to cooperate, and vice versa. This theoretical perspective carries huge implications for intercultural interaction in which identity issues are often salient. In fact, identity issues are thought to be major causes of miscommunication in intercultural interactions (Turner and Reynolds, 2003). We will come back to this topic again but for the time being, let us focus on production and perception of meaning.

Gudykunst's third operational factor for meaning production or perception is emotion. Emotion is generally regarded as the outcome of uncertainty and anxiety, and it is a factor that has strong leverage over perception and behaviour. A great many studies have been carried out regarding the psychological aspect of intercultural interaction, such as culture shock, which focuses on the conditions and process of sojourners' adaptation (Argyle 1982; Furnham and Bochner 1982). Uncertainty reduction theory (URT) examines the interplay between emotion and its causal factors (Stephan and Stephan 1992, 2002), and uncertainty/anxiety management theory (UAM), which is similar to URT, explores the causal factors that induce uncertainty and anxiety, but with an emphasis on keeping uncertainty/anxiety at a level where individuals would be sufficiently stimulated to act mindfully (Gudykunst 1995). The importance of these studies lies in the fact that they have revealed the important role emotion plays in influencing attitudes, cognition and behaviour. In intercultural interactions, our needs for security and sense of self are often challenged (Stephan and Stephan 1992) and that could lead to strong emotional responses, and subsequent misinterpretations and mishandling of situations.

Intercultural interaction is known to be difficult and emotionally charged, as mentioned at the beginning. As far as perception is concerned, negative affect such as discrimination, prejudice, or ethnocentrism often leads to distortion of meaning. The above discussion shows that personal construct, which comprises values, beliefs and social categories the individual holds in regard to social structure and social behaviour, has a major role to play in the way people make sense of their social environment. Very briefly, it operates through two cognitive mechanisms that are significant to perception of relationships and the subsequent emotional responses. Specifically, we differentiate between self and other and we make comparisons between self and others. Based on this self-other differentiation and the self-esteem rule, we categorise others and distinguish between out-group/s and in-group/s (Turner 1982; Operario and Fiske 2003) with favoured attitudes towards the latter. Perception of meaning is therefore likely to be affected by this difference in attitudes, as positive attitudes tend to lead to positive attribution of meaning or explanations, and vice versa (Jaspars and Hewstone 1982; Tajfel 1981).

What Does It Mean To Be Interculturally Competent?

We have just considered the three components of social interactive competence, i.e., attitudes, knowledge and skills, and what makes intercultural interaction more challenging than intra-cultural interaction. The main point highlighted is that to be efficient and appropriate in intercultural interaction, one has to be able to establish satisfactory relationships with the culturally different others, as well as to have the ability to overcome information shortage. However, it is important to note that what is required of a person in an intercultural context differs significantly from that of a mono-cultural context. That is, the expectations of them are very different with regard to cultural identities and mastery of knowledge and skills.

Given that IC is meant to be the ability to relate to or to interact with people from various cultures, not any one culture in particular; given that the way of acquiring the competence of a non-native culture (including language) is different from that of the native (Valdes 1998; Lantolf 1999), it is neither viable nor appropriate to expect as part of IC a full mastery of another culture, including the knowledge and motivation to identify with the members of the target culture. Rather, the issue is to have the abilities to engage with otherness and to gain cooperation in order to achieve mutual satisfaction in intercultural interactions. As pointed out by Bennett (1998), the main issue is to manage differences.

Focusing on the process of communication, Bennett (1998, 2-3) made the point that in contrast to mono-cultural communication, which is *similarity based*, intercultural communication is *difference-based*, and thus the key issue of intercultural competence is to deal with differences. Byram, takes the same position but from a different perspective by highlighting the power difference between the native and the non-native, and different ways of learning. He further elaborated this concept in his Intercultural Communicative Competence model (Byram and Zarate 1997; Byram 1997; Byram 2009) and in the construct of *intercultural speaker*, which he and his colleague originally came up with when contemplating the issue of IC development (Byram and Zarate 1997).

Although agreeing with Bennett about the difference-oriented nature of intercultural competence, Byram concerns himself more with the philosophical and educational aspects of power difference in the contexts of intercultural interaction and of cultural learning, especially from the foreign language learning perspective, taking the view that the learner should not be expected to imitate, and subsequently to achieve the same level of competence as the native speaker. Instead, they should develop the competence of an "intercultural speaker" (Byram 1997; Byram and Zarate 1994), whose position is in between the cultures with which they are in contact, and whose role is to mediate between different ways of thinking and behaving. Based on this view, Byram's (1997, 2009) Intercultural Communicative Competence model places more emphasis on fostering empathy and on the acquisition of the knowledge and skills needed to mediate between differences. Obviously, this difference-based approach can be expected to have a significant impact upon pedagogical issues related to the content of learning, teaching approaches and subsequently the assessment of levels of competence (1997, 2008), because the expected outcome not only differs, but also touches the innermost and emotion-charged issues of self-concept, personal beliefs and values. In a very general sense, being intercultural competent means to be able to meet the requirements of being both emotionally and cognitively flexible enough to deal with various cultural contexts, and of being curious and open-minded enough to learn about other cultures and to work with or coexist with people of various backgrounds. In the next part, we will look at how the concept of IC development has evolved.

Intercultural Competence Development

IC Development–Issues Concerning Theoretical and Pedagogical Development

To develop a better understanding of the conceptual content of IC development, it is more than useful to follow some current discussions on intercultural training and education. There has emerged a clear voice in recent years calling for the integration of a political element into the concept of intercultural competence development. The theoretical arguments are grounded in educational as well as social justice philosophies, and the call for the inclusion of social justice element and cultural awareness in intercultural learning is based on reflections upon the issues we are experiencing in the process of globalisation. Understandably, this theoretical inspiration carries important pedagogical implications, as expectations of competency development will inevitably have an impact on the selection of learning content, and then on the production and assessment of outcomes as suggested above. With regard to the conceptualisation of IC, the following discussion will enable us further to appreciate the fluidity and richness of the concept.

A brief look at some of the main issues discussed over the last three decades on intercultural contact and IC development will enable us to see that the current discussion covers a wider scope than, say, one or two decades ago, both in terms of the social issues covered and the competences needed for living in a multicultural society. In terms of social issues, what is meant here is that earlier discussions focused only on problems experienced by a relatively small number of immigrants and/or sojourners. In contrast to that, intercultural contact nowadays has become an everyday phenomenon for many people, and thus IC concerns much wider a population, in fact, it concerns all the members of the global community in a wide sense. At the same time, the contexts and purposes of contact differ as well. Generally speaking, as suggested earlier at several points, attention was previously on individuals' adaptation to their host environment, psychologically and behaviourally, but more recent discussion covers more wide-ranging issues that include the fair treatment of minority and sub-cultural groups in a multi-cultural society, the level of cultural awareness of the host society as well as that of the sojourner, social justice and social equality. For example, Dana and Allen (2008) point out that the gap between the needs of ethnic groups in the US and the lack of interculturally competent personnel in the social service sectors to meet these needs is a source of tension and a matter of social justice.

In terms of competency development, since the contexts and purposes of contacts vary greatly and the population concerned includes not only sojourners and ethnic groups, but also host members or cultural mainstream groups, there are inevitably new problems and new challenges, the consequences of which will have an impact not only on the individuals concerned, but on whole societies as well. One response to this change is the advocacy of political education to enhance our understanding of the human consequences of globalisation, and better training for skills to deal with the challenges in the global society in which multicultural contexts are the norm. The issues highlighted by this political approach include social justice and equality for the disadvantaged, social cohesion and stability, and education for global citizenship (Byram 2008; Dana and Allen 2008; Guilherme 2002).

The academic literature shows that earlier research on IC development focused mainly on effective functioning and psychological adjustment of sojourners or immigrants who have to live in a new cultural environment, either for a short or for a long period, and have to make adjustment in order to survive or to function. Attention therefore is paid to factors that are essential for adaptation, such as behavioural adaptation/shift, social skill development, uncertainty reduction and cultural learning (Berry and Sam 1997; Brislin, Landis and Brandt 1983; Furnham and Bochner 1986). This behavioural and psychological approach has led to the identification of various interrelated causal factors such as social contexts, behavioural traits, interpersonal and intergroup relationships, and the way these factors impact on individuals' IC development (Gudykunst and Bond 1997; Hall 1976; Hofstede 1980; Ruben and Kealey 1979). Current discussion, however, has expanded beyond these traditional approaches taking also into consideration social structuring and human rights issues, such as social justice and equality, social harmony and cohesion, and social responsibilities and entitlements of all the individuals who have to coexist in a world that is aptly described as the global village (Byram 2008; Alred, Byram and Fleming 2006; Dana and Allen 2008). While much attention of the world is directed to the economic side of the globalization nowadays, this voice reminds us of the need to understand the human side of the movement, and the long-term stability of the world peace and harmony.

For example, taking the view that educational aims should promote the qualities of self reflection, critical and independent thinking, and that foreign language learning encourages learners to explore different beliefs, values and behavioural norms, since they will inevitably come across different practices and perspectives between cultures in their learning, Byram (1997) has proposed the concept of "intercultural speaker" and advocated the notion of "intercultural citizenship". The former is defined as someone who is capable of mediating between different cultures and the latter as the ability "to act sensibly in and across political entities, at whatever level" (Byram 2008, 157), and of which the ability to question the status quo and to think and act critically and independently is thought to be an essential part. He argues (2008, 186) that intercultural citizenship experience "is a particular kind of intercultural experience", which "may include the promotion of change or improvement in the social or personal lives of the intercultural individuals or their fellows".

This is pertinent especially as individuals sometimes are caught in the moral dilemma of what to do when unethical deeds are carried out on the pretext of cultural tradition or cultural difference. Due to a consideration of respecting differences or avoiding appearing biased, sometimes people may feel difficult to take actions against what they see as wrong doings in a cultural context that is different from their own. Lack of clear guidance is a major problem, and this is precisely what is needed in regard to "promotion of change or improvement in the social or personal lives". One of the objectives of intercultural citizenship education is to encourage developing critical cultural awareness, which implies the competence to make independent and critical evaluations of events (Byram 2008). It also implies the skills to seek for cooperative and creative ways of problem solving. In defining "intercultural citizenship", Byram (2008, 187) suggests that it "has a specific nature that includes the obligation to judge values, beliefs, and behaviours according to agreed definitions of democracy and democratic principles". As he rightly points out, the application of the democratic principles is based predominantly on the western value orientation. In his recent work (2009) he took the stand that evaluation should be made on the basis of clear understanding of the different perspectives involved and of good reasoning instead of focusing on any particular evaluative option. Indeed, it is important that evaluation is made on a clear understanding of the issue concerned from different perspectives. He suggests (2009, 324): "Reasoning may lead a person to make an evaluation not according to criteria of rationality but of 'maximizing happiness' or 'communitarianism' or 'caring', to use Wringe's keywords – and to acting accordingly".

As globalisation brings the world communities closer to each other, contacts between nations and cultures are becoming increasingly frequent at every level. To be able to act sensibly and effectively across political and cultural boundaries becomes even more important than ever before, both at the level of individual achievement or personal satisfaction, and for social harmony and coherence in general. At the same time, with diverse practices and values systems being brought into closer contact, there is a likelihood of value conflicts and even moral confusion, and therefore it is important for individuals to be prepared to face conflict with open-mindedness and critical attitudes. It should be an important part of conflict-management skills to put into perspectives different views and events, yet not to lose sight of some fundamental values that are important for the common good of human society and the development of our human civilization. Being intercultural thus entails the abilities as well as the social responsibilities to make sensible and balanced evaluations or decisions on cultural related issues.

The political importance of multicultural, or cultural competence education, the preferred terms by Dana and Allen (2008), is raised from a somewhat different perspective. They pointed out that the lack of cultural competence was a major contributing factor to inequality in social service, as the needs of various minority groups were not recognised by the mainstream society in the US. Their view is that multicultural education is a means to address the social problems produced by the process of globalisation, particularly the psychological wellbeing of ethnic minorities. According to their studies, the change of demographic landscape in the US, where ethnic minorities have now accounted for about a third of the population, has given rise to social tension and psychological problems of the deprived ethnic groups. Because of the mono-cultural system, the disadvantaged are ill-served in their needs for social services, such as healthcare and education. Understandably, this could be a cause of resentment and racial tension. But more importantly, it is perceived as an issue of social justice and equality, as being denied of equal access to the social facilities is an infringement of the human rights of those concerned. For Weaver (2008, 144-5), an important step to improve the situation is to have effective multicultural competence training or education programmes for service professionals. But as they pointed out, current policies and educational structures are heavily loaded with the values and norms of the dominant group/s, thus it is necessary to raise cultural awareness on a much wider scale if real changes are to be made, because "a true realisation of cultural competence must go beyond the micro-level and requires transformation of programs and policies on the macro-level".

To integrate the political perspective into IC development, especially from the perspective of practical application, a few issues need to be taken into consideration. To start with, as the aim of this political dimension is to bring attitude change, to promote a strong sense of social justice in the learner or the trainee, it is necessary to encourage the learner to reflect on their own beliefs and values as well as to become aware of the existence of other, equally valid ones. But more importantly, as said above, it requires the learner to go beyond the extent of the knowledge and skills of engaging with otherness with respect and empathy. This political dimension entails a willingness to bring changes to undesirable realities or to seek for better solutions to improve social or individual's conditions in intercultural contexts. This is challenging in two aspects. First, clearly,

value judgment is assumed in this approach, so to avoid bias it is
important for the learner to be aware of the value standard being applied in
the evaluation and the potential conflicts between different value systems
or orientations. On the basis of that, the learner is to be encouraged to
develop the abilities of independent thinking and being critical in
analysing and reasoning. But to achieve this, different teaching
methodologies have to be adopted, along with assessment methods.

From a different standpoint, when facilitating attitude change, great
care has to be exercised in dealing with beliefs and values that individuals
hold, as they are integral parts of one's identities and thus emotion-
inducing. In regard to teaching and course management, Dana (2008, 109)
highlights the affective nature of moral or political aspect of intercultural
learning, and emphasises the importance of addressing issues like
ethnocentrism, prejudice carefully in education, saying that "ethical and
social responsibility issues are inherent in affective-experiential training
which requires careful preparation and mandatory evaluation of attempts
to remediate student attitudes and ethnocentric patterns of thinking." He
warns that if not carefully handled, attempts to bring about attitude change
could backfire, provoking intense emotional response and ending in
failure. This reinforces the point that education for attitude change should
be taken very seriously.

Political education aims at promoting attitudes supportive of social
justice, equality and respect of people of various social or cultural
backgrounds, and to develop the knowledge and skills for gaining access
to different perspectives and negotiating for consensus or cooperation.
Byram (2008) emphasises the ability to act interculturally, by which he
means having the attitudes, knowledge and skills necessary to mediate
between different views and to make sensible decisions in accordance with
a given context. As intercultural citizens play roles that are not directly
linked to any particular culture, we can say in the light of the discussion
above that an important part of their competence is to readily face different
values, beliefs, and states of emotional challenge. Being flexible and ready
to engage with others are essential basic orientations for this role. As far as
identity is concerned, such points echo what Adler (1998, 228) said about
the multicultural person: "The identity of multicultural person, far from
being frozen in a social character, is more fluid and mobile, more
susceptible to change, more open to variation. It is an identity based not on
a 'belongingness', which implies either owning or being owned by culture,

but on a style of self-consciousness that is capable of negotiating ever new formations of reality".

The broadening of the concept of IC will inevitably have some impact on the methodology and assessment of IC development. For instance, the qualities and social responsibilities that are to be cultivated for intercultural citizenship, such as being able to question the status quo, and being able to mediate between different or diverse views with the purpose to improve human conditions, are new to many educational programmes. Also, to address issues of this nature is very challenging for the teacher, as it could be emotional charged and there are often no ready answers for the questions being dealt with. Moreover, typical of intercultural education, assessing the outcomes of social justice education is not only difficult but problematic. Firstly, because of the subjective nature of attitude, it is difficult to apply clear objective measurements to assessment, which is deemed a necessary property of good psychometric evaluations. Secondly, as noted by Byram (2008), the subjective nature calls into question the desirability and practicality of assessing individuals' personality or political attitudes. Finally, one of the requirements of good assessment is that the instrument should adequately cover all the factors in the underlying construct, and as this article tries to show, IC covers a very broad spectrum, and therefore an reliable overall assessment has been, and will continue to be a challenge.

IC Development–Content and Approaches

The previous sections have paved the way for discussion about the content of IC learning, and we can now take a closer look at the components of IC learning models and different approaches, i.e., psychological, behavioural and educational political approaches that have been applied in IC development programmes.

As mentioned earlier, the three-component model proposed by Spitzberg and Cupach (1984) – motivation/attitudes, knowledge, and skills – is generally accepted as the fundamental structure of IC. On this basis there have been some variations, for example, Byram's Intercultural Communicative Competence Model (1997, 2008, 2009), contains a further element, namely, political education, which was discussed above. Similarly, Gamst et al (2004) included in their four-factor health professional education model the dimension called "Non-ethnic Ability", which refers to the "ability to work with a variety of diverse populations beyond people of color" (Weaver 2008, 145), recognising differences in age, poverty, gender, sexual orientation, and disability. What is common to these two perspectives is that they are highlighting some problems of a diversified society, such as inequality, conflict, and incompatibility of the social structure to accommodate different needs. These issues were not given due attention previously, whether it is social responsibilities or sensitivity to multi-identity needs in working environments.

Differing from the psychological and behavioural approaches to intercultural communication, the political education dimension and social justice approach have their roots in political ideology or educational philosophy – with the aim to achieve a better society. To have this additional dimension to the three-component competence model brings attention to the difficult intergroup relational issue linked to cultural identities in intercultural interaction, so that they will be treated seriously and carefully. But in terms of progression, development of competence in this regard can be interpreted under the three domains of attitude, knowledge and skills, because developing awareness of profound social justice and social responsibilities involves changes in attitudes towards unfamiliar values and perspectives as well as development in knowledge and skills to mediate between the differences. Having made this clear, we can now take a look at the three elements that form the main structure of IC.

Attitude refers to the desire to interact with culturally different others. It is the affective aspect of social interaction. Spitzberg and Cupach (1984) contend that whether one is motivated to engage interactions with others depends on various factors, contextual as well as objective-oriented. That is, whether to take the strategy of approach or the strategy of avoidance depends very much upon the purpose of interaction and to what extent one feels his/her objectives being met. The judgment, however, is based on continual appraisals of the progress of the interactions in terms of relationships, expectations, and the prospect of achieving the desired goals. As attitude is closely related to cognition and behaviour, it has been taken as a precursor or indicator of potential or stages of intercultural competence development in works such as the Multicultural Personality Questionnaire (Van Oudenhoven and Van der Zee 2002) and Bennett's Developmental Model of Intercultural Sensitivity (Bennett 1993).

It is believed that individuals' appraisals of their social interactions with people of different cultural groups is deeply affected by ethnocentrism, which refers to negative or biased attitudes towards culturally different others, as the term ethnocentrism means a belief of one's own cultural tradition being superior or *central* in relation to others. Unfortunately, we all tend to use our own culture as a "filter" (Begley 2003) to view the world around us, hence to interpret meanings in accordance with our own cultural frames of reference. So, reducing ethnocentrism is the key to attitudinal change. It is suggested that it is necessary that people are encouraged to engage with otherness and to discover different perspectives, in Byram's words, to have the willingness to "engage with otherness in a relationship of equality" (Byram 1997, 50), and to have the "curiosity and openness, readiness to suspend disbelief about other cultures and belief about one's own" (Byram 1997, 73).

However, it is only possible to decentre when one is aware of the existence of different perspectives and is willing to accept that different perspectives are equally valid. Horvath (1997, 174) points out that an important step to reduce ethnocentrism is to debunk the assumption of a single-reality of the world, which prevents us from exploring different world views or/and appreciating different cultural experiences.

For Ting-Toomey (1999), to decentre means to be mindful and respectful of cultural differences. She argues that it is essential to successful intercultural communication to have the willingness and abilities to accommodate the identity needs of others, such as security, inclusion, trust and connection, and being reflexively aware of one's own ethnocentric tendencies. What is emphasised in this approach is to practise mindfulness in reaction to cultural differences and to be active in discovering different cultural orientations. In other words, to be prepared to meet different views and practices with an open mind and flexible manner.

Bennett (1993) sees attitude change as a cognitive developmental process from being ignorant of differences at the one end of the spectrum to being able to make contextual evaluations of events on the basis of sufficient understanding of the different perspectives involved at the other end. This progress moves from ethnocentric stages – denial, defence, and minimization to that of ethnorelative – acceptance, adaptation, and integration. The idea of ethnorelativity, and indeed, the idea of multicultural education have been questioned by some critics for creating ethical multiplicity and being divisive of social unity of western societies (Bennett 1998; Banks 1998). In responding to this criticism, Banks argues that instead of dividing unified societies, the effort is in fact to unify diverging ones together, and that contextual evaluation is a process of learning and discovery, or a procedure of knowledge construction, not a practice of dual or multi-ethical standards.

In line with this notion of knowledge construction, the political education perspective places emphasis on the values of independent thinking and being critical of existing establishment. For example, Byram (1997, 50-3) maintains that education should encourage the learner to develop "an ability to evaluate critically and on the basis of explicit criteria perspectives, practices and products in one's own and other cultures and countries". This involves the willingness to explore unknown territory as well as to reflect upon one's own ways of thinking and behaving.

Knowledge is broadly conceptualised by Byram (2008, 163) as an understanding "of social groups and their products and practices in one's own and in one's interlocutor's country, and of general processes of societal and individual interaction". Our earlier discussion of meaning production indicates that successful communication is the outcome of knowing how to manage emotional factors, relationships, as well as knowing what script is to be enacted in a given social context. In other words, being able to act appropriately and effectively requires both culture-specific knowledge, such as social institutions, language, social rules of that cultural group, etc., as well as culture-general knowledge, the knowledge of how to handle the process of interaction, including being self-aware, understanding the consequences of social identification and social categorisation. The latter concerns more generally what happens during the process of interpersonal-intergroup interactions and is applicable to all sorts of cultural contexts. It is essential for the concept of being intercultural, which is the main theme of this book.

In addition, the advocacy of intercultural citizenship and critical cultural awareness encourages discovery of different socio-political realities. It is understandable that sound judgments and constructive critiques of social practices have to be based upon sufficient understanding of social issues, as well as on the determination to improve living conditions for and to bring justice to all the people in the world.

Our discussion indicates that the skills needed should include the ability to understand and mediate between different perspectives, to relate to others, and to make independent and well-founded judgments and decisions. Byram (1997) defines skills under two categories: skills of interpreting and relating – emphasising the abilities to empathise and to understand different perspectives, and skills of discovery and interaction – stressing the abilities to engage with people of different backgrounds and orientations, to find and learn different perspectives, and to negotiate and cooperate for mutually acceptable solutions.

Taking uncertainty and anxiety as major factors influencing communication activities, Gudykunst and Kim (2003) pay more attention on the psychological aspect, identifying five skills for effective intercultural communication, and they are: (1) ability to be mindful; (2) ability to manage anxiety; (3) ability to empathize; (4) ability to adapt one's behaviour; and (5) ability to make accurate predictions and explanations. Ting-Toomey (1999), from the perspective of identity negotiation, emphasises more on establishing rapport and being accommodative in action through exercising mindfulness. The skills that she identifies are relation-oriented, which include: mindful observation; mindful listening; verbal empathy; non-verbal sensitivity; mindful stereotyping; constructive conflict skills; and flexible adaptive skills.

Conclusion

In this chapter, we reviewed some discussions on the conceptualisation and development of IC covering the issues of how IC as a theoretic construct has evolved and what the construct of IC is about in terms of its nature, its social and educational implications. The first part of this chapter showed the wide scope and the elusive nature of IC. The second part focused on the effort made in promoting IC. It further illustrated the complex nature of IC as a construct, showing how the concept has broadened and been elaborated along with our deepening understanding of the process and consequences of globalisation. As we can see, the wide scope and the elusive nature of IC make it very difficult to define the term IC in a concise and precise manner. Precisely for that reason, the teaching and assessment of such a competence has remained a challenging task and unless we can come to some agreement, they will remain problems in the future. In regard to assessment, Dana (2008) has pointed out that although developmental models have been created to describe the progression from ethnocentric to ethnorelative stages, insufficient empirical data have been accumulated to define the characteristics of each stage of the progression with any certainty. Furthermore, there is still a shortage of evaluation tools to measure intercultural competence (Van de Vijver and Breugelmans 2008).

Bibliography

Adler, P. S. 1998. Beyond cultural identity: reflections on multiculturalism. In *Basic Concepts of Intercultural Communication: Selected Readings*, ed. M. J. Bennett, 225-45. London: Intercultural Press.

Alred, G., M. Byram, and M. Fleming, eds. 2006. *Education for Intercultural Citizenship: Concepts and Comparisons*. Clevedon, England: Multilingual Matters.

Argyle, M. 1982. Intercultural Communication. In *Cultures in Contact - Studies in Cross-Cultural Interaction*, ed. S. Bochner, 61-79. Oxford: Pergamon Press.

Banks, J. A. 1998. Multicultural Education: Development, Dimensions, and Challenges. In *Basic Concepts of Intercultural Communication – Selected Readings*, ed. M. J. Bennett. London: Intercultural Press.

Begley, P. A. 2003. Sojourner Adaptation. In *Intercultural Communication: A Reader*, eds. L. A. Samovar and R. E. Porter, 406-412. London: Thomson Learning.

Bennett, M. J. 1993. Towards Ethnorelativism: A Developmental Model of Intercultural Sensitivity. In *Education for the Intercultural Experience*, ed. R. M. Paige, 21-72. Yarmouth: Intercultural Press.

—. 1998. Intercultural Communication: A Current Perspective. In *Basic Concepts of Intercultural Communication – Selected Readings*, ed. M. J. Bennett. London: Intercultural Press.

Berry, J. W. and D. L Sam. 1997. Acculturation and Adaptation. In *Handbook of Cross-Cultural Psychology – Social Behaviour and Applications* (second edition), ed, J. Berry. London: Allyn and Bacon.

Bochner, S. 1982. The social psychology of cross-cultural relations. In *Cultures in Contact: Studies in Cross-Cultural Interaction*, ed. S. Bochner, 5-44. Oxford: Pergamon.

Brislin, R. W. and W. J. Lonner 1972. Preface. In *Cross-Cultural Research Methods*, eds. R. W. Brislin et al, xi-xiii. London: John Wiley & Sons.

Brislin, R., D. Landis and M. Brandt. 1983. Conceptualizations of intercultural behaviour and training. In *Handbook of Intercultural Training*, eds. D. Landis and R.W. Brislin, Vol.1 1-35. Elmsford, NY. Pergamon.

Byram, M. 1997. *Teaching and Assessing Intercultural Communicative Competence*. Clevedon, England: Multilingual Matters.

—. 2008. *From Foreign Language Education to Education for Intercultural Citizenship – Essays and Reflections*. Clevedon, England: Multilingual Matters.

—. 2009. Intercultural competence in foreign languages. In *The Sage Handbook of Intercultural Competence*, ed. D.K. Deardorff, 321-332. London: Sage Publications.

Byram, M. and G. Zarate. 1997. Defining and assessment intercultural competence: some principles and proposals for the European context. *Language Teaching* 29, 14-18.

Dana, R. H. 2008. Transitions in Professional Training. In *Cultural Competency Training in a Global Society*, eds. R. H. Dana and J. Allen., 95-111. NY: Springer.

Dana, R. H. and J. Allen. 2008. Globalization: psychological problems and social needs. In *Cultural Competency Training in a Global Society*, eds. R.H. Dana and J. Allen, 25-42. NY: Springer.

Deardorff, D.K. 2006. Identification and Assessment of Intercultural Competence as a Student Outcome of Internalisation. *Journal of Studies in International Education* 10, no. 3, 241-266.

Dinges, N. 1983. Intercultural competence. In, *Handbook of intercultural training 1*, eds. D. Landis and R. W. Brislin. Elmsford, NY: Pergamon.

Furnham, A. and S. Bochner. 1986. *Cultural Shock: Psychological Reactions to Unfamiliar Environments*. London: Methuen.

Gamst, G., R. H. Dana, A. Der-Karabetian, M. Aragon, L. Arellano, G. Morrow, et al. 2004. Cultural competency revised: the California brief multicultural competence scale. *Measurement and Evaluation in Counselling & Development*. 37, no. 3, 163-183.

Gudykunst, W.B. 1998. *Bridging Differences - Effective Intergroup Communication*. London: Sage Publications.

Gudykunst, W. and M. H. Bond. 1997. Intergroup Relations across Cultures. In *Handbook of Cross-Cultural Psychology* Volume 3 – Social Behavior and Applications, eds. J. Berry, M. H. Segall, and C. Kagiçibasi. London: Allyn and Bacon.

Gudykunst, W.B. and Y.Y. Kim 2003. *Communicating with Strangers: An Approach to Intercultural Communication*. Boston: McGraw Hill.

Guilherme, M. 2002. *Critical Citizens for an Intercultural World: Foreign Language Education as Cultural Politics*. Clevedon: Multilingual Matters.

Hall, E. T. 1976. *Beyond Culture*. Garden City, NY: Doubleday Anchor.

— 1998. The Power of Hidden Differences. In *Basic Concepts of Intercultural Communication   Selected Readings*, ed. M. J. Bennett. London: Intercultural Press.

Hofstede, G. 1980. *Culture's Consequences: International Differences in Work-Related Values.* London: Sage Publications.

Horvath, A. 1997. Ethnocultural Identification and the Complexities of Ethnicity. In *Improving Intercultural Interactions – Modules for Cross-Cultural Training,* eds. K. Cushner, and R. W. Brislin. London: Sage Publications.

Jaspars, J. and M. Hewstone. 1982. Cross-Cultural Interaction, Social Attribution and Intergroup Relations. In *Cultures in Contact - Studies in Cross-Cultural Interaction,* ed. S. Bochner 127-156. Oxford: Pergamon Press.

Johnson, F.L. 2003. Cultural Dimensions of Discourse. In *Intercultural Communication: A Reader,* eds. L.A. Samovar and R.E. Porter, 184-197. London: Thomson Learning.

Kim, Y.Y. 2001. *Becoming Intercultural: An Integrative Theory of Communication and Cross-Cultural Adaptation.* London: Sage Publications.

Lantolf, J.P. 1999. Second culture acquisition: cognitive considerations. In *Culture in Second Language Teaching and Learning* (Cambridge Applied Linguistics), ed. E. Hinkel, 28-46. Cambridge: CUP.

Lund, R. E. 2008. Intercultural competence – an aim for the teaching of English in Norway? *Acta Didactica Norge* Vol. 2 Nr. 1Art.9, 1-16.

McCann, C.D. and E. T. Higgins. 1990. Social Cognition and Communication. In *Handbook of Language and Social Psychology,* eds. H. Giles and W.P. Robinson, 13-32. Chichester: John Wiley & Sons.

Operario, D. and S. T. Fiske. 2003. Stereotypes, Content, Structures, Processes, and Context. In *Blackwell Handbook of Social Psychology: Intergroup Processes,* eds. R. Brown and S. Gaertner, 22-44. Oxford: Blackwell Publishers.

Ruben, B. D. and D. J. Kealey. 1979. Behavioural Assessment of Communication Competency and the Prediction of Cross-Cultural Adaptation. *International Journal of Intercultural Relations* 3, 15-47.

Spitzberg, B.H. and W. R. Cupach, 1984. *Interpersonal Communication Competence.* London: Sage Publications.

Stephan, C.W. and W. G. Stephan. 1992. Reducing Intercultural Anxiety through Intercultural Contact. *International Journal of Intercultural Relations* 16, no. 1, 89-106.

Stephan, C.W. and W. G. Stephan. 2002. Cognition and Affect in Cross-Cultural Relations. In *Handbook of International and Intercultural Communication,* eds. W.B. Gudykunst and B. Mody, 127-142. London: Sage Publications.

Tajfel, H. 1978. Social Categorization, Social Identity, and Social Comparison. In *Differentiation between Social Groups*, ed. H. Tajfel 61-76. London: Academic.

—. 1981. *Human Groups and Social Categories-Studies in Social Psychology*. Cambridge: Cambridge University Press.

Ting-Toomey, S. 1985. Toward a Theory of Conflict and Culture. In *Communication, Culture and Organizational Processes*, eds. W.B. Gudykunst et al., 71-86. Beverly Hills, CA: Sage Publications.

—. 1999. *Communicating across Cultures.* London: Guilford Press.

Turner, J.C. 1982. Towards a Cognitive Redefinition of the Social Group. In *Social Identity and Intergroup Relations*, ed. H. Tajfel, 15-40. Cambridge: Cambridge University Press.

Turner, J.C. and K.J. Reynolds 2003. The Social Identity Perspective in Intergroup Relations: Theories, Themes, and Controversies. In *Blackwell Handbook of Social Psychology: Intergroup Processes*, eds. R. Brown and S. Gaertner, 133-152. Oxford: Blackwell Publishers.

Valdes, J.M. 1998. *Culture Bound: Bridging the Cultural Gap in Language Teaching.* Cambridge: CUP.

Van Dijk, T.A. 1990. Social Cognition and Discourse. In *Handbook of Language and Social Psychology*, eds. H. Giles and W.P. Robinson, 163-183. Chichester: John Wiley & Sons.

Van de Vijver, F. J. R. and S. M. Breugelmans. 2008. Research Foundations of Cultural Competence Training. In *Cultural Competency Training in a Global Society*, eds. R. H. Dana and J. Allen, 117-132. New York: Springer.

Van Oudenhoven, J.P. and K.I. Van der Zee. 2002. Predicting Multicultural Effectiveness of International Students: The Multicultural Personality Questionnaire. *International Journal of Intercultural Relations* 26, 679-694.

Weaver, H. N. 2008. Striving for Cultural Competence: Moving beyond Potential and Transforming the Helping Professions. In *Cultural Competency Training in a Global Society*, eds. R. H. Dana and J. Allen, 135-55. New York: Springer.

Wiseman, R.L. 2002. Cross-Cultural Face Concerns and Conflict Styles. In *Handbook of International and Intercultural Communication*, eds. W.B. Gudykunst and B. Mody, 207-224. London: Sage Publications.

CHAPTER THREE

CONSTRUCTING AND DECONSTRUCTING INTERCULTURALITY[1]

JOSEP M. COTS AND ENRIC LLURDA

Introduction

In English at least, the notion of *interculturality*, or *interculturalism*, as a *thing* or an *object* (represented by a noun) is much less common than the notion of it as a quality (represented by the adjective *intercultural*). Indeed, a quick check on Google at the time of submitting this paper (17th November 2009) gives us the following counts: 108,000 entries for *interculturality*, 83,100 for *interculturalism*, and 6,320,000 for *intercultural* [2]. It seems obvious, therefore, that the notion of interculturality is more often discussed as an attribute of either an individual (e.g. intercultural speaker, intercultural competence) or as a type of human activity (e.g. intercultural education, intercultural communication), than as an entity.

In this paper we want to look at interculturality as a discursive construction, that is, a particular way of representing the world and structuring an area of educational knowledge and practice. With this purpose in mind, we report on the process of construction and deconstruction of the notion of *interculturality* as an *object* of educational

---

[1] The research reported in this article was funded by the Spanish Ministry of Science and Technology (SEJ2004-06723-C02-02/EDUC) and the Ministry of Science and Innovation (FFI2008-00585/FILO). Besides the authors, the team involved in this specific part of the project included the following researchers: Amaia Ibarrarán, Montse Irún, David Lasagabaster and Juan Manuel Sierra.
[2] We consider *interculturality* and *interculturalism* as synonyms, but in this particular paper we have chosen to use the former, for the simple reason that it appeared most frequently on the web.

debate that we followed in the context of a study involving the design and administration of a questionnaire to a group of 253 pre- and in-service secondary education teachers in Catalonia, Spain. The questionnaire was intended to learn about the teachers' views and practices in connection with multilingual learning and use, and interculturality. The different items constituting the survey can be grouped into four topics: languages, language teaching, immigration and intercultural education.

The main focus of this paper will be on the 20 items of the questionnaire that dealt with the topic of interculturality. After a review of the literature in connection with possible definitions of *interculturality*, the main body of the paper will be devoted to (a) presenting the different items included in the survey as well as the results obtained, and (b) reflecting critically on the notion of interculturality underlying specific items of the survey, by confronting them with the discourse of a group of teachers of different languages that were taking part in an in-service seminar.

The ultimate goal of this paper is to engage in critical reflection about the research process and, more specifically, about the way in which a particular research tool or method may contribute to constructing a discourse about a sensitive issue like interculturality.

Defining Interculturality

In line with what we said in the introduction to this chapter, it is not easy to find in the literature definitions of the notion of *interculturality* as such. The only definition of the concept that we have found is by Trujillo (2002, 107), for whom "interculturality is defined as a critical participation in communication, being aware that the assumption of culture as a watertight compartment related to nation-states or certain social groups is a fallacy whereas diversity is the feature that characterises reality". However, it is significant that immediately after this definition, the author introduces the concept of "intercultural competence", where interculturality becomes an attribute of a certain type of human ability. For Trujillo (2002, 107-108), intercultural competence "represents the development of our cognitive environment motivated by the appreciation of diversity and the recognition of critical awareness and analysis as means of knowledge and communication in a complex society". It seems therefore that in order to trace the meaning of interculturality, we have to make do with the adjectival expression of the notion *intercultural*, which is mostly associated with two main fields of research: communication and education.

The notion of *intercultural communication* arises from the fact that in our contemporary societies, it is increasingly common to take part in or witness communicative situations in which, as Gumperz (1982) points out, individuals with different cultural backgrounds come into contact, with similar or different degrees of communicative competence. In these situations, the different cultural backgrounds can have an impact on several aspects of interpersonal communication (Kramsch 2001):

- Interactional behaviour; e.g. roles, expectations about norms of interaction and interpretation, strategies for negotiation of meaning.
- Non-verbal and para-verbal behaviour.
- Face-saving strategies.
- Patterns of discourse organisation and their relationship with communicative goals.
- The reflection of attitudes, values, beliefs about 'the other' on deeper discourses.
- Speech act realisation; e.g. requests, apologies, greetings, etc.

Spencer-Oatey and Franklin (2009) point out that the problem of defining intercultural communication as any communicative situation in which the participants are members of at least two social/cultural groups is that since people tend to be simultaneously members of several social/cultural groups, practically all communication could be defined as intercultural. Therefore, the authors opt for a definition which is based not on the adscription of the interlocutors but on the cognitive/communicative effect of the interaction: "An intercultural situation is one in which the cultural distance between the participants is significant enough to have an effect on interaction/communication that is noticeable to at least one of the parties" (Spencer-Oatey and Franklin 2009, 3).

In the field of language education (especially foreign languages), the notion of intercultural communication is presented as a goal and, at the same time, as a challenge that needs to be met by both teachers and learners through the development of *cultural awareness* (Kramsch 1993, Tomalin and Stempleski 1993, Risager 2000, Roberts et al. 2001) side by side with the acquisition of multilingual competence. It is in this sense that in works such as those by Byram (1997), Byram, Nichols and Stevens

(2001) or Sercu (2002), we find the concept of "intercultural communicative competence", referring to a pedagogic programme intended to educate (not just to train) people so that they "can cross borders and can mediate between two or more cultural identities" (Sercu 2002, 63). This programme, according to Byram (1997, 42), involves the development of different types of knowledge, skills and attitudes, in addition to linguistic competence, which should result in "an ability to decenter and take up the other's perspective on their own culture, anticipating and where possible resolving dysfunctions in communication and behaviour".

From the point of view of education, in a special issue of the journal Intercultural Education entitled *Theoretical Reflections on Intercultural Education*, Portera (2008, 5) admits that even though the concept of intercultural education appears very often in many types of educational documents in Europe, "there is an on-going failure to provide a clear semantic definition or distinct epistemological foundation for the concept" and teachers and those responsible for school politics often misunderstand its basic principles, with practices such as an exclusive focus on celebration of exotic cultures or an excessive emphasis on differences.

This author makes a distinction between *multicultural* or *pluricultural*, and *intercultural* education. Whereas multicultural/ pluricultural education aims to promote knowledge and tolerance of people with different cultural backgrounds who form part of the same socio-political unit (e.g. a school, a city, a country, etc.), the aim of intercultural education is to promote relationships, interaction and exchanges among people in a global society, where the notions of identity and culture are not considered as a given adscription but as dynamic attributes which are constructed and re-constructed in interaction with the *other* in the course of our lives. Abdallah-Preitceille (2006, 480) summarises the perspective of intercultural education by saying that rather than presenting culture as determinant of behaviour, the emphasis is on "the manner in which individuals use cultural traits to speak, to express themselves verbally, bodily, socially and personally" and, ultimately, to relate to their physical and social environment.

Investigating Interculturality among Secondary School Teachers

From 2004 to 2007 the authors, together with four other researchers, were committed to exploring ways of developing interculturality among secondary school teachers. One of the instruments used in the project was a questionnaire that was administered to a total of 253 teachers and teachers-in-training of different areas of knowledge. This was envisioned to be an important source of information regarding the perceptions of teachers of different characteristics (age, subject matter, location, mother tongue, etc.) regarding the issues of interculturality and multilingualism in the school setting. The study was conducted simultaneously in Catalonia and the Basque Autonomous Community, two different geographical areas of Spain that each have two official languages: Spanish and the local corresponding language, either Catalan or Basque. This situation means that all schools must offer classes in Spanish and the local language, plus at least one foreign language, which in more than 90% of secondary schools is English.

The results and implications, as well as the technicalities of the questionnaire, are presented in Llurda and Lasagabaster (forthcoming). The relevant notion here is that in order to investigate teachers' beliefs regarding interculturality, it was rather inevitable for us to construct the concept through the questions that were going to be included in our questionnaire. Necessarily, such questions would somehow determine the outcomes of our study and convey the researchers' perspective into the data. We could simply not ignore the fact that by constructing the questionnaire we were already co-constructing the answers.

Designing a Questionnaire as a Research Tool

In order to better understand the process of questionnaire construction, we will describe here the different steps we took before reaching the final version that was used in our study. Since our focus was on the conceptualisation of interculturality in an educational context, it seemed logical to start looking into the literature dealing with aspects of intercultural education to find ideas that might turn useful in eliciting responses from teachers. In addition to the standard literature on intercultural communicative competence (including Byram 1997, 2000; Byram, Nichols and Stevens 2001; Sercu et al. 2005) a particularly rich source of inspiration was Jordán's (1994) work on the multicultural school, one chapter of which is specifically devoted a study on teachers' beliefs which the author himself carried out in Catalonia at a time when multicultural education was beginning to be felt as a need.

The questionnaire was part of a bigger project on the development of intercultural competence in secondary schools. This project also included a series of seminars with in-service teachers aimed at designing activities that promoted intercultural communicative competence among secondary school students in three curricular languages in schools in Catalonia: Catalan, Spanish and English. The seminar group, composed of two researchers and six language teachers (teaching a total of three different languages: Catalan, Spanish and English) met on five different occasions and discussed on issues pertaining to the broad area of interculturality. Those sessions were video-recorded and transcribed. The analysis of the transcripts provided relevant information about the topics those teachers were concerned about, and what they thought were the hot issues in dealing with interculturality in their classrooms.

Alongside the focus on teachers, the research project also aimed at investigating secondary school students' attitudes towards interculturality and the different languages that were present in the school setting. As with teachers, the methodology used with students was partly qualitative and partly quantitative. The latter involved a questionnaire, which shared some questions with the questionnaire implemented with teachers for the purposes of comparison. Some of those questions had been adapted from widely-used questionnaires on language attitudes (Baker 1992, Huguet and Llurda 2001, Lasagabaster 2003), and others had been simply created ad hoc by the researchers. Those questions reflected predetermined categories or aspects that the researchers felt strongly that they needed to be researched.

To sum up, the questionnaire was designed from an initial pool of questions that came from three different sources: external authoritative sources (bibliography, previous questionnaires), teachers' voices, and researchers predetermined interests and categorisations. That pool constituted the base from which the questionnaire was drafted, piloted and finally implemented. Questions dealt with personal data, use of languages, the perceived importance of different foreign languages, views on language teaching and learning, attitudes towards the languages present in the curriculum as well as the mother tongue of immigrant students, and beliefs about interculturality and intercultural practices in school, which is the focus of our current critical deconstructing approach to the construction of the concept of interculturality (see Table 3-1).

Table 3-1: The 20 items of the questionnaire dealing with interculturality and intercultural practices

Item 1: Schools should promote interculturality.
Item 2: Students should end up their Secondary Education with a good command of Basque/Catalan, Spanish and two foreign languages.
Item 3: It is necessary to accept that our society is ever more multicultural.
Item 4: Schools are the best place to promote the acceptance of interculturality in our society.
Item 5: Schools must respect their students' different cultures and identities.
Item 6: Our schools have enough means to work on interculturality.
Item 7: Language subjects (Basque/Catalan, Spanish, English, etc.) should establish connections and comparisons among them.
Item 8: The development of positive attitudes towards languages should be given more importance.
Item 9: Apart from English as a subject, this language should also be used to teach content.
Item 10: Immigration has had a negative impact on our students' language results.
Item 11: Interculturality should be dealt with in the language classes.
Item 12: Language Departments (Basque/Catalan, Spanish, and foreign languages) should coordinate themselves.
Item 13: Interculturality should be worked on in primary education above all, as all the efforts in secondary education should be devoted to deepening contents.
Item 14: It is necessary to adapt contents and teaching methods to these days.
Item 15: The learning of foreign languages fosters a wider view of the world.
Item 16: In the language classes more heed should be paid to written than spoken language.
Item 17: Former students were better than current students.
Item 18: Those who completed their secondary education before had a greater knowledge of languages.
Item 19: The more languages taught in secondary education, the worse the language competence attained in each of them.
Item 20: All teachers are responsible for the students' language competence, irrespective of the subject they have to teach.

Analysing the Questionnaire Results

The questionnaire was implemented with 253 teachers from two different cities, Lleida and Vitoria-Gasteiz, located in two different bilingual areas in Spain. Llurda and Lasagabaster (forthcoming) analysed the results of the questions dealing with interculturality in three different phases. First, they looked at the opinions expressed by the global sample in terms of whether they were mostly favourable, unfavourable or neutral regarding each of the items. A noteworthy result was that the highest rate of agreement occurred with items that referred to the importance of foreign language learning and the need to adapt current views and behaviours to an increasingly multicultural society. For instance, 95.6% of respondents agreed that "it is necessary to accept that our society is ever more multicultural" (item 3), 91.7% agreed that "schools should promote interculturality" (item 1), and 91.2% agreed that "the development of positive attitudes towards languages should be given more importance" (item 8). Conversely, those items that were presented in a negative sense, or which did not imply a positive conception of interculturality, were mostly disagreed upon. For instance, 68% of respondents disagreed with the idea that "those who completed their secondary education before had a greater knowledge of languages" (item 18), and 71.5% disagreed that "in the language classes more heed should be paid to written than spoken language" (item 16).

A second phase of data analysis involved performing a factor analysis that allowed researchers to cluster the different items in the questionnaire into the following six thematically related groups: (1) views towards the role to be played by schools regarding interculturality; (2) teachers' beliefs concerning their students' language competence and language teaching; (3) the coordination between the different languages and the work on the affective dimension of language learning; (4) the moment and situation in which interculturality has to be dealt with, and the effect of immigration on academic results; (5) expectations regarding language teaching in school; and (6) the perceived lack of resources in schools.

Finally, the third phase involved an ANOVA on the responses by the different groups of teachers in the study with the purpose of obtaining significant differences among those groups. With this idea in mind, teachers' responses were given a numerical value (1=totally agree; 5=totally disagree) and the responses were classified according to the following categories: (1) teaching experience (pre-service vs. in-service);

(2) mother tongue (Catalan vs. Spanish) (3) gender; (4) age (either older or younger than 40); and (5) subject taught (languages vs. other subjects). Although we expected pre-service teachers to have more positive views of intercultural issues, due to a hypothetical greater exposure to an intercultural discourse in their training, our results did not support such a claim, and the differences found between the two groups were more on a *practical-idealistic* dimension: pre-service teachers seemed to favour more idealistic views, whereas in-service teachers showed a more practical perspective on education. Thus, pre-service teachers were more in favour of maximalist principles such as the statement in item 2, "Students should end up their secondary education with a good command of Catalan/Basque, Spanish, and two foreign languages" as well as the statement in item 4, claiming that "schools are the best place to promote the acceptance of multiculturalism in our society", which in a rather paradoxical way combined with their preference for idea expressed in item 10 that immigration has had a negative impact on education. Experienced teachers, on the other hand, placed the emphasis more on more feasible and down-to-earth aspects, such as the need for teachers of different languages to work in a coordinated manner.

Another unexpected result came when we observed that L1 speakers of Catalan and Basque showed a somewhat defensive attitude against work involving interculturality, whereas Spanish L1 speakers were more in favour of it. Catalan and Basque L1 speakers appeared somewhat afraid of the consequences of immigration on the social use of their mother tongue, and were pre-emptively reacting to the idea that new languages and cultures may become part of the school curriculum. This was evident, for example, when they showed stronger agreement to the ideas that "immigration has had a negative impact on our students' language results" and "interculturalism should be worked on in primary education above all, as all the efforts in secondary education should be devoted to deepening contents". Gender did not yield any conclusive results, so we could not make any claims regarding differences between male and female teachers. Age yielded a clear pattern of results, which indicated that the older generation of teachers were more supportive of intercultural practices than younger ones, and the same happened with the "subject taught" variable, as language teachers were clearly more in favour of an intercultural approach than teachers of other subjects.

Problematising Interculturality as a Research Construct

Having presented a brief overview of some of the questionnaire results, we would like to take a step back and examine from a critical perspective the extent to which the research instrument we used, the questionnaire, can be subjected to a critical analysis. Our aim in this part of the study is to reflect upon the ambiguities of interculturality as a construct in educational research. We carry out this reflection by (a) focusing on the understanding of interculturality that can be derived from the twenty items included in question 14 in the questionnaire, and (b) confronting this particular way of understanding interculturality with elements of the discourse of language teachers, as constructed in the context of a series of seminars.

Following Green (1996, 72), we define presupposition as a proposition "whose truth is taken for granted in the utterance of a linguistic expression". There are two basic properties of presuppositions that are especially relevant when considering the limitations of a research instrument involving a series of statements with which readers are asked to express their degree of agreement/disagreement. The first of these properties is "constancy under negation" (Yule 1996, 26), which refers to the fact that a presupposition derived from a statement will remain true even if the original statement is denied. Thus, a statement like "schools should promote interculturality" presupposes the existence of something called *interculturality*. Even if we do not agree at all with that statement (i.e. schools should not promote interculturality"), the existence of *interculturality* is not questioned. In our case, this means that respondents are forced to admit that interculturality is something known to them and that they have a formed opinion about it. The second property of presuppositions relevant to our questionnaire is "defeasibility", which refers to the fact that "they are liable to evaporate in certain contexts, either immediate linguistic context or the less immediate discourse context, or in circumstances where contrary assumptions are made" (Levinson 1983, 186). The fact that the different items in the questionnaire are presented as isolated, decontextualised statements makes it impossible for their presuppositions to be further specified by the researchers, or questioned by the respondents.

One of the clearest presuppositions emerging from the twenty items is that of the existence of a social/educational phenomenon that we refer to as *interculturality*. This is evident in items 1, 4, 6, 11, 13 in statements in which the term "interculturality" is preceded by the definite article "the", which marks it as "something which can be identified uniquely in the contextual or general knowledge shared by speakers and hearer" (Greenbaum and Quirk 1990, 77).

After accepting its existence, the next problem respondents may have to face with *interculturality* is the definition of a somewhat abstract phenomenon as a *thing* (represented by a noun) rather than as a quality (represented by an adjective). As mentioned in sections 1 and 2 above, the latter is the most frequent way in which it appears, as is the case of expressions like "intercultural education" (Generalitat de Catalunya 1996), "intercultural competence" (Lustig and Koester 2005), "intercultural communication" (Scollon and Scollon 1995) or "intercultural discourse" (Kiesling and Paulston 2005). In order to search for a possible definition of interculturality, we could think of it as the quality of being intercultural, and we could then adopt the following definition of "intercultural speaker" suggested by Byram, Nichols and Stevens (2001, 5): "someone who has an ability to interact with 'others', to accept other perspectives and perceptions of the world, to mediate between different perspectives, to be conscious of their evaluations of difference". At this level of generalisation, it might not be easy for a (pre- or in-service) teacher-respondent, who has barely heard of the term, to imagine what interculturality involves from the point of view of education, in terms of the three basic elements in a pedagogic programme: knowledge, skills, and attitudes.

The fact that the notion of interculturality is often presented as an attribute of either an individual (e.g. intercultural speaker, intercultural competence) or a human activity (e.g. intercultural education, intercultural communication) allows its users to specify what they mean by concentrating on the individual or the activity itself, and by introducing particular ways of being or of doing something. In the case of the questionnaire employed in this study, this process of specification of what is meant by interculturality can be summarised into five main ideas that can be derived from the different items included in the questionnaire: (i) multilingualism, (ii) acceptance of cultural diversity, (iii) promoted through education, (iv) development of attitudes, and (v) a trans-curricular issue.

Multilingualism is present through items 2, 11, 15, 18, 19, all of which stress the importance of knowing more than one language; furthermore, items 11 and 15 suggest a possible association between languages and "interculturality" or a possibly related notion of a "more open-minded world view". Acceptance of cultural diversity can be found in items 3, 4, and 5, including the verbs "accept", "promote" or "respect" associated with the adjective "multicultural" or the noun "interculturality" or the noun phrase "different cultures". The idea that the educational system is a potential agent for promoting interculturality can be considered as a presupposition behind items 4, 6, 11, 13, which is especially true of the last three items, for which a denial of the proposition does not affect the basic presupposition. We can cite item 6 as an example: "Our schools have enough means to work on interculturality". In this case, even if we negate the proposition ("Our schools **do not have** enough means to work on interculturality"), the implicit presupposition that the school is responsible for the promotion of interculturality is not denied. The notion of interculturality involving attitudes appears explicitly only in item 8, but we consider that it is implicit in item 4, through the presence of the term "acceptance", and in item 15, through the expression "open-minded world view". Finally, the trans-curricular nature of interculturality is present in items 1, 4, 5, 6, 9, 11, 12, 20, which is achieved by the inclusion of collective agents: 'school' (items 1, 4, 5, 6), 'English plus some other contents subject' (item 9), 'lessons on languages' (item 11), 'departments of languages' (item 12), and 'all the teaching staff' (item 20).

These five ideas can be considered the components of interculturality, or one of the research constructs used in the questionnaire design. In order to attempt to understand the possible problems that respondents to the questionnaire may face in relation to the items dealing with the notion of interculturality, we are going to explore the discourse around these ideas as articulated by a group of eight secondary school language teachers, including teachers of Catalan, Spanish and English, who took part in an in-service training seminar aimed at developing and implementing materials around the notion of intercultural communicative competence (Byram 1997).

The teachers' discourse on multilingualism tends to be based on the idea that teaching Catalan or Spanish (first or second languages) is very different from teaching English (a foreign language). Therefore it is difficult for them to accept the idea of working together on some kind of common language learning programme. They also believe in the transfer of communicative competence from the first language onto other languages that are learnt later (Cummins 1979, Cummins and Swain

1986). They are aware of the gap between spoken and written language, and acknowledge that the school gives priority to written language and the idea of correctness, at the expense of communicative effectiveness, and that they still do not know very well how to assess spoken language. Bearing these ideas in mind, it is possible to understand one teacher's view that secondary school students are not competent in either their first or second language. Finally, there is some scepticism about the results of pedagogic action by the schools in terms of the development of communicative competence, as one teacher expresses her belief that children learn the language more in the street than in the school. These aspects of teachers' discourse on multilingualism may bring to question certain aspects of the items in the questionnaire dealing with multilingualism and language competence. Thus, the verb "speak a language" in item 2 may be ambiguous for teachers in terms of whether it refers strictly to spoken language or to the traditional definition of linguistic competence used by the school, and which includes spoken but especially written language. A similar case of ambiguity appears in item 18 with the notion of "knowledge of languages" and, in general, with those items including the notion of "linguistic competence" (19, 20) or "general performance" (10).

The idea of acceptance of cultural diversity, as a characteristic of interculturality also appears in the teachers' discourse, especially in the case of the foreign language teachers, for whom this is an essential premise of their work, which can already be seen in their teaching materials. For the teachers of Catalan and Spanish, this is not so obvious and they admit that their materials do not yet include much cultural diversity, in contrast to what happens with the English materials. They all admit that cultural diversity has entered their classrooms through the back door because the student population is already very diverse, and that students have adapted to it very well. However, some of them acknowledge that teachers have not adapted to this diversity, and they still teach as if they had culturally homogenous groups. One of the problems that may be derived from this discourse when confronting items on acceptance of cultural diversity (3, 4, 5, 15) may be related to the uncertainty on the part of the teachers about whether this acceptance requires specific action, or whether it simply involves a business-as-usual/laissez-faire attitude. Item 15 also implies that this may be an exclusive responsibility of foreign language teachers.

Questionnaire items 4, 6, 11 and 14 suggest that the promotion of interculturality is one of the responsibilities of the school. It is also suggested that this institution needs to adapt to a new social and cultural situation in which the student population has diversified, and the educational system not only has to deal with this diversity but also promote its acceptance. In front of this necessary adaptation, we find a discourse of resistance by the teachers. Thus, one of them sees it as implicitly involving a reduction of the traditional language curricula and, therefore, as incompatible with the upholding of academic standards. This same teacher expresses his view that the school cannot constantly adapt to the specific needs or demands of the students, and that while there are things that can be learnt outside the school, there is an important body of traditional academic knowledge, which is also useful and needs to be preserved. Another teacher considers that the promotion of interculturality is one of many new social responsibilities that have been assigned to the school, and that it is difficult for the teachers to cope with all of these new duties for which they have not been trained. We can see, therefore, that it is not at all clear that teachers may accept the assumption that interculturality is part of the curriculum side by side with traditional academic knowledge.

Attitudes play a key role in the definition of interculturality. Thus, Byram, Nichols and Stevens (2001, 5) associate interculturality with accepting "other perspectives and perceptions of the world", and the teachers who participated in the seminar also identified "respect towards other cultures" as being one of the implications of incorporating interculturality in their teaching. It is for this reason that the questionnaire includes two items in which the notion of attitude appears: 8 and 15 (in the latter, it is represented by the noun phrase "view of the world"). In the teachers' discourse, attitudes in the context of education are constructed as a somewhat elusive long-term goal which escapes any attempt to measure the impact of specific pedagogical action, as may be the case with the acquisition of specific types of knowledge or certain procedures. It is also acknowledged that, although the development of attitudes is always present in the design of the curricula, it plays a very minor role when it comes to their implementation. Taking the teachers' discourse into account, the responses to questionnaire items 8 and 15 may be interpreted as navigating in the ambiguity of the political correctness of having to pay lip-service to the role of attitudes in education and, at the same time, showing scepticism about the short-term impact of pedagogical action on attitudinal development.

The last component of the definition of interculturality that permeates the questionnaire is the idea that it is an educational issue that affects the curriculum as a whole and, as a consequence, it is not a responsibility that can be assigned to one of the curricular subjects. This can be seen in items 1, 4, 5, 6, in which the subject is "the school", and in items 9, 11, 12 and 20, in which interculturality is presented as the result of joint efforts from different curricular subjects, especially languages. The teachers' discourse in this case reflects again a somewhat sceptical attitude towards the real impact of trans-curricular actions initiated by the school or by the Department of Education. Although they think it unfortunate, they admit that it is very difficult, not to say impossible, to get language departments to collaborate and that, in general, languages are taught independently of each other. This is consistent with the idea expressed by a teacher of Spanish that teaching Catalan or Spanish has nothing to do with teaching English, and that they share very little in terms of goals and methods. This opinion is contested by a foreign language teacher for whom all the language subjects at secondary level should be academically organised into a single department.

Conclusion

The aim of this article is to reflect upon the ambiguities of interculturality as a construct in educational research. We did this by (a) focusing on the understanding of interculturality derived from a series of questionnaire items, and (b) confronting this particular way of understanding interculturality with some elements of the discourse of language teachers, as constructed in the context of a series of seminars.

The reflections presented in this paper lead us to draw a series of conclusions that bear special significance for future research. The first idea that needs to be emphasised is the fact that 'interculturality' is in itself a construct that we, among others, according to Portera (2008), have used and exploited without a sound semantic or epistemological grounding, without paying sufficient heed to the particular limitations of the method of research used for that purpose. In this chapter, we have shown how we have moved from one particular method, based on a quantitative analysis of the results obtained from a series of questions responded by pre-service and in-service teachers, to a reconsideration of the research premises using a qualitative discourse-analytic approach to the protagonists' voices, that is, the teachers who discussed the issue of interculturality in a series of seminars that dealt with it from different perspectives. Those voices supply a unique lens through which we can further understand the specific results obtained through the quantitative analysis of the responses given to the questionnaire. This reflection on the process of construction of a questionnaire on interculturality, and its subsequent deconstruction, shows us the need to work hand in hand with all the resources that are provided by different research traditions (Cots, Llurda and Irún 2008).

Teachers' voices add another relevant dimension to our study, which is the need to complement the emic perspective of the researchers with the etic perspectives of the practitioners. Interculturality, as a construct, needs to be co-elaborated by researchers and teachers, or it will risk becoming irrelevant as its connections with teacher experience are lost. The teachers' voices remind researchers of Lincoln and Guba's (1985, 37) axioms for naturalistic inquiry that realities are multiple and constructed according to contextual circumstances, which makes it difficult to make context-free generalisations.

Finally, underlying the exercise we have proposed for this section is the post-modern idea that the social world is the result of a multiplicity of permanent discursive constructions which can (and must) be contested. For applied linguistics, this view involves researchers problematising their own practices and the notions on which research projects are based. By showing how we constructed a questionnaire and how this questionnaire fares once it is confronted with teachers' own voices, we are exposing some of the limitations in our own study, but at the same time we are contributing to a higher level of understanding of research practice in applied linguistics. This idea is expressed by Pennycook (2001, 171-172) as one of the guiding principles that should be followed in order to make applied linguistics critical: "(…) a restive problematization of the given, (,,,) a constant questioning of our assumptions both within and beyond applied linguistics. (…) a way of thinking that is always reflective about itself, aware of the limits of knowing".

Bibliography

Abdallah-Preitceille, M. 2006. Interculturalism as a paradigm for thinking about diversity. *Intercultural Education* 17, no. 5: 475-483.

Baker, C. 1992. *Attitudes and language.* Clevedon, England: Multilingual Matters.

Byram, M. 1997. *Teaching and assessing intercultural communicative competence.* Clevedon, England: Multilingual Matters.

—. 2000. *Assessing intercultural competence in language teaching.* Sprogforum 18: 8-13.

Byram, M., A. Nichols and D. Stevens. 2001. *Developing intercultural competence in practice.* Clevedon, England: Multilingual Matters.

Cots, J. M., E. Llurda and M. Irún. 2008. Perspectivas de investigación en torno a la ideología lingüística del profesorado de lenguas de secundaria. In *Miradas y voces: Investigación sobre la educatión lingüística y literaria en entornos plurilingües,* ed. A. Camps and M. Milian, 61-74. Barcelona: Graó.

Cummins, J. 1979. Linguistic interdependence and the educational development of bilingual children. *Review of Educational Research* 49, 2: 222-251.

Cummins, J. and M. Swain. 1986. *Bilingualism in education.* New York: Longman.

Generalitat de Catalunya. 1996. *Educació intercultural.* Barcelona: Departament d'Ensenyament, Generalitat de Catalunya.

Green, G. 1996. *Pragmatics and natural language learning.* Mahwah, New Jersey: Lawrence Erlbaum.

Greenbaum, S., and R. Quirk. 1990. *A student's grammar of the English language.* Harlow, England: Longman.

Gumperz, J. 1982. *Discourse strategies.* Cambridge: Cambridge University Press.

Huguet, A. and E. Llurda. 2001. Language attitudes of school children in two Catalan/Spanish bilingual communities. *International Journal of Bilingual Education and Bilingualism* 4, no. 4: 267-282.

Jordán, J.A.1994. *La escuela multicultural: Un reto para el profesorado.* Barcelona: Paidós.

Kiesling, S., and C. Paulston. 2005. *Intercultural discourse and communication.* Oxford: Blackwell.

Kramsch, C. 1993. *Context and culture in language teaching.* Oxford: Oxford University Press.

—. 2001. Intercultural communication. In *The Cambridge Guide to Teaching English to Speakers of Other Languages*, eds. R. Carter and D. Nunan, 201-226. Cambridge: Cambridge University Press.

Lasagabaster, D. 2003. *Trilingüismo en la enseñanza. Actitudes hacia la lengua minoritaria, la mayoritaria y la extranjera.* Lleida: Milenio.

Levinson, S. 1983. *Pragmatics.* Cambridge: Cambridge University Press.

Lincoln, Y., and E. Guba. 1985. *Naturalistic inquiry.* Newbury Park, California: Sage.

Llurda, E. and D. Lasagabaster. An analysis of factors affecting teachers' beliefs about interculturalism. *International Journal of Applied Linguistics* (forthcoming).

Lustig, M., and J. Koester. 2005. *Intercultural competence: Interpersonal communication across cultures.* Boston: Allyn & Bacon.

Pennycook, A. 2001. *Critical applied linguistics.* Mahwah: Lawrence Erlbaum.

Portera, A. 2008. Intercultural education in Europe: epistemological and semantic aspects. *Intercultural Education* 19, no. 6: 481-491.

Risager, K. 2000. Cultural awareness. In *Routledge Encyclopedia of Foreign Language Teaching and Learning*, ed. M. Byram, 159-162. London: Routledge.

Roberts, C., M. Byram, A. Barro, S. Jordan, and B. Street. 2001. *Language Learners as Ethnographers.* Clevedon, England: Multilingual Matters.

Scollon, R., and S. Scollon. 1995. *Intercultural communication.* Oxford: Blackwell.

Sercu, L. 2002. Autonomous learning and the acquisition of intercultural communicative competence: Some implications for course development. *Language, Culture and Curriculum* 15, 1: 61-74.

Sercu, L., E. Bandura, P. Castro, L. Davcheva, C. Laskaridou, U. Lundgren, C. Méndez, and P. Ryan. 2005. *Foreign language teachers and intercultural competence: An international investigation.* Clevedon, England: Multilingual Matters.

Spencer-Oatey, H. and P. Franklin. 2009. *Intercultural interaction: A multidisciplinary approach to intercultural communication.* Basingstoke: Palgrave Macmillan.

Tomalin, B. and S. Stempleski. (1993). *Cultural awareness.* Oxford: Oxford University Press.

Trujillo, F. 2002. *Towards interculturalism through language teaching: Argumentative discourse.* Cauce, Revista de Filología y su Didáctica 25: 103-119.

Yule, G. 1996. *Pragmatics.* Oxford: Oxford University Press.

CHAPTER FOUR

BECOMING INTERCULTURAL:
A COMPARATIVE ANALYSIS OF NATIONAL
EDUCATION POLICIES

LYNNE PARMENTER

Introduction

The chapters so far in this book have provided various perspectives on the theories and practices of becoming intercultural. In this chapter, the focus turns to policies. The aim is to examine how intercultural aspects are treated in a variety of national education policy and curriculum documents, and to relate policy and curriculum statements to some of the theories discussed in earlier chapters. Education policy and curriculum documents from a range of countries in the Asia-Pacific region, Europe, Africa and the American region will be used for the purposes of analysis.

After a brief introduction to relevant theories of policy and curriculum, and a description of methodology, the main part of the chapter will be devoted to policy and curriculum analysis, discussing themes such as the prevalence of intercultural aspects in national policy and curriculum documents, rationales provided for becoming intercultural, the scope of interculturality, what it means to be intercultural and how this is to be achieved. It is hoped that this analysis will provide one comparative macro view of some of the current approaches to the intercultural dimension in education policy in a variety of political, social and cultural contexts.[1]

---

[1] Thanks to Mike Byram for comments on an earlier draft of this chapter.

National Policies and Curricula

Analysing education policy and curriculum documents is one way of exploring the link between theory and practice in a specific area of education. Education policy is a multi-faceted, multi-level, complex process, which is subject to negotiation at every turn (Bell and Stevenson 2006). At the same time, the products of these processes at the national level – Strategic Plans, Curriculum Frameworks, Courses of Study and the like – serve as a reflection not only of official knowledge (Apple 2003, 7), but also as a statement of official competences and values. These are the competences and values legitimised by the state as desirable, worthwhile, and to be aimed for. In the same way that official knowledge is increasingly being regulated through standardisation of outcomes (Young 2009, 11), officially sanctioned competences and values are increasingly being made explicit in national policies and curricula through *visions, statements of values* and *profiles of the learner*. For the purposes of this chapter, policy statements, plans, national curricula and nationally-authorized plans of study were used for analysis. There are obvious differences between policy and curriculum, but at the national level, both are used to provide explicit statements of officially validated competences and values, and it was these statements that were the subject of analysis.

This link between theory, policy and practice is made even more complex at the policy level by the introduction of *desirable* political discourses, which may or may not have anything to do with education. National level policy and curriculum documents are only one product of the highly complex policy process and, as Taylor et al (1997) point out, even analysis of the text is far from straightforward, as texts are open to interpretation and can say as much by what they leave out as by what they contain. The analysis of policy and curriculum documents in this chapter therefore makes no claim to represent what actually happens in schools, or to judge which theories of becoming intercultural are valid or workable. Neither does it make any attempt to analyse the processes of policy-making, nor the ways in which they are negotiated at various levels from the state to the individual classroom. It does not even manage to analyse the texts to the depth of examining what is left out in particular national contexts.

What the analysis in this chapter can show is which theories of becoming intercultural are influential at government level, and which aspects and approaches are promoted as desirable and officially validated.

The point of this analysis is to gain a macro view of global trends in official educational discourses of the intercultural. The ever-deepening relationship between globalisation and education requires this kind of view, in addition to in-depth analysis of specific local and national contexts. As Baker (2009, 958) has stated, "All policy issues are global". This is an observation supported by the analysis in this chapter, and by recent literature on influence of globalisation on education. Mok (2006, 18) provides a succinct summary:

> A close scrutiny of comparative education literature has well documented that there seems to have been a convergence of curricula on a global scale. International organizations such as UNESCO, the World Bank, the OECD, and research institutes such as the IEA, by virtue of their recommendations, funding power, and cross-national comparisons have inevitably influenced the way curricula are designed and changed the mindsets of education ministries in different parts of the globe. It is remarkable that reform rhetoric is becoming increasingly similar across different education jurisdictions: all education reform proposals talk about the importance of competition, global competence, diversity and choice, etc. ...

Again, closer analysis of these processes of convergence is a fascinating topic of research, but is beyond the scope of this chapter. For the purposes of this discussion of being intercultural, it is sufficient to note that global trends are having a significant impact on national education policies, not only in the well-publicised arena of academic standards, but also in the field of competences and values. As Rizvi and Lingard (2010: 8-9) comment:

> ...above all, policies are designed to ensure consistency in the applications of authorized norms and values across various groups and communities: they are designed to build consent, and may also have an educative purpose.

This applies at a whole range of levels, from local to global.

Access to nationally-sanctioned views of desirable competences and values has become remarkably easy in recent years, as more and more policy and curriculum documents are made available to the public through national Ministry of Education websites, databases of policy and curriculum documents maintained by UNESCO institutions such as the International Bureau of Education and the International Institute for Educational Planning, or databases of documents collected in regional initiatives, such as PADDLE, the Pacific Archive of Digital Data for Learning and Education.[2]

For the analysis in this chapter, websites of the Ministries of Education or associated government bodies for a total of 162 countries were located and searched. In cases where national policy/curriculum does not exist, regional or state bodies were used. Not all the websites provided access to information about education policies and curricula concerning being intercultural. There is also a language issue at various levels, as Ministries of Education have their own policies about what information to publish in what language. As with any act of publication, different information and perspectives are provided for different audiences. Some of the documents used in the analysis, for example, were education strategy plans written in or translated into English or French for an international audience, including donors from major international organizations such as the World Bank. These are quite different from national syllabi written for teachers and materials developers within the country, usually in the national or official language, but are treated together in this analysis as both provide a view of the official or authorised position of the education authorities on issues related to interculturalism. In practical terms, information available in English, French, Spanish, German, Portuguese and Japanese was accessed in the original languages, while information in other languages was translated.

Relevant information was found for a total of 65 countries. Geographically, the distribution was 10 countries in Africa, 13 in Asia, 20 in Europe, 15 in the Americas and 7 in Oceania. Relevant data were extracted from policy and curriculum documents in these countries and coded, and then themes were elicited, using standard qualitative data analysis methods (Creswell 2008, 243-266). Categories were then grouped into themes. Five major themes emerged, which can be broadly summarised in simple terms as (1) whether to be intercultural, (2) why to be intercultural, (3) the scope of being intercultural, (4) what being intercultural involves, and (5) teaching approaches to becoming

---

[2] The International Bureau of Education website (http://www.ibe.unesco.org/ en.html) provides links to information by country, including country profiles and curricular resources where available. The International Institute for Educational Planning (http://planipolis.iiep.unesco.org/basic_search.php) provides links to education plans, policies and reports by type or by country. PADDLE (http://www. paddle.usp.ac.fj/) provides a searchable database of education information on 15 Pacific Island countries.

intercultural. These five themes form the structure of the rest of the chapter, and will be treated in turn.

Throughout the analysis, the term *intercultural* and associated terms, such as *pluricultural* and *multicultural* were taken at face value as they appeared in documents. This means that the use of the term throughout this chapter tends to be imprecise, as it is used in so many different contexts and ways. Closer analysis of the exact meaning of the term in specific national contexts would be valuable, but is beyond the scope of this chapter.

To Be or Not To Be Intercultural

As mentioned in the previous section, this analysis was not designed to identify the silences of education policy and curriculum documents. In this case, only those documents which addressed intercultural issues were used as data for analysis, and in the vast majority of cases, documents addressing the issue of being intercultural did so in a positive way. In a few cases, reservations or ambivalence were apparent in the documents. The clearest case was from Saudi Arabia, where the 2004-2014 Ten Year Plan identified one of the challenges facing education as "the cultural invasion and its results", emphasising the need to adopt:

> ...a balanced approach that will allow students to enjoy the benefits of modern technology (which, in turn, will benefit the community) while maintaining the Kingdom's values and faith, and that is able to protect them from the risks that might harm them as individuals and groups and that might negatively affect Muslim society. (Kingdom of Saudi Arabia Ministry of Education 2005)

While not as explicitly stated, this issue of how to maintain the balance between the influence of other cultures and traditional cultural values and practices also appears occasionally in other countries, the Cook Islands being one example:

> The benefit of a more global understanding is significant for Cook Islands students as most are destined to travel and live in other countries and their own country is a significant tourist destination where people of many cultures come together. As the prospect of globalisation of culture and economy increases, awareness becomes the greatest means of protection for Cook Islands cultural independence. (Cook Islands Ministry of Education 2006)

In both cases, the significant term *protect* is used with implications of a cultural threat to the national culture. With a resident population of about 20,000, the Cook Islands has about three times as many nationals living overseas than on the Islands, and over four times as many annual tourists than residents (Cook Islands Government undated). In terms of context and scale, therefore, the Cook Islands are very different from Saudi Arabia, but the perception of cultural threat is shared, and ambivalence about the role of education in welcoming but *protecting* students from other cultures is apparent.

Although this kind of ambivalence is observable, it is only found explicitly in a handful of countries. In the policies and curricula of the majority of countries represented in this analysis, the concept of becoming intercultural was embraced wholeheartedly as positive and necessary. In global terms, it seems that the general trend in education policy has gone beyond *whether* to issues of *why* and *how*.

Why Be Intercultural?

Most documents dealing with interculturality, however it is defined, provided some rationale for its inclusion in policy or the curriculum. In broad terms, these rationales could be categorised into four main groups, namely, social ideals, political ideals, individual identity development and national interests.

By far the most common rationale given for educating students to be intercultural in the documents analysed was the social ideals of peace, betterment of humanity, social justice and sustainability. Among the constant international clamour about national standards, falling achievement, league tables, competition and short-term outcomes, the fact that policy/curriculum documents in at least 33 out of the 65 countries still include such ideals as an overarching rationale for intercultural education is reassuring for those who believe that education has a vital role in creating a better world (Boulding 1990, Freire 2004). Furthermore, these ideals are found as a rationale for intercultural learning in every region of the world. One example is the curriculum design document for initial (pre-school) education in Bolivia. One of the two key principles of this curriculum is intercultural education, and a strong link is made to social justice and peaceful coexistence:

[Intercultural education] requires the incorporation into the curriculum of diverse worldviews, forgotten or marginalized historical processes, different values and customs, contemporary themes and current issues, achievements and developments of different societies, everyday problems, analysis and transformation of unequal relations between people, and other elements which have long been ignored in Bolivian education. It is in this context that the intercultural axis [key area] aims to create a space within Bolivian education which promotes social relationships that:

- Establish respectful social coexistence between people and groups of different cultures.
- Recognize that the world is not homogenous and that each person and each group enriches and contributes to its diversity.
- Generate a social agreement whereby diverse social, cultural and ethnic groups work toward the construction of a just, equal and respectful society. (Bolivia Ministry of Education undated)

This description provides one of the clearest definitions of interculturality available in national policy and curriculum documents, with its reference to historical, geographical and political knowledge, prioritisation of minority and silent discourses, attention to diversity of values, worldviews and lifestyles, advocacy of positive relationships and co-existence, and commitment to social justice.

The second major rationale for intercultural education is political ideologies, specifically democracy. Although it is rarely defined, democracy is often cited as being one of the ideals, principles or aims of education in policy documents, and is often set alongside intercultural competence and/or associated terms. One of the more precise statements connecting intercultural learning with democracy can be found in the Czech Republic Framework Education Programme for Elementary Education:

The educational area *Man and Society* at elementary schools provides the pupil with the knowledge and skills necessary for his/her active engagement in the life of a democratic society. The instruction is aimed at the pupil's acquisition of the knowledge of the historical, social and cultural-historical aspects of human life in all its diversity, changeability and in mutual connections. ... The area focuses on the formation of positive civic attitudes, develops a consciousness of belonging to the European area of civilisation and culture and encourages the adoption of the values on which contemporary democratic Europe builds. An important part of the education in this educational area is the prevention of racist, xenophobic and extremist attitudes, education towards tolerance and respect for human rights... (Research Institute of Education (VUP) in Prague 2007)

This description of educating children to be intercultural is a good example of the *democratic package* apparent in education policy and curriculum documents from Namibia to Iceland to Panama, and is evidence of the globalisation of education referred to in the first section of this chapter. At the same time, it demonstrates the point made by Byram and Guilherme (this volume) in reference to the development of the Autobiography of Intercultural Encounters, namely that becoming intercultural is something which needs to be conceptualised beyond subject and curriculum boundaries, as part of a much wider trend in education.

The third rationale for intercultural learning is individual development. This appears much less frequently than the first two reasons, but is most commonly found in descriptions of the rationale or aims of foreign language education. The most common justification, and one very familiar to language teachers, is that intercultural learning expands the worldview of the student, opening up new horizons and ways of thinking and seeing. The description of language learning in the New Zealand curriculum adopts this view:

> Learning a new language extends students' linguistic and cultural understanding and their ability to interact appropriately with other speakers. Interaction in a new language... introduces them to new ways of thinking about, questioning, and interpreting the world and their place in it. Through such interaction, students acquire knowledge, skills, and attitudes that equip them for living in a world of diverse peoples, languages, and cultures. (New Zealand Ministry of Education 2007)

In the New Zealand case, this process of learning about others, which has long been a part of foreign language and social studies education, is taken a step further, with the argument that learning about others will lead to a questioning attitude and analysis of what is known from the perspective of the hitherto unknown:

> As they move between, and respond to, different languages and different cultural practices, they are challenged to consider their own identities and assumptions. ... As they compare and contrast different beliefs and cultural practices, including their own, they understand more about themselves and become more understanding of others. (ibid.)

A variation on this theme is that intercultural learning is essential in order to be able to adapt to living in a globalised world. In either case, this is the sense in which knowing how to be (Byram 1997) and knowing how to become (Houghton, this volume) take on paramount importance. Although this rationale is much less common than the previous two, especially in general statements of visions and aims, it is certainly not in conflict with the social and political rationales, which tend to be more prominent in policy documents.

The fourth rationale is that intercultural competence is necessary for the promotion of national interests. The clearest statement of this position is found in the foreign language section of the curriculum of Azerbaijan:

> Someone who has mastered a foreign language can directly access the international world to promote the national and moral values of his people, share achievements with others and exchange opinions and experience in the foreign language. (Azerbaijan Republic Ministry of Education undated)

Most countries do not place such explicit emphasis on promoting national cultural values abroad as a form of interculturality, but the same notion is certainly apparent in other countries, albeit in more subtle ways. In Japan, for example, Ministry of Education Guidelines for foreign language education (MEXT 1998) stipulate that materials should deepen understanding of Japanese culture and promote Japanese identity, which effectively means that textbook publishers will have difficulty getting their textbooks authorised for use in schools unless they adopt the same approach of "promoting the national and moral values of the people" as is advocated in Azerbaijan. Intercultural learning in the service of cultural nationalism has a long history, of course. A surprising finding of the analysis was how uncommon it is at the level of national policy and curriculum documents.

In national policy and curriculum documents, the question, "Why be intercultural?", therefore, is usually answered by appeal to social and political ideals of developing a more peaceful, just, sustainable and democratic world. Also apparent, but generally less emphasized, are reasons associated with national interests or individual development and opportunities. This leads to the issue of what it means to be intercultural, but a brief section on the scope of interculturality would be useful before embarking on this question.

The Scope of Interculturality

Cots and Llurda (this volume) have already pointed out that one of the problems inherent in any discussion of interculturality is the ambiguity of the term. This applies even more to the adjective, intercultural. In most national policy and curriculum documents, there is no attempt to provide a definition of the term, or to distinguish intercultural from related terms such as multicultural or pluricultural. In fact, the latter two terms are less often found in national policy and curriculum documents. It seems that intercultural has become the preferred term to cover a very wide range of meaning and of scope.

In the majority of national education policy and curriculum documents, the term intercultural is used first and foremost in discussions of cultural diversity within the nation. As in the Bolivian case above, the scope of intercultural education is primarily social cohesion and social justice within the nation. In many cases, however, the principles and content of intercultural education are easily extended beyond the nation, too, as this example from the objectives of basic education in Honduras shows:

> Promote interdisciplinary situations and flexible learning that promote ethical, civic, cultural and historical values, respect for human rights and understanding of intercultural situations in both the national and international spheres. (Honduran Ministry of Education 2003)

The apparent growing conflation between education for multicultural (within national borders) understanding and education for international (across national borders) understanding into the term *intercultural education*, together with the seeming lack of concern for such distinctions in education policy documents, may reflect the blurring of the "great divide" between domestic and international spheres (Baylis et al 2008, 24). At the political level, at least, this may be an aspect of education which is starting to reflect the reality of a borderless (in some respects, at least), globalised world.

Another important point to make regarding scope is that intercultural education is often linked explicitly to a transnational identity. This is most obvious in Europe, but is also apparent in other parts of the world. For example, one of the goals of primary education in Grenada is:

To develop perspectives, knowledge, skills and attitude needed to function as citizens of Grenada, the Caribbean and wider world community. (Grenada Ministry of Education 2006)

The same policy document states that education should be a major contribution in developing the "Ideal Caribbean Person" and a whole list of attributes of such a person, developed by the Caribbean Community (CARICOM) Heads of Government in 1998, is provided (ibid.). In a slightly different case, the Melbourne Declaration on Educational Goals for Young Australians, a joint declaration from all Australian Education Ministers, states that all young Australians should become active and informed citizens who:

...are able to relate to and communicate across cultures, especially the cultures and countries of Asia. (Australia Ministerial Council on Education, Training, Employment and Youth Affairs 2008)

This is a clear case of specifically-directed intercultural competence, bringing education policy aims into line with wider national political and economic policies, as Australia becomes increasingly integrated into Asian political and economic networks.

What Does Being Intercultural Involve?

The fourth theme emerging from the policy and curriculum documents related to the question of what being intercultural actually involves, or the aims, outcomes and content of intercultural education. In terms of attention, this was the question that seemed to preoccupy policy- and curriculum-makers most, as far more space was devoted to this than other themes in the majority of documents dealing with intercultural matters. Within this theme, five distinct categories of skills, knowledge, values and attitudes key to the development of an intercultural person were identifiable, and these will be treated in turn.

Recognition of Sameness

The first category was recognition of sameness across cultures. At the most basic level, this involves an awareness of the commonality of being human, and recognition of human dignity. The next step is recognition of human rights and equality, with many national policies going beyond mere recognition to require commitment. In the previous chapter, Houghton (this volume) problematised the role of education in changing students' values and attitudes, but most national policy-makers have no such qualms, Nepal's National Curriculum Framework being a good example:

> One of the main aims of education is to inculcate value among children. The traditional norms and values that are useful and helpful for the betterment of humanity should be preserved.... The values of humanity, social justice, democracy, child and human rights, equity and equality, peace and coexistence must be promoted through education. (Nepal Ministry of Education and Sports 2005)

As an extension of recognition of sameness as human beings, many national policy and curriculum documents also include references to solidarity, connectedness or fellow feeling, and commonality of cultures. The strong form of this is reference to belonging to the global village, which can be found in a number of countries. One of the core competences in the Taiwanese Curriculum Guidelines exemplifies this:

> Cultural learning and international understanding, which involves appreciating and respecting different groups and cultures, understanding the history and culture of one's own country as well as others', recognizing the trend of the globalization in which countries all over the world are integrated into a global village, and developing a global perspective with mutual interdependence, trust and cooperation. (Taiwan Ministry of Education undated)

Finally, recognition of sameness includes appeal to universal or transcultural values. References to universal values appear quite frequently in policy and curriculum documents, but are rarely defined. References to transcultural values include regional values (European, Latin American etc.) and religious values (Christian, Islamic etc.). For example, the cross-curricular area, "Thinking in European and Global Contexts" in the Czech Republic is described as follows:

> Education towards Thinking in European and Global Contexts... promotes in the pupil's consciousness and conduct traditional European values such as humanism, free human will, public morals, application of law and personal responsibility along with rational thought, critical thinking and creativity. (Research Institute of Education (VUP) in Prague 2007)

This recognition of sameness, across humanity or across specific groups of cultures, is thus one of the pillars of being intercultural.

Tolerance/Respect for Otherness

The second category covers a range of desired attitudes to otherness, from openness, through tolerance, to respect and appreciation. These attitudes form a continuum of neutral to positive attitudes to otherness. The negative end of the continuum is obviously not useful for intercultural engagement, and is not explicitly promoted in national education policies anywhere.

Openness to otherness can be defined as the starting point of intercultural competence, insofar as it is a prerequisite to any successful intercultural engagement. For example, one of the aims of education in Burkina Faso is:

> To perpetuate national values and affirm cultural identity while opening children to the outside world and to universal values. (Burkina Faso Ministry of Basic Education and Literacy, undated)

Openness to otherness requires awareness of diversity and recognition that there is value in finding out more about the other. Not far along the continuum from this point is tolerance. Tolerance necessitates some knowledge of the other, and a basic agreement that otherness is acceptable. As Byram (2009, 8) has commented, this is the "minimum standard" for intercultural engagement. In national policy and curriculum documents, however, tolerance is not usually treated as an aim in its own right, and is very rarely defined or discussed. Rather, it is included as part of a package, usually combined with human rights and democracy, as in this example from Lithuania:

> Education in Lithuania is based on the key values of the nation, Europe and global culture: the unrivalled value and dignity of an individual, love of our fellow, the natural equality of people, the human rights and freedoms, tolerance, and declaration of democratic relations in the society. (Lithuania Ministry of Education and Science 2003)

A bit further along the continuum of positivity of attitudes is appreciation. This appears very frequently in policy and curriculum documents, in a variety of contexts. In addition to tolerance, appreciation requires a positive reaction to otherness, together with recognition that one can learn or receive something of value from the other. For example, the secondary school social studies curriculum in Trinidad and Tobago states that students should be able to:

- explain, describe, and demonstrate an appreciation of the diversity of ethnic, religious, and social structures and the culture of Trinidad and Tobago;
- demonstrate an understanding and appreciation of the effect of change on individuals, institutions, and society, and become agents for positive change within the 21st century interconnected global village; (Trinidad and Tobago Ministry of Education 2008)

This seems to be a very common way of adding a value perspective to the knowledge and skills aspects of intercultural learning within subject studies.

A little further still along the continuum is respect. Byram (2009: 8) describes this as an attitude "where one does not simply tolerate difference, but regards it as having a positive value". In relation to being intercultural, policy and curriculum documents in many countries advocate respect for cultural diversity, respect for other people and groups, respect for other languages, respect for other beliefs and religions and respect for cultural heritage. A point which should be noted is that the use of various terms – openness, tolerance, appreciation, respect and others - in policy and curriculum documents may have a range of connotations, and this is something that needs to be understood much more deeply and in context – no judgments about commitment to intercultural engagement can be made purely through linguistic analysis of national policy documents.

Engaging with Otherness

Recognition of sameness and tolerance/respect for otherness can be seen as prerequisites to intercultural learning, or the foundations upon which intercultural competence can be built. A third category of what is involved in being intercultural that emerged from data was engagement with otherness. This covers knowledge, interpersonal and communication skills, affective involvement and action.

Knowledge of others has been a key element of the curriculum for a long time in most areas of the world, and this has not changed, although the content, methods and arrangement of learning and assessment are always subject to revision and refinement. Many countries are placing a renewed emphasis on interpersonal and communication skills in general, and this tends to filter through to intercultural learning too. More and more countries are including interpersonal and social skills as part of their national curricula, and many of these are relevant to intercultural

engagement. In the Seychelles, outcomes for social and co-operative skills
state that students will:

- Develop good relationships with others, and work in co-operative
  ways to achieve common goals;
- Participate appropriately in a range of social and cultural settings;
- Learn to recognize, analyse and respond appropriately to
  discriminatory practices and behaviours;
- Acknowledge individual differences and demonstrate respect for the
  rights of all people;
- Develop the ability to negotiate and reach consensus. (Seychelles
  Ministry of Education 2001)

These types of social skills, together with skills of communication – in
general and in a specific language or languages – are essential to
intercultural learning, and are highlighted in language education as well as
other areas of the curriculum and school life.

Affective involvement is another area of concern for policy and
curriculum developers dealing with issues relating to becoming
intercultural. Many policies and curriculum documents include reference
to empathy, and some go as far as compassion. The most detailed
description of the role of education in this respect is found in a section
entitled, "Understanding and compassion for others" in the Swedish
curriculum:

> The school should promote an understanding for others and the ability to
> empathise. Activities should be characterised by care of the individual's
> well-being and development. No-one should be subjective (sic) to
> discrimination at school based on gender, ethnic belonging, religion or
> other belief, sexual orientation or disability, or subjected to other degrading
> treatment. Tendencies toward harassment or other degrading treatment
> should be actively combated. Xenophobia and intolerance must be met
> with knowledge, open discussion and active measures. (Swedish National
> Agency for Education 2006)

Empathy here is invoked not just as a positive value, but as one which
has effects on behaviour within a society. This is then further justified by
reference to the fact that Swedish society itself has changed, leading to the
tension between being able to appreciate diversity and yet find anchor in a
traditional heritage.

> The internationalisation of Swedish society and increasing cross-border
> mobility place great demands on people's ability to live together and

appreciate the values that are to be found in cultural diversity. Awareness of one's own cultural origins and sharing a common cultural heritage provides a secure identity which it is important to develop, together with the ability to empathise with the values and conditions of others. The school is a social and cultural meeting place with both the opportunity and the responsibility to foster this ability among all who work there (ibid.).

Ultimately, engaging with otherness also involves action. This is actually less emphasised in policy and curriculum documents, perhaps reflecting the greater difficulty and lesser desirability of mandating specific action within a national educational programme.

Learning to Live Together

The previous category of individual attitudes and behaviours is sometimes made even more explicit in references to the societal level of learning to live together, which is the next category. This is strongly emphasised in many of the policy and curriculum documents. Some documents refer specifically to the "Learning: The treasure within" report (Delors 1996) in discussion of this issue, but many provide their own versions of the importance of co-existence, co-operation and harmony at interpersonal, intercultural and international levels. The general thrust of policy statements in this domain can be represented by the following quote from the Malta National Minimum Curriculum:

> In a society that is increasingly becoming multi-cultural, the educational system should enable students to develop a sense of respect, co-operation, and solidarity among cultures. Security and peace in the region depend on the ability of people to co-exist despite their differences. (Malta Ministry of Education, Culture, Youth and Sport 2000)

This is another area in which distinctions between the national and beyond-national tend to be blurred, with co-operation and co-existence applied to all spheres of interaction.

Transformation and Action

The final category within this general theme concerns transformation and action. Two forms of transformation are evident in national policy and curriculum documents. The first is self-transformation, which requires students to internalise the attitudes and values they have developed through intercultural learning and then actively employ them in some form. This most commonly appears in policy and curriculum documents in the form of active commitment to recognising and rejecting prejudice and discrimination. In the Junior Certificate Civic, Social and Political Education course, for example:

> ...pupils will be encouraged to recognise values and develop positive attitudes in relation to themselves, other people, the environment and the wider world. Among these attitudes and values are... a commitment to oppose prejudice, discrimination and social injustice at all levels of society. (Ireland National Council for Curriculum and Assessment, undated)

Such references to commitment and associated concepts indicate the expectation of deep change within the individual as a result of intercultural learning, change which is not limited to specific time or content limitations, but contributes to lifelong engagement in society as an active citizen.

There is also evidence of attention to transformation of society, connected to concepts of social responsibility and social justice. One example here is South Africa, where the social studies area of the curriculum:

> ...aims to develop a sense of agency in learners. It is important that young people understand that they are able to make choices in order to make a difference for positive change. They should be encouraged to do this not only in an historical context of learning from the past, but also to make choices in the present and for the future, for the development of an ethic of sustainable living... Respect for and appreciation of all cultures and languages is integral to this Learning Area. It promotes critical questioning as a basis for developing responsible citizens in a democracy. (South Africa Department of Education 2002)

In a similar way, the concepts of agency and making a difference referred to here go beyond the acquisition of knowledge, skills and attitudes, advocating the development of students who engage in and transform societies in positive ways.

National policies and curricula thus pay considerable attention to the question of what being intercultural involves, identifying the recognition of sameness, tolerance and respect for otherness, engagement with otherness, learning to live together and transformation as key elements of becoming intercultural. While these elements are liberally sprinkled through policy and curriculum documents in many parts of the world in general terms of ideals, vision and aims, there seems to be little coherence in many countries when it comes to the concrete policies of how to achieve the goal of becoming and being intercultural. In this respect, there needs to be much greater comparative in-depth study of a whole range of countries and contexts, following through from general policy statements to curricula, syllabi, materials, classroom practice and teacher and student identities. This echoes and would complement UNESCO's recommendation for "a global comparative study of educational content and methods… with particular reference to the recognition and accommodation of cultural diversity" (UNESCO 2009, 118).

Teaching Approaches to Becoming Intercultural

The final theme that emerged from analysis of the policy and curriculum documents concerned approaches to teaching students how to be intercultural. There is not enough space to look at this in detail here, but two key points can be made.

The first issue is the actual arrangement of the curriculum itself. In some countries, the subjects of social studies and foreign languages adopt all or most of the responsibility for intercultural matters. In other countries, cross-curricular approaches are favoured, and this is probably the most common option, usually in combination with subject teaching. In other countries, intercultural competence may be classed as a key competence or core skill. In a few countries, intercultural learning is a key principle of the entire education policy and curriculum, and these are the cases where intercultural learning is expected to infuse every subject and cross-curricular theme, beyond content to methods of teaching and purposes of education.

The second issue, which has already been examined by Yamada (this volume) and Houghton (this volume) is the marriage of intercultural learning with critical awareness. This is evident in many countries, but policies of several Latin American countries stand out in particular. The Colombian curriculum guidelines for ethics and human values provide a taste of the dominant approach in this region, the key concepts being autonomy, critical responsibility and the interplay between being rooted in the familiar and yet being able to distance oneself from it:

A constant task of schooling at all levels should be the development of autonomy in students. Educating people to think for themselves, to act from personal conviction and to have a critical sense of taking responsibility requires recognizing their capacities to assume values, attitudes and norms transmitted through different areas of socialization, while also recognizing their ability to actively appropriate these cultural aspects, recreate them and construct new values. This means encouraging the development of an autonomous moral conscience, which emphasizes the deep-set roots and dependence of human beings on the cultural context in which they are formed, while simultaneously recognizing their capacity for reason and abstraction, which allows them to distance themselves from the taken-for-granted, judging it critically from the perspective of values and principles reflecting universalizable content, an example of such content being human rights. (Colombia Ministry of Education, undated)

Most policy and curriculum documents outside Latin America do not provide any explanation of how teaching for interculturality and critical consciousness are linked, but the development of critical awareness is often mentioned in passing in descriptions of intercultural learning. The connection and its implications are issues which are increasingly being addressed in the theoretical literature, for example, by people such as Parker (2010) in the field of social studies, and people such as Guilherme (2002) in the field of foreign language education.

Conclusion

What implications does this analysis of education policy and curriculum documents have for the theories and practices of becoming and being intercultural? This is only a partial, superficial analysis of what is happening around the world, of course. A great deal more research needs to be done to really understand how the theories of interculturality are being played out in and beyond classrooms in Africa, Europe, the Americas and the Asia-Pacific. A great deal more research needs to be done to find out how policies related to the intercultural are implemented, and how they are negotiated by schools, teachers and students.

What this analysis can prove is that intercultural learning is a real concern of many education policy-makers around the world, and that it is seen as a positive trend by the majority. It also shows that the big ideals – peace, social justice, democracy and sustainability – remain the dominant rationale for intercultural learning in schools, at least at policy and curriculum level. What is also evident is that there is a blurring between the *national* and the *foreign* or *international* in discussions of intercultural education, with basic aims, principles and content being transferred easily between the two. There is also little, if any, concern with the distinction between intercultural education and intercultural training examined by Byram and Guilherme in the first chapter of this book. The concern with theory, where it exists at all, is not to find which theories of interculturality are most valid or reliable, but which theories fit into national priorities and provide concrete ideas for how to attain political goals of social cohesion and global integration, or economic goals involving intercultural interaction between individuals or groups.

The analysis of what is involved in being intercultural suggests that many policy-makers are happier producing lists of key words and phrases than working out a coherent framework of how these fit together and how to achieve them, but this is a feature that is probably not unique to issues of being intercultural. There is still much work to be done on producing robust policy and curriculum frameworks based on substantive theory – social, psychological and political - for becoming intercultural in specific socio-politico-cultural contexts, but most of the raw ingredients are already there in the policy and curriculum documents.

Once a coherent framework has been developed, implementation, negotiation and evaluation become key issues. Most policy documents do not yet include clear guidelines in this respect, but with the increasing global interest in cultural diversity and interculturality (Council of Europe 2008; UNESCO 2009), this is surely a matter of time.

Perhaps the best conclusion to this analysis would be the proverb, "Where there's a will, there's a way". The political and social will for becoming intercultural in the sphere of education policy exist at national level in many countries all over the world, as this chapter has shown. Working out the way is the next job of policy-makers, curriculum developers, researchers, educators and students around the world.

Bibliography

Apple, M. 2003. *The state and the politics of knowledge.* New York: Routledge Falmer.

Australia Ministerial Council on Education, Training, Employment and Youth Affairs. 2008. *Melbourne declaration on educational goals for young Australians.*
http://www.curriculum.edu.au/verve/_resources/National_Declaration_on_the_Educational_Goals_for_Young_Australians.pdf.

Azerbaijan Republic Ministry of Education. Undated. *National curriculum for primary education: Foreign languages.* http://kurikulum.az/en/curricula/general-education/primary-education/foreign-language.

Baker, D. 2009. The invisible hand of world education culture. In *Handbook of education policy research,* ed. G. Sykes, B. Schneider and D. Plank, 958-968. New York: Routledge.

Baylis, J., S. Smith and P. Owens. 2008. *The globalization of world politics: An introduction to international relations.* Oxford: Oxford University Press.

Bell, L. and Stevenson, H. 2006. *Education policy: Process, themes and impact.* Abingdon: Routledge.

Bolivia Ministry of Education. Undated. *Curriculum design for the level of initial education.* http://www.oei.es/linea3/Educacion_Inicial_Bolivia.pdf.

Boulding, E. 1990. *Building a global civic culture: Education for an interdependent world.* New York: Syracuse University Press.

Burkina Faso Ministry of Basic Education and Literacy. Undated. *Lettre de Politique Educative.* http://www.meba.gov.bf/SiteMeba/plans/politique-educative.html.

Byram, M. 1997. *Teaching and assessing intercultural communicative competence.* Clevedon, England: Multilingual Matters.

—. 2009. *Multicultural societies, pluricultural people and the project of intercultural education.* Strasbourg: Council of Europe.

Colombian Ministry of Education. Undated. *Curriculum Guidelines: Education for Ethics and Human Values.* http://www.mineducacion.gov.co/cvn/1665/articles-89869_archivo_pdf7.pdf .

Cook Islands Government. Undated. *The Cook Islands.* http://www.cook-islands.gov.ck/cook-islands.php.

Cook Islands Ministry of Education. 2006. *Kura Apii Ora'Anga 'Iti-tangata o te Kuki Airani/Social science in the Cook Islands.* http://www.education.gov.ck/docs/curriculum/Curriculum_Social_Science.pdf.

Council of Europe. 2008. *White paper on intercultural dialogue: Living together as equals in Dignity.* http://www.coe.int/t/dg4/intercultural/Source/White%20Paper_final_revised_en.pdf.

Creswell, J. 2008. *Educational research: Planning, conducting and evaluating quantitative and qualitative research.* Upper Saddle River, NJ: Pearson.

Delors, J. 1996. *Learning: The treasure within.* Paris: UNESCO.

Freire, P. 2004. *Pedagogy of indignation.* Boulder: Paradigm.

Grenada Ministry of Education. 2006. *Strategic plan for educational enhancement and development, 2006-2015.*
http://planipolis.iiep.unesco.org/upload/Grenada/Grenada%20Speed%20II.pdf.

Guilherme, M. 2002. *Critical citizens for an intercultural world: Foreign language education as cultural politics.* Clevedon, England: Multilingual Matters.

Honduran Ministry of Education. 2003. *Curriculo Nacional Basica.*
http://www.se.gob.hn/content_htm/pdfs/cnb/cnb.pdf.

Ireland National Council for Curriculum and Assessment. Undated. *Junior certificate civic, social and political education syllabus.*
http://www.curriculumonline.ie/uploadedfiles/PDF/jc_civics_sy.pdf.

Kingdom of Saudi Arabia Ministry of Education. 2005. *The executive summary of the Ministry of Education ten-year plan 1425-1435H (2004-2014).* http://www.moe.gov.sa/pdf/english/moe_e.pdf.

Lithuania Ministry of Education and Science. 2003. *The national education strategy, 2003-2012.*
http://planipolis.iiep.unesco.org/upload/Lithuania/Lithuania_National_Education_Strategies_Provisions_2003-2012.pdf .

Malta Ministry of Education, Culture, Youth and Sport. 2000. *National minimum curriculum.*
http://www.education.gov.mt/ministry/doc/pdf/curriculum_english.pdf.

MEXT (Ministry of Education, Culture, Sports, Science and Technology, Japan). 1998. *Course of study for junior high schools.*
http://www.mext.go.jp/a_menu/shotou/new-cs/youryou/chu/chu.pdf.

Mok, K. H. 2006. *Education reform and education policy in East Asia.* Abingdon: Routledge.

Nepal Ministry of Education and Sports. 2005. *National curriculum framework for schools (pre-primary-12) in Nepal.*
http://librarykvpattom.files.wordpress.com/2009/06/ncf_nepal.pdf

New Zealand Ministry of Education. 2007. *The New Zealand curriculum for English-medium teaching and learning for years 1-13.*
http://nzcurriculum.tki.org.nz/Curriculum-documents/The-New-Zealand-Curriculum.

Parker, W. ed. 2010. *Social studies today: Research and practice.* New York: Routledge.

Research Institute of Education (VUP) in Prague. 2007. *Framework education programme for elementary education.*
http://www.vuppraha.cz/soubory/RVP_ZV_EN_final.pdf.

Rizvi, F. and B. Lingard. 2010. *Globalizing education policy.* Abingdon: Routledge.

Seychelles Ministry of Education. 2001. *The Seychelles national curriculum.*
http://www.education.gov.sc/menu_files/CurriFramework.PDF.

South Africa Department of Education. 2002. *Revised national curriculum statement grades R-9 (schools).*
http://www.education.gov.za/Curriculum/GET/doc/social.pdf.

Swedish National Agency for Education. 2006. *Curriculum for the compulsory school system, the pre-school class and the leisure-time centre. Lpo 94.* http://www.skolverket.se/sb/d/493/a/1303.

Taiwan Ministry of Education. Undated. *General guidelines of grade 1-9 curriculum of elementary and junior high school education.* http://english.moe.gov.tw/ct.asp?xItem=391&ctNode=784&mp=1 .

Taylor, S., F. Rizvi, B. Lingard and M. Henry. 1997. *Educational policy and the politics of change.* London: Routledge.

Trinidad and Tobago Ministry of Education. 2008. *Secondary school curriculum forms 1-3: Social studies.*
http://www.moe.gov.tt/Curriculum_pdfs/Socal_Studies_Curriculum.pdf

UNESCO. 2009. *UNESCO world report: Investing in cultural diversity and intercultural dialogue.* Paris: UNESCO.

Young, M. 2009. What are schools for? In *Knowledge, values and educational policy: A critical perspective*, ed. H. Daniels, H. Lauder and J. Porter, 10-18. Abingdon: Routledge.

PART II:

BECOMING INTERCULTURAL THROUGH EXPERIENCE

CHAPTER FIVE

FROM INTERCULTURAL LEARNING TO INTERCULTURALITY AND SECOND/ FOREIGN LANGUAGE ACQUISITION: HOW AND WHY?

YAU TSAI

Introduction

Although the complexity of intercultural competence (IC) development and the lack of consensus about the term *interculturality* are discussed in previous chapters of this book, this chapter provides a different perspective on the feasibility of becoming intercultural and achieving success in second or foreign language acquisition via intercultural learning in a natural environment. The view that intercultural learning easily takes place in the global society of the twenty-first century arises from the fact that due to the recent trend toward globalisation and internationalisation, people all over the world have more and more opportunities to communicate and interact with each other by using English as an international language. It is especially easy for people who are immersed in the target culture, such as students studying abroad, to experience intercultural learning in which they have to communicate with native speakers, and negotiate the differences between their own cultures and the target culture through English as a shared language in daily life. Recent research has shown that studying abroad is a good approach to enhancing intercultural learning (Weber 2005) and promoting the development of intercultural competence and intercultural communicative competence (Sercu 2002). Studies have also found that intercultural learning in a study abroad context can be the key factor that enables people to develop a new way of reasoning and thinking in order to succeed in the global society (Vigneron 2001).

When students who speak English as a second or foreign language (ESL/EFL) can experience intercultural learning through face-to-face communication and interaction with native speakers in a study abroad context, they may be affected by intercultural learning and become intercultural in daily life. More importantly, they are very likely to be affected by intercultural learning whilst acquiring English as a shared language more effectively and efficiently. The question then arises as to whether and how the experience of intercultural learning enables students studying abroad to become intercultural and also facilitates their second or foreign language acquisition. Drawing upon a range of theories and the results of recent empirical studies, this chapter thus proposes the intercultural-learning effect model to explain how and why intercultural learning leads to interculturality and second/foreign language acquisition (SLA) in a study abroad context.

The intercultural-learning effect (ILE) model, which helps to understand the impact of intercultural learning on interculturality and SLA in this chapter, is based on the experience of intercultural learning among international students studying abroad in an English-speaking country. While emphasising that socio-psychological factors (i.e. attitudes, motivation and cross-cultural adaptation) are essential to identifying the impact of intercultural learning on interculturality and SLA, the ILE model claims that under the influence of intercultural learning, social-psychological factors such as motivation, attitudes and cross-cultural adaptation can make a change to enable students studying abroad to develop different learning modes and thinking systems, which lead to interculturality and greater success in SLA. More importantly, it is claimed that the frequency of communication and interaction with native speakers plays a role in determining how students studying abroad experience intercultural learning and why they can actually benefit from intercultural learning in developing interculturality and achieving greater success in SLA.

The Process of Intercultural Learning

According to Gudykunst and Mody (2002), *being intercultural* refers to encounters where individuals are immersed, either temporarily or permanently, in cultures other than their own. Intercultural learning is thus a process of interaction in a particular linguistic and cultural context (Paige and Stringer 1997). Such a learning process also refers to living in a new culture or temporarily experiencing intense exposure to different cultural products and materials (Sen Gupta 2003). The process of intercultural learning, which is based on the predominant factors of attitudes and knowledge, involves the function of interpreting, relating, discovering and interacting skills from one culture to another (Byram 1997). According to Sercu (2000, 74), "the intercultural learning process thus can be described in terms of maintenance of integrity of identity as a constant process of negotiation between what is one's own and what is foreign, what is part of one's identity and what is new and challenging". Roberts, Byram, Baro, Jordan and Street (2001) maintain that this kind of learning can be seen as something that enables people from different cultures to act as intercultural speakers and use a shared language to communicate with each other in their everyday lives.

ESL/EFL learners can be viewed as intercultural speakers (Byram and Zarate 1997) who may have two or more cultural identifications (Byram 2008). A person as an intercultural speaker not only has sensitivity to cultural differences but also knows how to adjust himself to those differences (Roberts et al. 2001). This kind of learning is practically and psychologically challenging to ESL/EFL learners (Harder 1980). However, the most critical element in intercultural learning is not how fully a person knows each culture but the degree to which he or she gets involved in the process of intercultural communication and human relations (Hoopes 1981). In other words, intercultural learning can have a greater effect on those who get more actively involved in the target culture. Whether or how people can understand themselves and others and learn to be intercultural depends on their ability to be open to others and to get involved in the activities of meaningful communication (Müller-Hartmann 2000).

The Role of Socio-Psychological Factors in Intercultural Learning and SLA

Socio-psychological factors such as motivation, attitudes and cross-cultural adaptation are the factors that can not only affect SLA but also involve intercultural learning. According to Alred (2003), psychology provides a common point of reference for understanding intercultural development. For example, cross-cultural adaptation is a complex and dynamic factor that is definitely essential to intercultural communication which leads to SLA (Begley 2003). Watson-Gegeo (2004, 339) points out that "language learning and acculturation are part of the same process". In fact, the adjustment to a second or foreign language is usually considered as part of acculturation to the host culture (Schumann 1978). This sheds light on the fact that the adjustment to both the target culture and the target language can reflect the impact of intercultural learning on interculturality and SLA in the process of intercultural learning. In addition, motivation to acquire the second or target language (L2) is considered the factor that is beneficial for facilitating SLA (Dornyei et al. 2006) and experiencing intercultural learning. As intercultural learning in itself involves communication and interaction with native speakers, whether or not people can be motivated to communicate and interact with native speakers is usually the key to determining how much they can be affected. According to MacIntyre, Donovan and Standing (2004), motivation to acquire a second or foreign language includes the willingness to communicate (WTC) which is defined as both the ability to initiate communication and the ability to make learners achieve communicative competence. This indicates that such motivation in itself enables individuals to show a consistent tendency in their predisposition toward or away from intercultural communication. Dornyei (2005) points out that L2 motivation is often associated with the concept of the ideal L2 self and can be considered as the desire to shorten the distance between the ideal L2 self and the ought-to-be self in order to achieve language learning tasks. Lamb's (2004) empirical study aimed at learners who speak English as a foreign language and come from Indonesia has shown that L2 motivation is helpful to developing cultural identity. Houghton (this volume) also explores such processes in relation to the self-development. Since L2 motivation is essential to developing cultural identity, the ideal L2 self and the willingness to communicate and interact with native speakers, it definitely helps students studying abroad to actively experience intercultural learning and in turn achieve interculturality and SLA.

Attitudes as a social factor can not only reflect the success of SLA but also be linked to the encounters with the target culture. According to Garrett, Coupland and William (2003), language attitudes function as both input and output of social interaction and enhance SLA. More favourable attitudes toward the target language group as input enable learners to have better performances in acquiring the target language (Baker 1992). Attitudes toward the other culture are also the key factor of determining how successful learners can be in a language course (Gardner 1985). In fact, cultural awareness consisting of one's insight into understandings of the self and otherness (Byram 1997), cultural identity referring to the ability to negotiate the conflicts between two cultures and adapt to the host environment (Kim 1988) and intercultural competence defined as "the ability to imagine and share the thoughts, feelings and point of view of other people" (Richards et al. 1985, 91).are part of learning outcomes and also appear in one's attitudes in the process of intercultural learning. According to Richards and Weber(1985), empathy which enables learners to imagine, understand and share the thoughts and feelings of other people is one of the elements in intercultural competence and can contribute both to the positive attitudes toward people with a different language and culture and to the degree of success in SLA.

The Importance of English to Learners in Intercultural Learning

Since English as an international language is becoming increasingly important to people in the twenty-first century, SLA, which refers to learning another language after the learning of the native language (Gass and Selinker 2001), often involves the use of English as a shared language for communicating and interacting with people from different countries. According to Block (2003), SLA should not be limited to the superficial meaning of the second language, as is the focus of linguistics, but rather be viewed more widely from the perspective of applied linguistics and related to the ways in which people acquire the second, third or fourth language for interaction with native speakers. Especially when globalisation has produced "a new society, in which English is shared among many groups of non-native speakers rather than dominated by the British or Americans" (Warschauer 2000, 512), the distinction between a second language and a foreign language in SLA lies mainly in the number of opportunities that learners have to use the language as an instrument in the environment (Gardner 2001). On the one hand, a cluster of economic, military, political and technological factors has led to the world-wide dominance of English as a language of wider communication in the global society (Bruthiaux 2002). On the other hand, "English is now redefining national and individual identities worldwide, shifting political fault lines, creating new global patterns of wealth and social exclusion and suggesting new notions of human rights and responsibilities of citizenship" (Graddol 2006,12). Under such circumstances, no matter English is one's second or foreign language, it has been commonly considered a tool of communication and interaction with other people in the global society of the twenty-first century and thus essential to experiencing intercultural learning.

Intercultural-Learning Effect (ILE) Model

The ILE model introduced in this chapter is rooted in Krashen's monitor model (1978), Gardner's socio-educational model (1985) and Schumann's acculturation model (1978) insofar, as the three models highlight the importance of socio-psychological factors such as motivation, attitudes and cross-cultural adaptation in SLA. More importantly, the three models point to the concepts of *integrativeness, acculturation* and *comprehensive input in a natural environment*, each of which can also support an impact of intercultural learning on interculturality. This ILE model was developed through the analysis of quantitative and qualitative data (Tsai 2009), which were gathered from international students studying in an English-speaking country, to compare their experience of intercultural learning in which they communicate and interact with native speakers by using English as an international language in daily life. It was found that intercultural learning in a study abroad context can have an impact on the development of interculturality and the achievement in SLA. According to wide ranges of theories and empirical studies, the ILE model was developed to illustrate how and why intercultural learning can lead to interculturality and SLA (See figure 1).

The ILE model makes three claims, each of which will be discussed in more detail below:

(1) Intercultural learning can affect the three variables of attitudes, motivation and cross-cultural adaptation;

(2) The three variables of motivation, attitudes and cross-cultural adaptation are predictable from the frequency of communication and interaction with native speakers and

(3) Changes caused by intercultural learning can be shown in the three variables of motivation, attitudes and cross-cultural adaptation and enable students studying abroad to make further changes in both thinking systems (i.e. internal processing mechanisms) and learning modes (i.e. subconscious and conscious learning modes) in which students develop different language learning strategies to become intercultural and achieve success in SLA.

Figure 5-1 Intercultural Learning-Effect Model

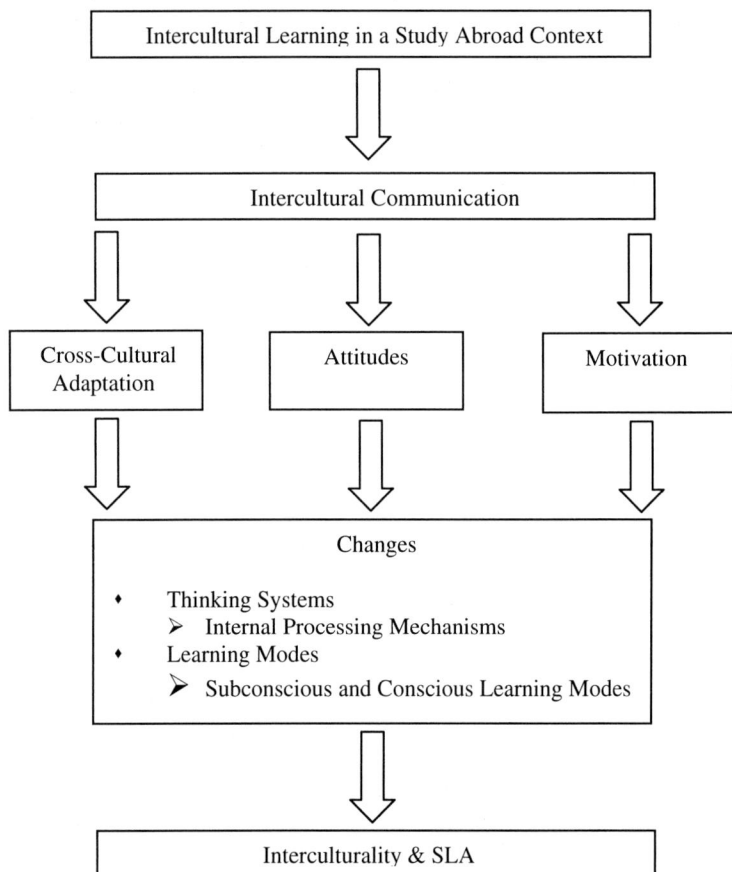

```
┌─────────────────────────────────────────────────────┐
│       Intercultural Learning in a Study Abroad Context │
└─────────────────────────────────────────────────────┘
                          ⬇
┌─────────────────────────────────────────────────────┐
│              Intercultural Communication              │
└─────────────────────────────────────────────────────┘
        ⬇                  ⬇                  ⬇
┌──────────────┐   ┌──────────────┐   ┌──────────────┐
│ Cross-Cultural│   │  Attitudes   │   │  Motivation  │
│  Adaptation  │   │              │   │              │
└──────────────┘   └──────────────┘   └──────────────┘
        ⬇                  ⬇                  ⬇
┌─────────────────────────────────────────────────────┐
│                      Changes                          │
│                                                       │
│   •   Thinking Systems                                │
│        ➢  Internal Processing Mechanisms              │
│   •   Learning Modes                                  │
│        ➢  Subconscious and Conscious Learning Modes   │
└─────────────────────────────────────────────────────┘
                          ⬇
┌─────────────────────────────────────────────────────┐
│                 Interculturality & SLA                │
└─────────────────────────────────────────────────────┘
```

Social-Psychological Factors as a Reflection on the Impact of Intercultural Learning

The ILE model firstly claims that under the impact of intercultural learning, students studying abroad are affected and make a change in their motivation to acquire the target language, attitudes toward native speakers and the target culture and cross-cultural adaptation to the host culture. Students who are affected by intercultural learning may have mixed motivation that consists of both the integrative and instrumental motives and desires. In other words, the two motivational orientations (i.e. integrative motivation and instrumental motivation) proposed by Gardner's socio-educational model (1985) not only exist among students studying abroad concurrently but also enable them to develop two learning modes (i.e. subconscious and conscious learning modes) which are claimed as two different kinds of knowledge in Krashen's monitor model (1978). With these two orientations, students possess different learning modes and also develop various language learning strategies. For instance, students with integrative motivation tend to acquire the target language naturally and subconsciously from the interaction with native speakers or their internal processing mechanisms, which are developed by students themselves to achieve SLA in a natural setting (Ellis 1990) and also lead to interculturality. In contrast, those who have instrumental motivation consciously grasp every opportunity to practice the target language and in turn acquire it through activities which are also beneficial for developing interculturality in daily life. The two motivational orientations in the ILE model enable students studying abroad to develop two learning modes and different language learning strategies to achieve greater success in SLA and also develop interculturality. As Cohen, Paige, Sively, Emert and Hoff (2005, 17) have mentioned, language and culture learning strategies can be defined "the conscious and semiconscious thoughts and behaviours used by learners to improve their knowledge and use of the target language".

Students studying abroad are also considered to be affected by intercultural learning in their attitudes toward native speakers and the target culture. With a change in attitudes, culture shock, cultural awareness and cultural identity are found to take place among students who understand more about the target culture. More importantly, intercultural competence as one component of interculturality can be identified from empathy, tolerance as well as open-mindedness and may be shown in students' attitudes. Culture shock, cultural awareness, cultural identity, intercultural competence and intercultural communicate competence, accompanied by the change in attitudes, are thus considered as the effects of intercultural learning that symbolise interculturality and benefit SLA.

For students immersed in the target culture, they are also considered to be easily affected by intercultural learning in cross-cultural adaptation. Cross-cultural adaptation shown among students studying abroad commonly involves both social adaptation and psychological adaptation proposed by Schumann's acculturation model (1978). However, both social adaptation and psychological adaptation in the IEL model are considered to be different from each other in the origins of problems, the solutions to problems and the length of development. For instance, the problems in psychological adaptation originate from personal factors such as stress or emotion, while those in social adaptation are related to language and cultural barriers. The problems in psychological adaptation may be controlled and solved by students themselves through the help of friends and families in a short time, whereas the extent to which social adaptation can be achieved takes time and depends on language proficiency, the knowledge of the target culture and the attitudes of the hosts toward foreign students.

Frequency of Communication and Interaction with Native Speakers as a Predictor

Tracing the effects of intercultural learning on interculturality and SLA may start with understanding the degree to which students studying abroad experience intercultural learning. Secondly, the ILE model thus claims that the frequency of communication and interaction with native speakers is the filter that determines how much intercultural learning students studying abroad can experience. The more students studying abroad communicate and interact with native speakers, the better they experience intercultural learning. However, students also need communicative strategies to communicate and interact with native speakers well. Communicative strategies such as the negotiation of meaning can help students studying abroad become alert to different communicative situations and keep communicative channels open to native speaker in the process of intercultural learning. As Byram (1997) has emphasised, one needs to learn to "decentre" in order to achieve intercultural communication. The better students studying abroad adopt communicative strategies to communicate and interact with native speakers, the more they benefit from intercultural learning in interculturality and SLA.

Transformation from the Impact of Intercultural Learning to Interculturality and SLA

The third claim of the ILE model is that intercultural learning can cause changes in the three variables of motivation, attitudes and cross-cultural adaptation. This enables students studying abroad to make further changes in their thinking systems and learning modes in which they develop different language learning strategies to become intercultural and acquire the target language more efficiently and effectively. In other words, one's thinking system or learning modes play a role in the development of interculturality and the achievement in SLA. The systematic development of interculturality and the achievement in SLA may gradually change with interaction with people in a natural environment and through one's internal processing mechanism.

Intercultural learning in the ILE model is an ongoing process which enables students studying abroad to alter their motivation to acquire the target language, attitudes toward native speakers and the target culture and cross-cultural adaptation to the target culture. Since a study abroad context offers students many opportunities to communicate and interact with native speakers, it is natural for them to experience intercultural learning and make changes in the three variables. Once there are changes in students' motivation, attitudes and cross-cultural adaptation, further changes in their thinking systems or learning modes can be found. With changes in thinking systems and learning modes, students studying abroad are more likely to develop intercultural competence, intercultural communicative competence and different language learning strategies to achieve greater success in SLA. The more intercultural learning students studying abroad can experience, the more likely they change their thinking systems and learning modes. These changes may take time but should enhance the development of interculturality and the achievement in SLA. Without any change in those variables, however, it is less likely to find the effects leading to interculturality and SLA in the process of intercultural learning.

The variable of motivation in the ILE model should include two motivational orientations that consist of integrative and instrumental motives and desires in acquiring the target language. This is different from the perspective of Gardner's socio-educational model (1985) that integrative motivation is more important to learners who attempt to acquire the target language than instrumental motivation. In fact, the two motivational orientations in the ILE model are considered to be equally important to students studying abroad and also incorporated into one component of L2 motivation for developing different functions in students' thinking systems and learning modes. Cross-cultural adaptation in the ILE model involves both social adaptation and psychological adaptation, but two kinds of cross-cultural adaptation should be distinguished from each other. Social adaptation and psychological adaptation are very different from each other in the origins of their problems, the solutions to their problems and the length of their development. The notion that two kinds of cross-cultural adaptation in the ILE model should be viewed separately and also identified from different viewpoints seems to be apart from the perspective of Schumann's acculturation model (1978) that two kinds of cross-cultural adaptation should be combined together. While emphasising the close links among the three variables of motivation, attitudes and cross-cultural adaptation, the ILE model claims the interrelationship among the three variables as the key to reflecting the impact of intercultural learning on interculturality and SLA.

Conclusion

Although intercultural learning might take place everywhere in a study abroad context and students studying abroad seem to be unable to resist the impact of intercultural learning, this does not mean that everyone can feel it and also benefit from it. It can thus be concluded that students studying abroad need to understand the degree to which they experience intercultural learning through the frequency of communication and interaction with native speakers. Especially when students who are immersed in the target culture have to communicate and interact with native speakers by using English as an international language in daily life, we conclude that the development of interculturality and the achievement in SLA can be identified through their motivation to communicate and interact with native speakers, attitudes toward native speakers and the target culture and cross-cultural adaptation to the host culture.

As noted by Barron (2006), students usually lack adequate awareness of language and culture learning strategies and do not make good use of the learning opportunities that a study abroad context offers them. We thus emphasise that more motivation to communicate and interact with native speakers, more positive attitudes toward the target culture and native speakers and stronger cross-cultural adaptation to the host culture are definitely helpful to determining the degree to which students studying abroad experience intercultural learning and also benefit from it. While providing researchers with a new model to draw attention to the facts that intercultural learning is a trend which younger generations in the twenty-first century are very likely to experience and that this kind of learning definitely plays a role in becoming intercultural and achieving greater success in SLA, we conclude that with the trend toward globalisation and internationalisation, EFL/ESL teachers across the world should reconsider a new direction in which they can train students to become intercultural and also acquire English effectively and efficiently through the experience of intercultural learning outside the classroom.

Bibliography

Alred, G. 2003. Becoming a 'better stranger': A therapeutic perspective on intercultural experience and/as education. In *Intercultural Experiences and Education*, eds. G. Alred, M. Byram and M. Fleming, 14-29. Clevedon, England: Multilingual Matters.

Baker, C. 1992. *Attitudes and Language.* Clevedon, England: Multilingual Matters.

Barron, A. 2006. Learning to say 'you' in German: The acquisition of sociolinguistic competence in a study abroad context. In *Language Learners in a Study Abroad Context,* ed. M. S. Dufont and E. Churchill, 59-88. Clevedon, England: Multilingual Matters.

Begley, R. A. 2003. Sojourner adaptation. In *Intercultural Communication*, eds. L. A. Samovar and R. E. Porter, 406-411. Belmont, CA: Wadsworth/Thomson Learning.

Block, D. 2003. *The social turn in second language acquisition.* Edinburgh: Edinburgh University Press.

Bruthiaux, P. 2002. *Predicting Challenges to English as a Global Language in the 21st Century Language Problems & Language Planning* 26, no. 2: 129-157.

Byram, M. 1997. *Teaching and Assessing Intercultural Communicative Competence.* Clevedon, England: Multilingual Matters.

Byram, M. and G. Zarate. 1997. *Defining and assessing intercultural competence: Some principles and proposals for the European context.* Language Teaching 29: 239-243.

Byram, M. 2008. *From Foreign Language Education to Education for Intercultural Citizenship--Essays and Reflections*. Clevedon, England: Multilingual Matters.

Cohen, A. D., M. R. Paige, R. Sively, L. H. Emert, and J. Hoff. 2005. *Maximizing Study Abroad through Language and Culture Strategies: Research on Students, Study Abroad Program Professionals, and Language Instructors.* Minneapolis: Centre for Advanced Research on Language Acquisition, University of Minnesota.

Dornyei, Z. 2005. *The Psychology of Language Learning: Individual Differences in Second Language Acquisition.* Mahwah, NJ: Erlbaum.

Dornyei, Z. K. Csizer and N. Nemeth. 2006. *Motivation, Language Attitudes and Globalisation.* Clevedon, England; Multilingual Matters.

Ellis, R.1990. *Understanding Second Language Acquisition.* Oxford: Oxford University Press.

Gardner, R.C. 1985. *Social Psychology and Second Language Learning— The Role of Attitudes and Motivation.* Victoria, Australia: Edward Arnold.

—. 2001. Motivation and second language acquisition. In *Motivation and Second Language Acquisition*, eds. Z. Dornyei and R. Schmidt, 1-19. Honolulu, HI: University of Hawaii Press.

Garrett, P. B., N. Coupland and A. William. 2003. *Investigating Language Attitudes.* Cardifff: University of Wales.

Gass, S. and L. Selinker. 2001. *Secondary language acquisition: An Introductory Course.* Mahwah, NJ: Lawrence Erlbaum.

Graddol, D. 2006. *English Next.* London: British Council.

Gudykunst W. B. and B. Mody 2002. *Handbook of International and Intercultural Communicaiton.* Thoudsand Oasks, CA: Sage.

Harder, P. 1980. Discourse as self expression: On the reduced personality of the second language learner. *Applied Linguistics* 1: 212-270.

Hoopes, D. S. 1981. Intercultural communication concepts and the psychological education. In *Multicultural Education: A Cross-Cultural Training Approach*, ed. M. D.Pusch. 10-38. Yarmouth, ME: Intercultural Press.

Kim, LY. Y. 1988. *Communication and Cross-Cultural Adaptation.* Clevedon, England: Multilingual Matters.

Krashen, S. 1978. The monitor model. In *Second-Language Acquisition and Foreign Language Teaching,* ed. R. Gingras, 1-26. Arlington, Virginia: Centre for Applied Linguistics.

Lamb, M. 2004. Integrative motivation in globalisation world. *System* 32, no.1: 3-19.

Maclntyre, P.D., L. Donovan. and L. Standing. 2004. Extroversion and willingness to communicate in second language learning. Paper presented in the Annual Conference of the Canadian Psychological Association, Saint John's NL June 2004.

Müller-Hartmann, A. 2000. The role of tasks in promoting intercultural learning in electronic networks. *Language Learning & Technology* 4, no. 2: 129-147.

Paige, R. M. and D. Stringer 1997. *Training Design for International and Multicultural Programs.* Intercultural communication Institute: Portland, OR.

Richards J., J. Platt. and H. Weber 1985. *Dictionary of Applied Linguistics.* London: Longman.

Roberts, C., M. Byram, A. Baro, S. Jordan and B. Street. 2001. *Language Learners as Ethnographers.* Clevedon, England: Multilingual Matters.

Schumann, J. H. 1978. The acculturation model for second language acquisition. In *Second Language Acquisition and Foreign Language Teaching,* ed. R. Gingras, 27-50. Arlington, VA: Centre for Applied Linguistics.

Sen Gupta, A. 2003. Changing the focus: a discussion of the dynamics of the intercultural experience. In *Intercultural Experience and Education*, ed. G. Alred, M. Byram and M. Fleming.155-178. Clevedon, England: Multilingual Matters.

Selinker, L. 1972. Interlanguage. *International Review of Applied Linguistics* 10: 209-231.

Sercu, L. 2000. *Acquiring Intercultural Communicative Competence from Textbooks: The Case of Flemish Adolescent Pupils Learning German.* Leuven, Germany: Leuven University Press.

—. 2002. Autonomous learning and the acquisition of intercultural communicative competence: Some implications of course development. *Language, culture and curriculum* 15, no. 1: 61-74.

Tsai, Y. 2009. Intercultural Learning in the Context of Study Abroad: A Role in Second/Foreign Language Acquisition. *Ed, D, Thesis*, Durham University, England.

Vigneron, F. 2001. Study of landscapes as an approach to openness to others. In *Developing Intercultural Competence.* ed. M. Byram, A. Nichols and D. Steven. Clevedon, England: Multilingual Matters.

Warshauer, M . 2000. The changing global economy and the future of English teaching. *TESOL Quarterly* 34, no. 3: 511-535.

Watson-Gegeo, K.A. 2004. Mind, language and epistemology: Toward a language acquisition paradigm for SLA. *The Modern Language Journal* 88, no. 3: 331-350.

Weber, S. (2005). *Intercultural Learning as Identity Negotiation.* Frankfurt: Peter Lang.

CHAPTER SIX

A STUDY OF THE PSYCHOLOGICAL EXPERIENCE OF INTERNATIONAL STUDENTS THROUGH THE IMAGERY AND METAPHOR OF JAPANESE STUDENTS IN ENGLAND

MARI AYANO

Introduction

According to the Japanese Ministry of Education, Culture, Sports, Science and Technology (2007), nearly 83,000 Japanese went to study abroad in higher education in 2004, 70 % of whom chose the United States and European countries as their destination. In 2008, they also reported that after the "Plan to Accept 100,000 Foreign Students," the number of international students in Japan was increasing dramatically and numbered approximately 117,000 in higher education in 2004 (The Ministry of Education, Culture, Sports, Science and Technology-Japan, 2008).

The recent globalisation in education has seen the characteristics of Japanese international students change dramatically (Hayashi 2000; Ward, Bochner and Furnham 2001). "Economic growth after World War II in Japan and the Japanese government's policy in the light of recent worldwide movements towards globalisation made studying abroad accessible for more young Japanese" (Ayano 2006a, 12). In Japan, studying abroad used to be only for the elite few, but it is now also accessible for ordinary people who have the desire and the financial background such as language learners studying at a Japanese university, which has a branch in a foreign country or a Year Abroad programme as a course requirement (Hayashi 2000). The majority of the participants in the study reported in this chapter come under this new group.

Numerous studies on the adjustment processes of international students have been carried out from different research perspectives partly because of the increase in the number of international students and partly because of a growing interest in multicultural issues. However, few studies have focused in depth on the nature of students' psychological experience.

Traditionally, intercultural adjustment was discussed within the context of so-called culture shock and some well-known theories have influenced some studies to some extent. Examples include stage theory (Oberg 1960; Adler 1975), the U-curve/W-curve hypothesis (Lysgaard 1955; Gullahorn and Gullahorn 1963) and the ABC of intercultural experience (Ward, Bochner and Furnham 2001), some of which remain influential in their fields and have inspired further research. Although they provide useful information and carry important implications, the following three weaknesses were identified:

- Research studies in sociology and social psychology focuses on behavioural changes and psychological states rather than the psychological experiences of individuals.
- Research studies from clinical psychology, counselling and psychiatry focus on the negative aspects of the psychological experiences of individuals viewing them only as problematic reactions to intercultural experiences, rather than as opportunities for change.
- Since the characteristics of international students have been dramatically changing due to the recent globalisation in education, a factor, which influences intercultural adjustment, is not sufficiently taken into account (Hayashi 2000; Ward Bochner and Furnham 2001).

In order to support international students to learn, to make friends and to challenge various kinds of activities in different cultural settings, effectively, it seems crucial to reveal what is actually happening in detail and in depth while they consciously feel happy or sad, for example. As a counsellor who was trained in the person centred approach, my view of human beings has been deeply influenced by Carl Rogers who views human organisms as being full of natural potential and inherently trustworthy in terms of "actualising tendency", which motivates our behaviour and provides "one central source of energy" in life. It regulates even our most basic behaviours like the seeking food or sexual satisfaction and also directs development, fulfilment, enhancement, constructive and reproductive outcomes and wholeness (Rogers 1977, 242-3).

As mentioned, the primary aim of the study reported in this chapter was to reveal what is happening in the minds of international students' while they are tackling the challenges presented by living in a different environment to establish a new way of living rooted in their actualising tendency. The focus of the present study is thus twofold. Firstly, it focuses on the manifestations of the psychological adjustment of Japanese international students in the host country. Secondly, it focuses on the significance of the support system that enables them to be as effective as students and residents abroad, since international students have to keep making continual efforts to cope with a life in a different culture besides the academic work.

The Study

The research participants were Japanese students who were studying in England for one academic year. They were divided into two groups. The first group of students belonged to a branch of a Japanese university attached to a British university, which had its own campus and followed a different curriculum from the British university. However, the students lived in several colleges of the British university with other students and had opportunities to join various kinds of activities, such as sports clubs, an orchestra, formal dinners and a ball with host students and other international students. The classes they took whilst studying in England included English language classes and European culture and politics.

During the holidays, they were required to leave the college under regulations of the British university. During this time, they joined holiday programmes planned by their university such as ski tours, English language school programmes, European tours, home stays, and independent travel with friends, although in fact most of them travelled with a group of close Japanese friends. From this group, the number of participants for the questionnaire research was 43 and of those, 12 students volunteered for an interview. The second group consisted of exchange students at the same British university, who had attended the pre-sessional English course for one to two months prior to the main academic course at the university. They attended several classes at the university with host or other international students and lived in the university colleges. The number of research participants from this group was 6, all of whom agreed to attend the interview.

I conducted a one-year longitudinal research project with these students by questionnaires and interviews from 1999 to 2001. The questionnaires focused on students' background, experiences, feelings and emotions before and during their study abroad. I adapted some questions from other questionnaires. The questions concerning the states of homesickness were taken from the Dundee Relocational Inventory (DRI) (Fisher 1989). For absent mindedness, the Cognitive Failures Questionnaire (CFQ) was used (Broadbent et al 1982). For psychological well-being, a standardised test based on sub-questions of the General Well-Being Schedule (GWS) was chosen (Fazio 1977 (cited in Robinson, Shaver and Wrightsman, 1991)).

Data were collected three times. The first phase of data collection took place approximately one month after the students' arrival, the second one was during the second term and the final phase was before their departure. The number of the informants who completed three questionnaires totalled 78 (female 49, male 29). The data from questionnaire research were mainly analysed quantitatively using SPSS in order to establish the evidence of students' experiences during the year such as home-sickness, psychological fatigue, psychological well-being and relationships with other people.

Semi-structured interviews applying imagery and metaphor approaches used in counseling were conducted. The interviews covered similar questions to those covered in the questionnaires, but in more depth. The imagery and metaphor approach was appropriate for my research since "metaphors can be used to describe experiences and emotions for which, at least at that time, there are no words; they are too abstract, intense, complex or ethereal" (Bayne and Thompson 2000, 48), and "metaphors seem to be a useful marker for psychotherapeutic change, as the 'burdened' theme in the good-outcome was transformed into an 'unloading' theme, a change which was not evident in the poor outcome" (Levitt, Korman and Angus 2000, 33).

In my past experience of interviewing Japanese students, some of them seemed to find it very difficult to hold an image in their mind and talk about it, so I used a method invented by Ishiyama (1988) to facilitate the generation of student imagery and metaphor, which originally derived from counsellor training using metaphors. I modified some questions to make them more appropriate for my research but the basic meaning of each question remained true to the original.

Regarding the data analysis of interview material, I used thematic analysis and grounded theory analysis (Strauss and Corbin 1990) when analysing interview transcripts. The former is a widely known qualitative analysis method developed by Boyatzis (1998) who defines it as follows:

> ...thematic analysis, is a process that many have used in the past without articulating the specific techniques. It is a process used as part of many qualitative methods. In this sense, it is not a separate method, such as grounded theory or ethnography, but something to be used to assist the researcher in the search for insight (Boyatzis 1998, vi).

As for grounded theory, Strauss and Corbin (1990) define it as follows:

> A grounded theory is one that is inductively derived from the study of the phenomenon it represents. That is, it is discovered, developed, and provisionally verified through systematic data collection and analysis of data pertaining to that phenomenon. Therefore, data collection, analysis, and theory stand in reciprocal relationship with each other. One does not begin with a theory, then prove it. Rather, one begins with an area of study and what is relevant to that area is allowed to emerge.(Strauss and Cohen 1990, 23)

Ayano (2006a, 2006b) argues that thematic analysis and grounded theory compensate for each other's weaknesses. That is to say, thematic analysis helps reduce a vast amount of data to a manageable size and grounded theory enables the researcher to analyse data in depth. Although those two methods have different characteristics, the analytical processes they use are similar since they both involve coding, categorising and linking data by making comparisons (ibid.).

Findings

In this section, I will present some data relevant to the research questions focusing firstly on the general psychological states of Japanese students and secondly on their concerns. Further, remembering that the research project mixes quantitative and qualitative research methods, and noting Fielding and Fielding's (1986) comment that it is necessary to link the findings from both sets of data to illustrate the whole picture relevant to my research questions, I will summarise the findings from questionnaires already reported in previous studies (Ayano 2006a; 2006b) and focus more on interview findings in this study.

When I met the students for questionnaire research and interviews, I noticed that many of them looked very tired. Their eyes were not so bright, although they were where they had chosen to be and were doing what they had wanted to do. In this section, I will describe their psychological states during their year of study in England focusing on the psychological conditions affected by the transition to a different country.

The Arrival Stage

Activities and experiences at the arrival point appearing in students' stories are listed below:

· Moving in and changing accommodation(s)
· Sightseeing
· Language training
· Making friends
· Collecting information about a new environment
· Shopping
· Academic work

From this list, we can see that students were busy working to settle into a new environment in various ways that included moving in and changing accommodation, sightseeing, shopping and making friends, alongside academic work and language training since they were all students. Students' views of such experiences were expressed using the following metaphors: *josoo kikan*[1] *and kinryoku toreeningu,* translations of which are presented in table 6.1 below.

Table 6-1 Translations of the Japanese metaphors *josoo kikan* and *kinryoku toreeningu*

Interview transcription	English translation[2]
Josoo kikan	Approaching period
Kinryoku treeningu	Muscle training

---

[1] Interview transcription
[2] Japanese transcriptions were translated by the researcher

The Japanese students who participated in my research also said that they expected the main part of the study abroad programme would be coming soon, implying that they were preparing for it at that point. From the two metaphors above, we can see that they saw study abroad as something challenging like doing the high jump or some difficult sport that required big strong muscles.

Other students said that *Shokkaku ga katahoo torete dokoni ittara iika wakaranai ari ga, onaji basho o guruguru mawatte iru.* (An ant with only one tentacle is going round in circles not knowing where to go.) The use of this ant metaphor and/or imagery clearly shows that the student was working very hard to settle into a new place by trial and error, feeling lost and confused in an unfamiliar environment.

When we encounter a new environment, we recognise things that are different or strange to us through all of the five senses that we do not normally notice in a familiar environment. Then we make an effort to understand the meanings and values of the new aspects by comparing them with old, familiar things and start feeling secure and comfortable when we can interpret new things in their own context.

More than a few students said that they tried to rearrange the furniture in their college rooms or put up curtains that were similar to those in their own rooms back in Japan. Others put up posters of artists such as famous singers or movie stars on the wall of their rooms to feel as secure as they felt in their own rooms back in Japan.

Establishing daily routines was another major concern because it enables us to move around more freely without having to think things through or checking whether or not we are doing things correctly and effectively.

When I asked students about the reason for studying abroad, most of them said that they wanted to master English, by which they meant they wanted to speak fluently and communicate easily with native-speakers. Making good friends with host people was another priority. Having actually arrived in England and faced up to reality, they realised that it was not so easy to achieve the goals they set previously set for themselves and that they needed to set new ones that were more realistic and achievable.

Considering the points made above, the arrival point seemed to be a demanding period and the results of the three psychological tests, i.e., DRI, CFQ and GWS, noted earlier supported this view.

Students' self-images were also expressed using imagery and metaphor. They often saw themselves as younger or small animals such as fish, puppies, whales, birds or ants, and as flying, floating or airy objects such as basketballs, balloons, frisbees or birds. When I asked them why they used such kinds of imagery and metaphor, they said that on the one hand, younger and small creatures are vulnerable, useless and need care. But on the other hand, they were growing and were full of potential. Further, the flying, floating and airy object imagery and metaphor seemed to carry two covert meanings for them. It showed firstly that they felt unstable in an unfamiliar environment, and secondly, that they felt free from their parents and from the small world of Japan.

The Middle Stage

Activities and experiences mentioned by the students in this period are listed below:
·   Holiday and Moving out of college
   ➢ Trip to Europe
   ➢ Home stay
   ➢ Visit friends' home
   ➢ Language school
   ➢ Working holidays
·   Academic work
·   School activities
   ➢ School festival
·   Socialising
·   Daily routines
·   Unpleasant incidents
   ➢ Being expelled from college, becoming sick
   ➢ Being a victim of racial discrimination

Although the students had had many different kinds of exciting experiences by the middle of the year, they did not seem too excited. Consider the typical example presented in table 6-2 below.

Table 6-2 An example of how students were feeling mid-year

Interview transcription	English translation
Shuyo sareteru mitaina kanji. Oware ba kaereru.	It is like that being kept in a prison. I can go home when I finish my term in prison.

Students had many challenging experiences every day in England such as walking around the city, shopping with friends, trying to speak in English, doing a home-stay with a stranger for a few weeks and overcoming problems. Whilst this had all helped them develop survival skills in a new place, they still felt far from independent living. Having familiarized themselves with and explored their new environment, their interest seemed to shift towards making friends with host students and international students from other countries whilst maintaining relationships with friends.

Table 6-3 Sandy's story[3]

Interview transcription	English translation
Honto-wa moo, doppuri tsukat-te, koo, kaerou-to omot-tetanda-kedo, nanka...Nante-yun-daro. Aisoreeto-sare-terut-te yuuka... (Guruupu-ni hairo-to doryoku-sita-noka?) Un, sita sita. Sita-kedo yappa- nanka, soremadet-te yuuka... Issen-o hika-rerut-te yuuka...[...] Igirisujin-no naka-deno tukiai-kata-o, watashi-ni taisi-te, onaji-yoo-ni si-tekure-nai. [...] Tatoeba kurabu-toka-ni it-temo, hanashi-kake-tari site-kureru-kedo, minna, yappa, jibun-no motto kyomi-no-aru hitotati-to, atumat-tec-chau-kara, jibun-wa, don-don, don-don, oite-ika-re-chau. Karera- wa sooyuu-fuu-ni, isikiteki-ni yat-terun-ja-nai-to omou-ndakedo. Nanka, jibunteki-niwa imaichi sononaka-ni hait-te ike-nainat-te yuu...	Honestly, I wanted to be immersed into British students' groups. But, the reality is...I feel isolated. (Did you try to join a British students' group?)[4]Oh, yes, yes, I did. But, I felt they put a border between them and me. For example, if I went to a club meeting, they came to talk to me kindly but they soon left me and went to someone else with whom they can talk about something more interesting. So, I felt left behind by them. They may have not noticed but I felt I couldn't join them.

---

[3] All names used in this chapter are pseudonyms
[4] Sentences in brackets are questions asked by the interviewee.

As noted earlier, making friends with host students was one of the main purposes of studying abroad. Before going England, they had dreamed of themselves being surrounded by host students and had tried very hard to realise that dream for several months by then but despite their enormous effort, most students reported that they were not satisfied with their relationships with host students and non-Japanese international students. Let us consider another story in which the student established a close relationship with host students.

Table 6-4 Nancy's story

Interview transcription	English translation
[…] Yappari sugoi tukare-tandesu-yo. Moo, sutoresu-mo tamat-te ki-te, uun, tanosii-kedo yappari nihonjin-tomo iru-koto-mo ooi-desu-kedo, eigo shabera-nakucha naranaikoto-mo ookute… Sutoresu-toka, shiranai-hito-to ikki-ni ippai at-tari-sita-nde, moo… Hito-to sonna-ni zut-to issho-ni irut-tekoto-ga, nihon-dewa nakat-ta-kara. Jikka-dat-tan-de. Ima-wa, nani-ka asa-kara ban-made, dareka-ni awa-nakucha ikenai-kara, soyu-node, sugoi sutoresu-ga tamat-tet-te. Moo, kekko, sakunen kaeru chokuzen-gurai-wa, kekko, bakuhatsu-sisoo-na hodo-ni tsukare-tete, de, nihon kaet-ta-kara, nihon-wa iinaa-to omot-te. Zut-to, kaet-tekuru-no sugoi iya dat-tanndesu-kedo.	I felt so tired. The stress was cumulating and …it's fun, of course, I spent a lot of time with Japanese friends, but I had to speak in English a lot…that was stressful and I've had met a lot of strangers at once and…I haven't previously spent so much time with someone without my family because I was living with my parents back in Japan. Now, I have to meet people from morning to night. That is stressful, too. Then, I was so exhausted that I was almost bursting with my emotion, before I went back home in Japan during the holidays. I felt so relaxed in Japan that I really didn't want to come back here.

Unlike most research participants, Nancy (pseudonym) had become very friendly with host students. She said that it was very exciting to meet someone for the first time and speak English with them but she said it was also stressful and tiring. She went out for a drink almost every night with host students in her college, although she dislikes drinking alcohol. She was unable to refuse, since she also wanted to develop close relationships with host students. She ignored her psychological and physical conditions and when she was too tired to continue this lifestyle, she decided to return to Japan for a while. Although she had succeeded in making good friends with host students on the surface, her underlying psychological experience had not been so enjoyable.

The Final Stage

Activities and experiences in the end of the year were as follows:

- Holidays
  - ➢ Trip to Europe
  - ➢ Home stay/staying at a friends' home
  - ➢ Cerebrating Christmas and New Year
  - ➢ Travel within the UK
  - ➢ Going back to Japan
- Academic work
  - ➢ Exams
  - ➢ English
  - ➢ Discussion
- Daily routines
- Coping with stress and homesickness
- Preparing for going home

Approximately eight months after their arrival, I interviewed the participants for the last time for the purposes of data collection. Since the winter holidays had just finished, the holidays were a common theme. As I mentioned before, students had to vacate their accommodation during the holidays and for this reason, the Japanese university offered students different kinds of activities. Although leaving the city was unusual and exciting, travelling around and staying at hotels and strangers' homes seemed exhausting. This is clear in the example presented in table 6.5 below.

Table 6-5 Ted's story

Interview transcription	English translation
...yappa, ichi-ban taihen-datta-naa to omou-koto ga, fuyu, 3-shuu-kan...date, 1-shuu-kann ga sukii no ryokoo itte, 2-shuu-kan ga, jibunn wa jiyuu-ryokoo o erandan-desu-yo. De, jibun-ra de yotei tatete, jibun-ra ga hoteru tottari-shinakya ikenai kara, yappa, sore ga taihen-datta-kanaa.	So, what I thought the hardest thing was, in winter, for three weeks, one week for a ski trip and two weeks for a free trip which was my choice. And we made a plan for ourselves, which means we had to book hotels for ourselves, it was difficult.

By then, they had become more used to living in the host environment and could even manage to arrange a trip for themselves but considering their English proficiency, even this kind of activity must still have been a challenge for them and being so unsettled for three weeks must have been be very tiring. Counter-intuitively, however, such experiences seemed to increase their confidence.

Table 6-6 Mary's story

Interview transcription	English translation
Soo-desu-ne. motto nanka, nihon-datta-ra, motto minnna gaman-sezu...tte yuu ka, moo, sono, tannin wa doo-demo iikara, jibun no miti o iku-tte-yuu kanji wa shita to omou-kiedo, kono D-city ni ite, onaji basho ni nihon-jin ga katamatte-iru to, nanka, otagai-ni, nanka, minna, onaji senjoo ni irukana toka, minna nani shiterundaroo tteiu, nanka, soosaku-shichau-yoo-na, sensaku? Umaku ienai-kedo, sono. "Are? Heya ni inai-kedo, kyoo wa dooshichattanda-roo toka. Tatoeba, Moshi, Tomodati de, eigo o nobashi-tai. De, gaijin ni ippai aitai-tutte, maikai, maikai ai-ni itteru-to, aa, inai to omoi-tutu-mo, moshi sonotugi no toki ni, sono-ko ni atta-ra, mata kyoo mo ai-ni iku-no? toka, nanige-naku, jibun de shitumon shiteru-n-desu-ne. sore wa warui imi wa motteinai-n-dake-do, atode yoku kangae-reba, puraibashii no koto...puraibeeto na koto-da-shi, kikanaku to mo ii noni, kiichatta.ri	Well, I suppose if we are in Japan, we could go on our own way without worrying about other people. But now, we Japanese are in D-city stuck together, well, each other, we check whether we stand at the same line or not, or sniffing or prying about what other people are doing. For example, I might think, "Well, s/he wasn't in her/his room. Where did s/he go, today?" For example, if my friend who wants to improve her/his English proficiency and go to see foreigners (British people), I envy her/him and I found myself asking her/him, "Are you going to see foreigners (British people) today, again?" It is her/his privacy...I can be too nosy without noticing it. I didn't have to ask it but I asked such questions.

In their daily life, establishing a relationship with host students and non-Japanese international students still seemed to present a challenge and during this period, only a few students succeeded. Whether or not they had host and/or non-Japanese friends and if they did, how often they met them seemed to become a major concern for them since they thought this would influence the development of their English proficiency.

Table 6-7 Jack's story

Interview transcription	English translation
Dakara, nanka...anmari gohatto-desu-toka-yu-kanji-no (laugh)[5]. Nihongo-gakka-de manna-deru hito-to tomodachi-ni naru-to, nihonjin-ga 3,4-nin atsumaru-kara, butsukaru-wake-desu-ne. ...Tomodachi-tokat-te 2-tai-1-ja-naku-te, 1-tai-1-janai-desu-ka, akiraka-ni...ano...hanasu-toki. Demo, aru-teido-no nihonjin-dousi-no kiyaku...kiyaku-kankei-ppoku, futari-de hitori-no tokoro-ni ikut-te yuno-ha, akiraka-ni, ano, sore-wa kizuke-nai-desu-ne, tomodati-kankei. ...toriai-toka. ..."nani hanasi-ten-da-yoo aitsu"...toka, nari-kane-nai-desu-ne.	...So, it's something like a taboo...to make a friend with a (British) student in the Japanese language course. Because...because if you make a friend with a (British) student in the Japanese language course, 3 or 4 Japanese students interact with one (British student). It is obvious that a conversation goes better if you are a pair (with a British student), not two (Japanese) to one (British). It's not good to come between other people's one to one relationships by tacit agreement within the Japanese students' group. It disturbs other's friendship. [...] Scrambling for a British friend [...] or searching how others are doing...something like, "Hey! What are they talking about together?"

As Jack said above, it seemed crucial yet difficult for them to establish a close relationship with host and/or non-Japanese students on the one hand whilst maintaining friendships with other Japanese students on the other hand. Ayano (2006a; 2006b) suggested that having a host and/or a non-Japanese friend often sparked jealousy in other Japanese students, which often led to exclusion from the Japanese network. Furthermore, the students without any host and/or non-Japanese friends seemed to develop a negative self-image by contrasting to those who go out to see a host and/or a non-Japanese. Since this was the end of the period, they only had a limited time to build up a friendship with host and/or non-Japanese people, it seemed natural for the tension between participants to increase. During this period of time, the students started missing the host environment on the one hand, and started thinking of going back home on the other hand.

---

[5] Words in brackets are added by the researcher.

Table 6-8 Matthew's story

Interview transcription	English translation
Kawatta koto to ieba...ima, igirisu ni irukoto ni nare-chatte, gaikoku-jin ga, moo, mawari ni iru-koto ga atarimae ni nacchatte, nihon ni kaetta toki-ni, nanka, sugoi, sabishii-ki ga surun-ja nai-kanatte....	What changed in me is...now, I have got used to be in England, it is natural for me to have foreign (British or other) people around me. I think I may feel lonely when I go back to Japan (because there are few of them in Japan)[6].

Talking about the changes in him while studying abroad, Matthew started talking about how natural it felt to be surrounded by British and/or non-Japanese people in daily life. Then, his story shifted to his future life in Japan after his return. During this period of time, students were busy preparing to leave the host country and to start a new life in Japan whilst completing academic work. They had to tidy and pack things up to send back home whilst saying good-bye to people they had met in the host country and doing whatever they could to minimise regret. Anna's story exemplifies how the students felt during this period of time. They seemed to have mixed feelings about their experience and were becoming impatient. They were struggling with psychological conflict over their home and host countries.

---

[6] A phrase is added by the researcher to convey the intended meaning of the interviewee.

Table 6-9 Anna's story

Interview transcription	English translation
…2-shuukan-gurai mae dattanda-kedo, nanka, sono-mae kara. Nanka, fuyu-yasumi ga atte, sore-de, karendaa mite, kooyatte kazoeru-janai-desu-ka. Sono-toki ni, "waa, ato…moshi, fuyu-yasumi ga owattara, ato, 1-kagetu naijann toka…ato, 1-kagetu shika nai-ya toka, minna de kutiguti ni ii-dashite…. De, dokka ikanakya toka, igirisu, zenzen, mawatte nai kara, ikanakya toka, sooyuu hito ga dete kita-ri toka shite, jibun mo asette…. Aa, nanka, "A, kaerunda!" to omou to chotto…. Ureshii hanbun, samishii hanbun desu ne. Nanka, saisho wa, D-city nante, nani-mo nai-shi…to omotte, hayaku kaeri-tai, hayaku kaeri-tai…iya na koto mo ippai atta-kara, hayaku kaeri-tai to omotte-tanda-kedo, yappari, iza kaeru to naru to, aichaku-tte-yuu-ka, nanka…un, sabishii desu ne. nanka, chotto, D-city o hanareru-no-ga….	About 2 weeks ago or so, we had the winter holidays. Before that, I looked at a calendar and counted how many days we have. When I did it, I thought "Oh, we have only less than one month here after the winter holidays." Others also recognised it and started talking about that. One said eagerly, "Oh, I have to visit a place or two, because I have not visited anywhere really!" Then, I started feeling uneasy. Well…, I realised that I was going home. I have a mixed feeling, half happy and half sad. Well, when I came here, I thought there was nothing interesting in D-city and so, I wanted to go home soon…well, because I had a lot of troubles with my friends too. But now, I am actually going home soon and I found I am attached here. So, I miss here. I don't want to leave here.

Self-evaluation of the year abroad was one of the most common and important topics dealt with at this stage and Tom used the metaphor of a star to describe it.

Table 6-10 Tom's story

Interview transcription	English translation
Hoshi desu ne. Te ni haira-nai hoshi ga...sora ni kagayai-teru hoshi wa, te o nobashi-te-mo, te ni haira-nai-ja-nai-desu-ka. Sore ga, ikki ni tikaduita-ka-naatte. Kyori-kan-tte yuun-desu-ka, "Te ni haira-nai-jan"tte omotte-te-mo, nanka, "A, sugee, nanka, tikazuita-kanaa"tte yuu-no-ga arimasu ne. Tada hoshi ga tikazuite-kita-dake kamo-shirenain-desu-kedo, jibun ga seichoo-shita-tte yuu-no-mo sukoshi aru-kamo-shirenai-desu-ne...(...hoshi-tte nan-desu-ka.)* hoshii-mono-tten-desu-ka. Kodomo no koro hoshikatta mono. Ano, sora toka sugoi sukidattan-desu-yo. Uchuu toka. Sorede, ichiban saisho ni hakkenn-shita-hito ga namae tukerareru-janai-desu-ka. Mada, hakken-sarete-nai-yatu o. Sorede, sono hoshi ga hoshikattan-desu-yo. jibunn de, mitukeru-monotte-yuuno-ka, kyuushuu-suru-mono ga fueta-kanaa-tte omotte...	A star which I can't get...we can't get a shining star in the sky. I feel like it became closer to me. It became closer to me, like, "I never be able to get it," turns "Wow! It's coming closer!" It is only the star came to me but I may have developed and moved to the star. (What do you mean by a star? What is a star to you?") [7] I can say, it is what I want. It is what I wanted when I was a child. I liked the sky and was interested in the space. If someone discovers a star, then, that person can put a name on it, right? I wanted to have that. The star is something I will discover. I came to this country and I met a lot of people. The new world was open to me I found more new things and absorbed them.

As we can see, Tom's story involves self-evaluation of the year abroad and personal development was a typical aspect of students' positive self-evaluations. Next, let me provide an example of students' negative self-evaluation that expresses negative feelings about study abroad.

Table 6-11 Andrew's story

Interview transcription	English translation
Nagai shugaku ryoko. "Shugaku ryoko, ikanakya yokatta.	It has been like a long school trip. I might want to say, "I shouldn't have gone on a school trip" now.

[7] Questions by the interviewee.

In fact, many students said that they felt depressed and/or they feel physically tired in the interviews during this period of time. Whilst a school trip itself can be an exciting and wonderful opportunity for the students, it can be exhausting and overwhelming if it is too long. For some students, the experience of studying abroad for a year seemed to be overwhelming and they seemed to need some more time to extract meaning from their experience and recover from fatigue.

The Implications for the Support System

In this final section, I will present some implications summarising the findings. From the data above, it can be seen that study abroad was a challenging experience for the Japanese international students who took part in the present study. For many international students, adjusting to an unfamiliar environment is not as easy as suggested in the traditional theories (Oberg 1960; Lysgaard 1955) and many students reported that they experienced psychological difficulties over the year as well as enjoyable experiences of various kinds. This was also reported by other research (Abe, Talbot and Geelhead 1998; Ayano 2006a and 2006b; Sonoda 2008). Despite the difficulties, however, I would like to argue that intercultural experience should not only be seen in terms of disaster. Students still seemed to cherish the hope and desire to grow up or move to another part of the world which implies they had a more developed self. For example, Ted said that he had grown very much since he came to England, in terms of changing in his way of thinking.

Table 6-1 Ted's story

Interview transcription	English translation
...yappa, mono no kangae-kata no kawari-kata dayo ne. Moo, jibun ga ugoka-nakya, doo-nimo naranari-tte yuuno to.... Ato, aredayo-nee. Jibun ga, yo-no-naka miru-me ga dekaku natta yonee. Soo-yatte, kangaeru yooni natteru-tte- koto wa, iro iro, un. Bucchake, dakara, kita-toki-yori wa, zettai, deka-ku natteru-ki ga suru-ne.	...So, a way of thinking has changed in me. And now, I know that I have to move otherwise nothing happens. And also, my view towards the world has become wider. I started thinking so. So, I can say, I definitely have grown very much than I was when I came here.

In daily life abroad, students may have developed more self-awareness than when they were in their home environment perhaps because they had more opportunities to compare themselves and their lives in many ways with people in and aspects of the host country. Ash's story below is one of the examples:

Table 6-13 Ash's story

Interview transcription	English translation
...Igirisu-jin no hoo-ga, motto jibun no kimoti-tte-yuu-no o, sugu, jibun de hyoomen ni dasu-ja-nai-desu-ka. Nihontte-yuu-no wa, Nihon-da-to, dasu hito ga iru kedo, yappa, aru-teido osae-tari nanka shitari suru-kedo, kotti wa moo, sonna-no naku-te, ma, nante yuun-da-roo. Honto-ni mukatuita-toki wa, honto-ni sugoi okoru-shi, yorokobu toki, honto-ni yorokonde-ru-shi, motto jibun ni sunao-da-naatte-yuu-fuu-ni. (Jibun mo soo-yuu-fuu-ni) yatte-mitai to omou. Sukoshi wa natterun-ja-nai-desu-ka?	British people express their emotions, don't they? In Japan, we Japanese, well…some don't, but most of us usually suppress our emotions. When they really get, they express their anger. When they are happy, they shows their happy feelings. They are honest themselves. I want to do it like them. I think I can do it a little, now.

Another explanation may be that, as some students said, they had more time to think about themselves because they had less of a social life and were generally less occupied with familiar things than in their own country. The process of being intercultural is not as simple as just learning a way of behaviour in a different culture and learning a language of a host country. It is a process of braking down and reconstructing the own value system, which occurring continuously. Therefore, I would like to argue that a support system should be developed to support the personal development of the international students to make their experiences more meaningful to them. In other words, it will help them to be intercultural individuals.

Conclusion

In this chapter, the psychological adjustment process of Japanese international students mainly through their stories focusing on imagery and metaphors was discussed. Contrary to the traditional theory of culture shock, the psychological conditions of Japanese international students were rather negative throughout of the year but by exploring students' stories, a variety of factors clearly influenced their psychological conditions.

According to Rogers, the process through which individuals explore themselves and become aware of the self "is a painful, vacillating one (1961, 531)." However, after going through such a process, they become "free from internal strain and anxiety" and "represent the maximum in realistically oriented adaptation (ibid.: 532)." Having examined Japanese students' experience of studying abroad, it is found that encountering a different culture seems to share some similarities with this psychological process, which implies in turn that a person-centred approach can be useful in helping international students explore their inner experiences.

I argue that being intercultural is not only experiencing and being influenced by a different culture, but also integrating what they learned from different cultures and their own ones. When this process is succeeded in each individual, the capacity and tolerance of their mind towards the difference may increase, and such individuals can behave more flexibly in intercultural settings.

Further research should include analysis and support for students on their return to their country, since the phenomenon of *reverse culture shock* has been noticed and it seems to be a process of integration of the old and the new culture, but not sufficiently researched.

Acknowledgements

An earlier version of this chapter was published in Ayano (2009).

Bibliography

Abe, J., D.M. Talbot and R.J. Geelhead. 1998. Effects of a peer program on international student adjustment. *Journal of College Student Development*, vol. 39, No. 6, 539-547.

Adler, P. S. (1975). The transitional experience: An alternative view of culture shock. *Journal of Humanistic Psychology. 15,* no. 4, Fall: 13-23.

Ayano, M. 2006a. Japanese students in England. In *Living and Studying Abroad: Research and Practice*, eds. M. Byram and A. Feng, 11-37. Clevedon, England: Multilingual Matters.

—. 2006b. Intercultural Experience and the Process of Psychological Adjustment: A Case Study of Japanese Students in England. PhD Thesis, Durham University.

—. 2009. A Study of the Psychological Experience of International Students through the Imagery and Metaphor of Japanese Students in England. *Journal of Liberal Arts*, no.5 : 33-59. Seijoh University Nagoya, Japan.

Bayne, R. and K.L. Thompson. 2000. Counsellor response to clients' metaphors: an evaluation and refinement of Strong's model. *Counselling Psychology Quarterly* 13, no. 1: 37-49.

Bochner, S. 1982. The social psychology of cross-cultural relations. In *Cultures in Contact: Studies in Cross-Cultural Interaction*, ed. S. Bochner, 5-44. Oxford: Pergamon.

Bochner, S., N. Hutnik and A. Furnham. 1985. The friendship patterns of overseas and host students in an Oxford students residence. *The Journal of Social Psychology* 125, no. 6: 689-694.

Boyatzis, R. E. 1998. *Transforming Qualitative Information: Thematic Analysis and Code Development.* Thousand Oaks: Sage Publications.

Broadbent, D. E., Cooper, P. F., FitzGerald, P. And Parkes, K. R. (1982). The Cognitive Failures Questionnaire (CFQ) and its correlates. *British Journal of Clinical Psychology. 21, 1-16*

Fazio, A. F. 1977. *A Concurrent Validational Study of the NCHA General Well-Being Schedule. (Dept. of H.E.W. No. HRA-78-1347).* Hyattsville, MD: National Center for Health Statistics.

Fielding, N. G. and J.L. Fielding. 1986. *Linking Data: Qualitative Research Methods Series* 4. Beverly Hills: Sage.

Fisher, S. 1989. *Homesickness, Cognition, and Health*. Hove and London: Lawrence Erlbaum Associates, Publishers.

Gullahorn, J. T. and J.E. Gullahorn. 1963. An extention of the U curve hypothesis. Journal of Social Issues 19, no. 3: 33-47.

Hayashi, S. 2000. Study abroad and change of self: An Interview study of vocational school students. *Jinbun Ronso: Bulletin of the Faculty of Humanities and Social Sciences* 17: 59-83.

Ishiyama, F. I. 1988. A model of visual case processing using metaphors and drawings. *Counsellor Education and Supervision* 28: 153-161.

Levitt, H., Y. Korman and L. Angus. 2000. A metaphor analysis in treatments of depression: metaphor as a marker of change. *Counselling Psychology Quarterly* 13, no. 1: 23-35.

Lysgaard, S. 1955. Adjustment in a foreign society: Norwegian Fulbright grantees visiting the United States. *International Social Science Bulletin* 7: 113-127.

Oberg, K. 1960. Cultural shock: Adjustment to new cultural environments. *Practical Anthropology* 7: 177-182.

Robinson, J. R., Shaver, P. Rl and Wrightsman, L. S. (1991) (Eds.). Measures of Personality and Social Psychological Attitudes: Volume 1 in Measures of Social Psychological Attitudes Series. San Diego: Academic Press.

Rogers, C. R. 1961. *Client-Centered Therapy.* London: Constable.

—. 1977. *Carl Rogers on Personal Power.* New York: Delacorte Press.

Sonoda, T. 2008. A Study on feature of consultation for international student. *Gunma Daigaku Ryuugakusei Sentaa Ronshuu* 7: 1-9.

Strauss, A. and J. Corbin. 1990. *Basics of Qualitative Research: Grounded Theory Procedures and Techniques.* Newbury Park: Sage.

The Ministry of Education, Culture, Sports, Science and Technology-Japan. 2007. Waga kuni no ryuugaku seido no gaiyoo−ukeire oyobi haken. http://www.mext.go.jp/a_menu/koutou/ryugaku/07062723.htm

The Ministry of Education, Culture, Sports, Science and Technology-Japan. 2008. Promotion of International Student Exchange. http://www.mext.go.jp/English/org/struct/046.htm

Ward, C., S. Bochner and A. Furnham. 2001. *The Psychology of Culture Shock.* East Sussex: Routledge.

CHAPTER SEVEN

LINGUISTIC COMPETENCE VS. INTERCULTURAL COMPETENCE?

YUMIKO FURUMURA

Introduction

Tests administered worldwide to evaluate linguistic proficiency include the Test of English as a Foreign Language (TOEFL) and the Test of English for International Communication (TOEIC). Whilst the former focuses upon testing general English language skills and is often used for university admission purposes, the latter focuses on testing English for business purposes. If the purpose of learning English is to get high scores on such tests, there are surely many successful learners of English in Japan who have developed their skills through e-learning and on intensive courses specifically geared towards achieving that end. And of course, holding such qualifications is of benefit to students when they start job-hunting or apply to study abroad. The question to be addressed in this chapter, however, is whether learners with linguistic competence *alone* can be considered successful language learners in today's increasingly multicultural world, when the importance of developing good relationships with people from other countries using English, and indeed with people from one's own country, cannot be denied.

The most recent theories have stressed that when a foreign language is used for oral communication between living individuals in real time, linguistic competence (knowledge of the grammar and of the dictionary meanings vocabulary) is insufficient. Learners need both linguistic competence in order to produce grammatically correct and meaningful speech and also the ability to speak appropriately, to choose the language that suits the occasion, the topic and the person with whom one is speaking (Byram 2008, 78-79).

Everything may seem to go well between speakers and their interlocutors in the absence of conflict but disagreements naturally arise from time to time when people need to reject suggestions or refuse requests, for example, perhaps causing offence in the process. When choosing appropriate attitudes in English, how useful is the linguistic competence of Japanese speakers of English (JE) who have attained high scores in tests such as TOEFL and TOEIC when they attempt to resolve such conflict?

Maynard (1993, 27) notes that when they want to refuse, "Japanese tend to refuse indirectly, with statements of excuses that are not offensive, or with long sentences because refusing often means that the result of it doesn't meet an addressee's expectation (my translation)". This attitude is known as high-context communication, while people from English-speaking countries such as the U.S.A. and the U.K. are said to use low-context communication.

> High–context [systems] make greater distinction between insiders and outsiders than low-context cultures do. People raised in high-context systems expect more of others than do the participants in low-context systems. When talking about something that they have on their minds, a high-context individual will expect his [or her] interlocutor to know what's bothering him [or her], so that he [or she] doesn't have to be specific. The result is that he [or she] will talk around and around the point, in effect putting all the pieces in place except the crucial one. Placing it properly - this keystone - is the role of his [or her] interlocutor (Hall 1976, 98).

Tsuruta, Rossiter and Coulton (1988) also note that while Japanese tend to prefer indirect expressions, native-speakers of English (NSE) are said to prefer more direct expressions. Having learned about this difference in communication style between Japanese and NSE, some JE might decide to use direct expressions when communicating in English with NSE. According to Beebe, Takahashi and Uliss-Weltz (1990), when Japanese people make refusals in English, some tend to transfer indirect strategies from Japanese into English, but others tend to say "no" directly without considering the situation.

The purpose of this chapter is to explore the relative importance of linguistic competence and intercultural competence for English language learners in relationship-development with English-speaking people. More specifically, the question to be addressed is whether or not a JE with linguistic competence can successfully reject his/her interlocutor's suggestion in English, whilst maintaining a good relationship with him/her at the same time. An open-ended role-play will be presented below, illustrating one of the two tendencies mentioned above, in which a JE uses an indirect strategy when communicating in English with a NSE. It will be examined in detail to clarify the reasons why the JE chose to take this approach and to explore the influence of his behaviour upon his relationships with his interlocutor.

> The intercultural speaker can use their explanations of sources of misunderstanding and dysfunction to help interlocutors overcome conflicting perspectives; can explain the perspective of each and the origins of those perspectives in terms accessible to the other; can help interlocutors to identify common ground and unresolvable difference (Byram 1997, 61).

According to Byram's (1997) description of the competence(s) required of intercultural speakers, the JE in this study needs to help the interlocutor overcome conflicting perspectives, with explanation, to solve the problem when refusing, without offending the interlocutor in order to maintain a good relationship. NSE evaluations of the refusal role-play will suggest how effective the JE's intercultural communication style might be in this conflict situation.

The Study

Four groups of research subjects took part in the study; Japanese speakers of Japanese (JJ), English speakers of English (EE), Japanese speakers of English (JE), and native-speakers of English (NSE). While EE are also native-speakers of English, this group was convened to make role-plays in twelve situations to enable comparisons to be made with the role-plays conducted by JJ to highlight differences and similarities between EE and JJ. Thirteen JE who scored over 750 points in the TOEIC test, and over 500 points in the TOEFL (PBT) test participated in oral open-ended role-playing tasks in English with a British lady in five situations, and were specifically asked to try not to cause offence. The research subjects were all over twenty-two years old and had studied abroad in the U.S.A or Australia for more than ten months. Forty-two NSE later evaluated selected role-plays having listened to the recorded conversations and read the transcripts. They were all living in Japan, had worked as English teachers for more than ten months and came from the U.K., Canada, and the U.S.A.

The conflict situations involved refusals and rejections of various kinds including requests, invitations, suggestions, and offers from a friend, and made by people of higher or lower status in the workplace. JEs were asked to role-play five situations that were modified from those used in the research of Beebe, Takahashi and Uliss-Weltz (1990). Data were collected to identify some of the defining characteristics of the JE's attitude when communicating in English, which seemed to differ from those of NSEs who were also categorised as EE. One hundred and sixty-five role-plays conducted in English between JEs and a British lady were compared with one hundred and ninety-two role-plays conducted between EEs and EEs and one hundred and seventy-four role-plays between JJ to identify Japanese attitudinal features when communicating in both Japanese and English. Speaker B role-players were instructed to refuse speaker A requests etc. whilst trying to maintain a good relationship with him or her.

In this chapter, an overview of the results will be presented before a special focus is placed upon one role-play in which a JE was asked to reject his boss's suggestion in the workplace without causing offence, to highlight the distinguishing features of the interaction.

Overview of Results

Refuser utterances were analysed by semantic formulas ranging from direct ("No", or "Inability") to indirect ("Apology", "Excuse", "Suggestion of alternative" etc.) so that the differences and similarities among JJ, EE, and JE could be found by using Fisher's exact test. The non-refusal rates and the direct refusal rates are shown in table 7-1 and table 7-2 below. Characteristics of JE attitudes when communicating in English, detailed in Furumura (2004), were as follows:

1.   Despite the fact that JEs wanted to refuse in some situations, many JE, e.g. about 77% of them in #1 were unable to refuse in the end (see Table 7-1). Instead of refusing, they compromised, made concessions or postponed their answers. JE attitudes resembled those of JJ, while JE's attitudes were different from EE's in two situations in refusals of requests, as can be seen in table 1 below.

Table 7-1 Non-refusal rate

Stimulus Type	JJ (N=14)		EE (N=16)		JEE (N=13)	
	N	%	N	%	N	%
#1 (request : lower)	10	71.4	2***	12.5	10***	76.9
#2 (request : equal)	5	33.3	0**	0	6**	46.2
#9 (offer : equal)	1	6.7	0	0	0	0
#4 (invitation : upper)	7	50.0	4	25.0	6	46.2
#6 (suggestion : upper)	5	35.7	2	12.5	3	23.1

#1: increase in pay, #2: lending a notebook, #9: offer of cake after lunch,
#4: invitation of a party on Sunday, #6: suggestion of little notes as a reminder.
*: p < .05 **: p < .02   ***: p < .001   Fisher's exact test (p: level of significance,
the less p gets, the more significant the statistics would be.)

2.   Fewer JEs used direct formulas than EEs; JEs were similar to JJs in attitude, that is, more JEs tended to use indirect formulas than EEs (see Table 7-2).

Table 7-2 Direct refusal rate

Stimulus Type	JJ (N=14)		EE (N=16)		JEE (N=13)	
	N	%	N	%	N	%
#1 (request:lower)	3	21.4	8	50.0	7	53.9
#2 (request : equal)	4	26.7	10*	62.5	4*	30.8
#9 (offer : equal)	11	73.4	14	87.5	10	76.9
#4 (invitation : upper)	3	21.4	10*	62.5	3*	23.1
#6 (suggestion : upper)	2	14.3	3	18.8	2	15.4

#1: increase in pay, #2: lending a notebook, #9: offer of cake after lunch, #4:
invitation of a party on Sunday, #6: suggestion of little notes as a reminder.
*: p < .05   Fisher's exact test (p: level of significance, the less p gets, the more
significant the statistics would be.)

Special Focus on One Role-Play

It was found that Japanese people seem likely to transfer their Japanese communication patterns to communication in English; that is, Japanese people either use indirect formulas or are unable to refuse, especially when they think that their refusal may cause problems for their interlocutor, such as failing an examination because they could not borrow the notes.

A role-play conducted in English is presented below in which a JE used indirect refusals. The male JE was a thirty-nine year old English teacher at high school in Japan, who had scored over 600 in the TOEFL (PBT) test, which meant that his linguistic competence could be considered high. He had studied in the U.S.A. for a year and a half for teacher- training purposes.

In the role-play, speaker A (NSE) and speaker B (JE) were asked to play the roles of language teachers at a private school in Britain, where speaker A was the head of speaker B's department. The specific situation they were asked to role-play was that speaker B was at his desk trying to find a report that speaker A had just asked for. While speaker B was searching through the mess on his desk, speaker A walked over and then two speakers were asked to role-play the conversation that ensued. Only the first part of the role-play was scripted in advance for speaker A by the author, but having read that, both speakers were left free to say anything they liked until their conversation came to an end. However, the JE (speaker B) was specifically asked to refuse speaker A's request whilst attempting to maintain a good relationship with the boss. Their role-play ran as follows:

> Speaker A1 (NSE): You know, maybe you should try to organize yourself a little better. And I always write myself little notes to remind me things. Perhaps you should give a try.
>
> Speaker B1 (JE): Nnhh, oh …o.k. uhhhhh I don't want to have any trouble with you, so uhhm..I try. I'll do my best to organize.
> Speaker A2 (NSE): Nnhh o.k. Find those
> minutes, and then soon you find them. Please come through and give them to me.
>
> Speaker B2 (JE): OK.
>
> Speaker A3 (NSE): OK. Thanks.

How did the JE explain himself in this role-play when he was interviewed about it afterwards? He claimed that he had used indirect language because he intended to be polite and wanted to avoid causing trouble with the interlocutor when communicating in either English or Japanese. However, he also claimed that he intended to refuse his boss's suggestion about taking notes by not responding to the suggestion at all. Accepting the blame for not being able to find the minutes on his messy desk, he said he would try to organise himself better, despite the fact that he did not actually intend to follow her advice.

In both English and Japanese role-plays, he adopted similar strategies that would enable him to organise himself in his own way. According to him, he usually didn't change his attitude depending on the language he was using or the ethnicity of the interlocutor, which suggested that he didn't consciously use intercultural competence in intercultural communication.

After the JE had been interviewed about the role-play, forty-two NSEs who had lived in Japan for over ten months and who were working as assistant English teachers at the high school level, were then asked to evaluate it on a scale of one to five (one was low, three was neutral and five was high) in terms of how direct, assertive, different, close or appropriate the JE's attitude seemed to them to be. NSE answers are presented in table 7-3 below, which shows variety of combinations of each NSE's answers for all questions not found in the statistic data as to the mean of their evaluations, and the questions ran as follows:

1. How direct is the Japanese refusal of the suggestion?
2. How assertive is the Japanese refusal of the suggestion?
3. How different is this refusal from the kind that you would use in the same situation?
4. If you were the suggester, how would you expect the relationship between you and the Japanese refuser to develop in the future?
5. How appropriate is the way of refusing?

Table 7-3 Five-grade evaluation by NSE (N=42)

Na./Eth./s.	Age	Direct	Assertive	Different	Close	Appro-priate
Br.wh. F	23	1	2	2	3	3
Br .wh. F	23	1	1	3	1	1
Br. Wh. F	24	1	1	4	2	1
Br. Wh. F	24	1	2	4	1	2
Br.wh. F	26	1	1	3	1	2
Br.wh. F	29	2	2	2	2	3
Br.wh. F	23	1	1	5	2	2
Am.wh. F	24	1	1	2	2	4
Am.wh. F	25	2	3	5	3	3
Am.wh. F	29	1	1	4	2	3
Ca.wh. F	24	2	2	3	1	2
Ca.wh. F	24	2	2	5	2	1
Am.Ja. F	22	2	1	2	1	5
Am.Ja. F	22	1	1	5	2	5

Am. Ja. F	23	2	1	2	2	5
Am.Ja. F	24	2	2	3	3	3
Am.Ja. F	24	1	1	5	3	1
Am.Ja. F	25	1	1	5	1	1
Am.Ja. F	29	2	1	3	3	3
Am.Ch. F	25	2	2	5	3	1
Ca.Ja. F	25	1	1	5	3	1
Ca.Ja. F	26	1	1	5	2	3
Br.wh. M	23	3	3	5	4	2
Br.wh. M	23	2	1	5	2	2
Br.wh.M	24	4	4	2	2	4
Br.wh.M	24	2	1	4	2	2.5
Br.wh.M	24	2	3	5	3	3
Br.wh. M	25	1	2	4	2	2
Br.wh.M	22	2	2	2	3	4
Am.wh. M	23	1	1	5	3	2
Am.wh. M	24	2	1	3	2	2
Am.wh.M	24	1	1	4	2	3
Am.wh.M	28	2	2	3	3	3
Am.wh.M	29	2	2	5	2	3
Am.wh. M	31	2	2	4	2	2
Am.wh.M	34	3	3	2	4	2
Am.wh.M	36	2	2	4	4	2
Ca.wh. M	23	2	4	5	4	2
Am.Ja M	23	2	2	2	2	2
Am.Ja.M	23	2	2	3	2	2
Am.Ja.M	31	4	5	5	1	4
Am.Ko. M	23	4	3	5	1	5

Note: Br.= British, Am.= American, Ca.= Canadian, Wh.= White, Ja.= Japanese, Ch.= Chinese, Ko.= Korean, F= Female, M= Male

Table 7-4 shows the mean values of NSE evaluations of the role-playing above. The whole NSE group was divided into several sub-categories including "white-British", "white-American", "Asian-American", "female" or "male".

Table 7-4 Mean of evaluations by NSE ethnic groups (N=42)

Ethnic	Sex	Age	Direct	Assertive	Different	Close	Approp-riate
Br. wh.(n=14)	F/M	24.1	1.7	1.9	3.6	2.1	2.4
Am.wh.(n=14)	F/M	27	1.8	1.9	3.9	2.6	2.4
Am.asia(n=14)	F/M	24.6	1.9	1.7	3.9	2.1	2.9
Mean		25.2	1.8	1.8	3.8	2.3	2.6

All NSE groups tended to evaluate the JE's attitude in this situation as indirect (M=1.8), less assertive (M=1.8), and different from their attitude (M=3.8). Concerning the 'close' element, it was found that NSEs expected the relationship of the JE with his interlocutor to become more distant in the future. However, of the three NSE groups, Caucasian Americans evaluated this element highest (M=2.6) British and Caucasian Americans evaluated the way of refusal as being a little less appropriate (M=2.4), but Asian Americans felt neutral about this element.

Table 7-5 Mean of evaluations by NSE gender (N=42)

Sex	Age	Direct	Assertive	Different	Close	Appropriate
Female(n=22)	24.7	1.4	1.4	3.7	2.0	2.5
Male(n=20)	25.9	2.3	2.3	3.9	2.5	2.7
Mean	25.2	1.8	1.8	3.8	2.3	2.6

Table 7-5 (above) shows differences in evaluations between females and males, regardless of ethnic group. Concerning the elements of "direct", "assertive" and "close", differences higher than 0.5 of grades in evaluations were found in the males when compared to the females (see Table 7-5), which suggests that male NSEs seemed to think the JE's attitude were more direct and assertive, and they expected closer relationships to develop in the future.

Pearson's product-moment correlation coefficient was used to find out which among five elements would correlate positively or negatively in which subcategory groups (see Table 7-6). It was also found that the "appropriate" element correlated positively with the "direct" and the "assertive" elements, that is, the more directly speaker B behaved, the more appropriate all the members of the male group of NSE might consider that person to be, and especially the members of the British group might regard the JE as acting more appropriately when he or she sounded assertive.

Table 7-6 Correlation: Pearson's product-moment correlation coefficient; r (N=42)

Mutually related elements	Group	Coefficient
Direct, Appropriate	All (N=42)	r= 0.367*
	Male (N=20)	r= 0.601**
Different, Appropriate	All (N=42)	r= - 0.309*
	Female (N=22)	r= - 0.503*
Close, Appropriate	American (N=28)	r= - 0.388*
	Male (N=20)	r= - 0.468*
Assertive, Appropriate	British (N=14)	r= 0.639*
Direct, Assertive	All (N=42)	r=0.762 (p < .00000001)
	American (N=28)	r=0.781 (p < .000001)
	White (N=28)	r=0.712 (p < 0001)
Direct, Close	White (N=28)	r=0.406*
Direct, Different	Asian American Female (N=10)	r= - 0.791**
	Asian American Male (N=4)	r=0.962*
Assertive, Close	White (=28)	r=0.535**
Different, Close	Asian American Male (N=4)	r= - 0.962*

Note: *p < .05   **p < .01 (p: level of significance, the less p gets, the more significant the statistics would be.)

It was also found that the "appropriate" element correlated negatively with the "different" and "close" elements. In other words, when the NSEs felt the JE was behaving differently from them, the JE decisions may have been considered less appropriate. However, it seems counter-intuitive that when the NSEs regard the JE's attitude to be appropriate, their relationship was expected to become more distant in the future.

Let us examine the evaluations of the JE in more detail. There appear to be two main patterns. Firstly, seven NSEs evaluated the JE's attitude as being more appropriate and expected more distant relationships to develop between them in the future. Secondly, and in contrast, four NSEs evaluated the JE's attitude as being less appropriate and expected closer relationships to develop between them in the future. The former group consisted of three Asian American females, a Caucasian American female, a British male and two Japanese American males. It is assumed that although they seemed to regard the JE's indirect attitude as being appropriate, his indirectness was expected to cause distance in their relationship. The latter group consisted of three Caucasian American males, and a British male. They did not seem to expect his indirect attitude to have a negative impact upon the relationship, even though it was less appropriate. Their comments will be reported in the next section.

Next, let us focus on the relationship between the "close" element and the "direct", "assertive", and "different" elements to examine what kind of competence may be needed to maintain good relationships between NSEs and JEs in conflict situations. Table 7-6 above shows that the "close" element correlated positively with the "direct" and "assertive" element among the white group (N=28) in this situation. In other words, the more direct or assertive the JE's attitude was considered to be by the members of the Caucasian group, the closer they expected the relationship between them to be in the future. It can also be seen that the "close" element correlated negatively with the 'different' element in the Asian male American group, which suggests that when they perceived the JE's attitude to differ from theirs, the relationship between them was expected to be distant.

In sum, the "direct" element was positively related to the "assertive" element, both of which were also positively related to the "close" element, especially in the Caucasian group. This suggests that adopting a direct and assertive attitude in this situation may have been preferable to an indirect attitude but notably, four Caucasians expected the future relationships to be 'close'.

Next, let us consider comments about the JE's behaviour made by forty-two NSEs. Concerning the "direct" element, thirty-seven NSEs (88.1%) evaluated the JE as being very indirect (1) or indirect (2). Their responses were as follows:

He says "o.k." "I don't want to have any trouble with you", and "I try", these "utterances" can be construed as agreeing with the British teacher, and is quite indirect (Japanese American / female).

He says that he will try her suggestion, but it is his hesitance that sends the message that he doesn't really want to (Japanese American / female).
He never said no (Caucasian British / female).

He said "I'll do my best to organise" — not that he will do what she asked, just very general and long pauses (Caucasian British / male).

Request is to use notes: reply is not at all related to request, yet the refusal is somewhat clear (Caucasian Canadian / male).

The data presented above can be categorised into two types. Some NSEs thought that the JE sounded like he was agreeing with his boss, but others thought he was rejecting the advice.

Concerning the "assertive" element, thirty-four NSEs (81%) evaluated the JE as being either not assertive (1) or less assertive (2). The data presented below focus on the parts of his utterance that sounded less assertive. In sum, according to the following responses it seemed that the JE didn't sound like he was either disagreeing with his boss or rejecting her advice.

He says practically nothing to disagree with anything she says. He does not express his opinion at any point even though she is actually being a little rude (Japanese American / female).

When he gave in and said I will try, I don't want any trouble. If he didn't want to write notes to himself, he should have said —I have my own system, but thanks for your suggestion (Japanese American / female).

Never refused, never agreed, I think he will not do the suggestion, but he never makes a firm decision (Japanese American / male).

How he pauses in his sentence, for example, "….so uhhm" in the sentence. It didn't sound like a refusal. It seemed like he would agree to everything she said (Japanese Canadian / female).

Concerning the "different" element, twenty-five 25 NSEs (59.5%) evaluated the JE as being different (4) or very different (5). The data presented below focus on the parts of his utterances that sounded different.

I would state how I keep things organized and ask the other person not to worry and promise to do what they are asking for (Japanese American / female).

"I try... I'll do my best"—I won't use these phrases in refusal (Chinese American /Female).

> The first part may be similar "I don't want to have any trouble with you", but I would say that even though it looks messy, I can usually find everything because I know where I put things (Caucasian American / male).

> I would not hesitate and tell her that I would look for it now (Caucasian British / female).

> I wouldn't refuse a suggestion from my boss (Caucasian Canadian/ female).

> I would suggest an alternative solution to the problem if I really didn't agree (Japanese Canadian / female).

About 60 % of NSEs considered the JE's attitude to be different or very different from them, but nine NSEs (21.4%) considered it to be very similar (1) or similar (2).

> Because she is his boss, it is hard to refuse, so I would say something with about the same meaning, but in a different way. For example, I wouldn't say "I don't want to have any trouble with you", but I would say "I'll try" (Caucasian American / female).

> I wouldn't want to make a fuss in the middle of the office. Though I don't really want to follow the suggestion, I'll say something similar mostly. So the person will leave me alone (Japanese American / female).

> Kind of agree, but not definitely agree (Caucasian British / female).

> Try not to have a confrontation (Caucasian British / male).

In addition, eight other NSEs (19%) were found to evaluate the JE's attitude as being half way between "different" and "similar". One of their comments ran as follows:

> If it is a boss you're speaking to, you wouldn't want to offend them. So agreeing to just trying out the suggestion would mean a direct refusal. (Japanese American / female).

In sum, while more than a half of the NSEs considered the JE's attitude to differ from theirs, about 40% of them seemed to understand his indirect strategy. Indeed, many NSE comments indicated that they were also wary of rejecting their boss's advice.

Concerning the "close" element, twenty-seven NSEs (64.2%) expected the relationship between the JE and the NSE to become distant (1) or very distant (2) in the future, for the following reasons:

> Through such (vague/indirect) miscommunication, frustration and animosity will build (Caucasian American / female).

> I would get irritated because the Japanese person was not telling me how he felt—he is thinking that he is refusing but he is communicating that he will try (Japanese American / female).

> The Japanese person is saying what he thinks I want to hear and not what he really feels. It is difficult to be close with someone who is not honest with you (Caucasian British / female).

> I would become increasingly confused by his responses (Caucasian British/ male).

Eleven other NSEs (about 26 %) evaluated this "close" element half way between "close" and "distant" (3) and their comments ran as follows:

> I don't think the suggester's approach was too direct at all ─she merely said this is what I do ─why don't you try it. She didn't demand anything ─ so I feel the relationship shouldn't be strained (Japanese American/ female).

> Both were very polite & sensitive to each other's feelings (Chinese American / female).

> They're both trying to get on with each other, but miscommunication (Caucasian British / male).

Although the number was small, about a quarter of the NSEs did not think the JE's attitude was so bad, although this did not mean that they thought his strategy would help him develop a good relationship with his boss in the future. Concerning the "appropriate" element, twenty-three NSEs (54.8%) evaluated the JE's response as being very inappropriate (1) or inappropriate (2), for the following reasons:

> I feel that the response was very unprofessional. The Japanese man is not in Japan, but England. Maybe you can get away with misplacing minutes or sloppy work, but in a western culture it could be grounds for dismissal. Also, it's his boss doing the suggesting (Japanese American / female).

Needed to be more assertive & obvious (Caucasian American / male).

It's not a very "appropriate" refusal because he doesn't clearly admit or take ownership of the situation that's been addressed (Caucasian American / male).

Never say to someone, "I don't want to have any trouble with you." It implies that the other person is not a good person (i.e.—you expect to have trouble with them). It is rude (Caucasian British / female).

Somewhat inappropriate: a western office demands western communication, which the refuser will learn to apply over time (Caucasian Canadian / male).

Eleven NSEs (26.2%) evaluated this "appropriate" element as being neutral (3), for the following reasons:

It's a neutral safe answer (Caucasian American / female).

He did not give a rude reply (Japanese American / female).

It was an o.k.-response, but the situation could get worse (Caucasian British / female).

I think the Japanese man handled the situation in neither a bad or good way (Caucasian British /female).

So-so — if you don't want to offend your boss—it is appropriate reply, but it does not sound like a refusal—so it does not seem to accurately express the action of refusing (Japanese Canadian / female).

Only eight NSEs (19%) evaluated the JE's attitude as being appropriate (4) or very appropriate (5), for the following reasons:

Because she is his boss, it is difficult to choose the "appropriateness" of his refusal. Given the situation, and the fact that he doesn't want to follow her suggestion, I feel his answer was as good as mine would be (or close) (Caucasian American/female).

He politely listened to her suggestion without making any promises (Japanese American/female).

Very subtle and reserved (Korean American/male).

He basically told her to "mind her own business" (Caucasian British/male).

Quite appropriate for professional relationship (Caucasian British/male).

In short, the NSE evaluations can be categorised as describing the JE's attitude as being either inappropriate (about 55%) or neutral/appropriate (about 45%), and the JE's attitude can broadly be described as ambivalent. The range of opinions does not seem to depend on gender and ethnicity. Both female and male NSEs evaluated the JE's attitude as being either inappropriate or appropriate, as did both Asian and Caucasian NSEs.

To illustrate, while one Japanese American female considered the JE's response to be very unprofessional and a Caucasian American male considered it to be rather inappropriate, a Caucasian British male considered it to be quite appropriate for a professional relationship. A Caucasian British female also considered his attitude to be rude but a Japanese American female did not. In addition, concerning the JE's statement "I don't want to have any trouble with you", one Caucasian American male claimed that he would use a similar statement, but a Caucasian British female said she never would because it sounded rude and critical of the other person. Thus, the reasons for the differences between NSE evaluations do not simply depend on either gender or ethnicity.

Discussion and Conclusion

Having scored highly in the TOEFL test, the JE in this study can be considered to have high linguistic competence. Insofar as getting high test scores is the mark of a successful learner, he can be considered to be a successful learner of the English language. However, in the real world, we cannot deny the importance of also being able to develop good relationships with people from other countries as well as people in our own country in an increasingly multicultural world. To this end, we need to develop intercultural competence as well as linguistic competence as we learn foreign languages.

In the study described in this chapter, it is clear from both the statistical results and the NSE evaluations of the JE's communication style that his communication style, as evidenced in the role-play and his explanation of it, carries the potential to cause misunderstandings when communicating with NSE. Furthermore, having considered the role-play, the NSEs seemed to expect the relationship between the JE and the NSE to become more distant in the future, which was not at all what the JE claimed he intended. Therefore, we can conclude that more intercultural competence is needed in intercultural situations such as the ones described in this chapter to minimise miscommunication and prevent relationship deterioration.

In the role-play, the JE's rejection of his boss' advice was considered to be "indirect" by about 88% of NSEs. However, according to NSE evaluations and as can be seen in table 7-6, the "direct" element correlated positively with the "close" element, especially in the "white" group. It can be inferred from this result that the JE's indirect attitude may impede the development of a good relationship with his boss in this situation, even though he claimed he intended to avoid causing offence through his indirect attitude. In fact, it's evident from NSE comments that many NSEs also avoid offending their boss when rejecting suggestions, but they would have used different expressions from those used by the JE. Clearly, linguistic competence is necessary to deliver the message the speaker wants to convey to the interlocutor but in cases of disagreement, some tactics seem to be required to avoid causing offence, which relates more to intercultural competence. When the tactics used in other cultures differ from those used in our own, we need to know what they are to become interculturally competent and to avoid unexpected negative results.

According to Gudykunst (2004, 173), "our personalities influence the way we make attributions. Three personality characteristics—category width, uncertainty orientation, and cognitive complexity—affect the flexibility of our cognitive systems". Category width is relevant to this discussion insofar as it involves making attributions about strangers. "Category width refers to the range of instances included in a cognitive category" (Pettigrew 1982, 200).

> Narrow categorizers also tend to have a high degree of confidence in their predictions of and explanations for strangers' behaviour, but their predictions and explanations tend to be inaccurate. Broad categorizers tend to make more accurate predictions of and explanations for strangers' behaviour than narrow categorizers. (Gudykunst 2004, 174)........ . These tendencies, however, can be managed cognitively by becoming mindful when narrow categorizers communicate with people who are different (ibid, 175).

As Gudykunst (2004) notes above, narrow categorizers might predict other people's behaviour inaccurately because of their cognitive tendency.

Without any education or training to help them develop intercultural competence, such people may continue misjudging the behaviour of strangers causing miscommunication in the process, especially in intercultural encounters. In this increasingly globalising world, we will all meet people from different cultural backgrounds as we go through life. At such times, both linguistic and intercultural competences are needed for people to recognise correctly what is happening, and what the interlocutor's behaviours mean in intercultural communication.

In Japan, intercultural matters should be handled carefully in foreign language education, but this does not mean that teachers should impose the communication style of native speakers of target languages upon students. Actually, anecdotal evidence suggests that some Japanese students ask why they need to imitate the communication style of NSEs claiming they would like to use their own communication style, even when communicating in English, because they are Japanese. To persuade them to reconsider, the negative results caused by miscommunication or misunderstanding in intercultural situations need to be shown to these students to help them understand what Gudykunst (2004) means about how cognitive systems function when we communicate with people who are different.

As noted by Byram (1997) above, to be intercultural speakers, people need to be able to explain the sources of misunderstanding and dysfunction to help interlocutors overcome conflicting perspectives. So, they should at least develop their knowledge of different values and communication styles, and notice the impact they can have upon on their relationships with people from other countries while practicing and experiencing communicating with foreign people. In this way, intercultural competence can be developed.

In the study described in this chapter, data were only collected from people from the U.K., the U.S.A. and Canada, but the Japanese are communicating increasingly in English with people who have more diverse cultural backgrounds than are represented in this study. In the future, then, data from English speakers from other areas should be collected to explore the evaluations of Japanese attitudes when communicating in English, or the situations in which they may behave similarly to Japanese people.

Moreover, it is hoped that NSEs will also develop intercultural competence as English is increasingly used as a *World English* by a considerable number of people from various cultural backgrounds around the world. The differences in communication styles described in this chapter between NSEs and JEs, when speaking English, hint at the need for increased mutual understanding to overcome intercultural conflict rooted in misunderstanding.

Bibliography

Beebe, L., T. Takahashi and R. Uliss-Weltz. 1990. Pragmatic transfer in ESL refusals. In *On the development of communicative competence in a second language*, ed. R.C. Scarcella, E. Andersen, and S. Krashen, 55-73. New York: Newbury House.

Byram, M. 1997. *Teaching and assessing intercultural communicative competence*. Clevedon, England: Multilingual Matters.

Furumura, Y. 2004. Ninohjin eigowasha to eigo bogowasha tono taijinkattou taishohouhou no hikaku: Comparative study of interpersonal conflict management between Japanese speakers of English and native speakers of English. *Language Education & Technology* 41: 157-178.

—. 2005. Nihonjin Eigowasha no nihongo /eigo ni okeru taijin koudou youshiki no henyou ni tsuite: About Japanese changing their interpersonal communication patterns between in English and Japanese. *Language Education & Technology Kyushu-Okinawa Bulletin* 5: 1-12.

Gudykunst, W. B. 2004. *Bridging differences: Effective intergroup communication*. Thousand Oaks, CA: Sage.

Hall, E. T. 1976. *Beyond culture*. New York: Doubleday.

Maynard, S. 1993. *Kaiwa bunseki: Conversational analysis*. Tokyo: Kuroshio Shuppan.

Pettigrew, T. F. 1982. Cognitive styles and social behavior. In *Review of Personality and Social Psychology* 3, ed. L. Wheeler, 199-223. Beverly Hills, SA: Sage.

Tsuruta, Y., P. Rossiter, and T. Coulton. 1988. Eigo no social skill: Politeness system in English. Tokyo: Taishukan Shoten.

PART III:

BECOMING INTERCULTURAL THROUGH EDUCATION

CHAPTER EIGHT

DEVELOPING CRITICALITY THROUGH HIGHER EDUCATION LANGUAGE STUDIES

ETSUKO YAMADA

Introduction

Byram (1997, 63) defines "critical cultural awareness" as "an ability to evaluate, critically and on the basis of explicit criteria, perspectives, practices and products in one's own and other cultures and countries." It is a central concept of intercultural communicative competence (ICC) and is assumed to play an important role in ICC. But what exactly does *criticality* mean in the context of foreign language education, and how is it related to the intercultural dimension of language learning?

The study to be described in this chapter explores criticality at work in the everyday practice of foreign language education. The study, conducted in two parts in beginner's Japanese language courses in a British university, showed that whilst critical cultural awareness can develop on its own without targeted instruction even in foreign language classes at the beginners' level, its development can be intensified through targeted instruction in focused lessons.

The study was initially inspired by the Criticality Project at the University of Southampton, whose members took as their theoretical base the concept of criticality outlined by Barnett (1997). This highlighted the importance of fostering criticality and setting appropriate educational aims in line with it, in opposition to the current inclination towards skill-development in higher education. The project aimed to bridge Barnett's theoretical framework and everyday practice in higher education. Having conducted empirical research on Modern Languages[1] degree courses, the project leaders concluded that the "content" elements of intermediate-advanced level language studies and academic content subjects have a significant contribution to make to the development of criticality (Brumfit et al. 2005). However, they also questioned "the precise role of the language element itself" (ibid, 160).

The study described in this chapter focuses on two aspects of Modern Languages Studies which have not been explored by the Criticality Project at the University of Southampton or elsewhere: beginners' language courses and a non-European language course. First, the criticality model developed in the study will be presented, and the fundamental concept of criticality and factors contributing to its development will be explored. Then, a pedagogical approach that can be used to promote criticality development that was developed in the study will be presented, before the basic criticality model is further discussed in relation to other models proposed by Barnett (1997) and by the Criticality Project at the University of Southampton.

The Criticality Model[2]

Beginner-level language studies tend to incline towards the instrumental phase of language learning because of the steady introduction of new grammatical structures in communicative language teaching and the limitation of dealing with abstract topics in written texts. Barnett's (1997) concerns about higher education highlighted in the previous section are particularly evident in beginner-level language studies: there is an over-emphasis on practical skill-development. The Criticality Project at the University of Southampton concluded that the "content" elements of intermediate-advanced level language studies can make a contribution to the development of criticality (Brumfit et al. 2005). The possibility of criticality development at the beginner-level, if any, was assumed not to lie mainly in the study of the "content" of written texts.

While traditional methods test previously established theories and develop and modify them in the light of new data (Greenwood and Levin

---

[1] This article follows the usage of the term "modern language" in UK which refers to "foreign language study" such as French and German in contrast to the study of Greek and Latin.

[2] Yamada (2009), which was published prior to this book, was modified and integrated into this chapter.

1998; Heron and Reason 2001; McNiff and Whitehead 2002; 2005; Reason and Bradbury 2001; Wadsworth 1998), action research was thought to be suitable for the study described in this chapter as it aims to generate new theory or knowledge in relation to practice (action). The study was conducted by the author of this chapter as teacher-researcher in two stages of lower and upper beginner-level courses in four-year Japanese degree programmes at a British university, where the author (of this chapter) was teaching. The course syllabus was based on textbooks, which were based on grammatical structures and integrated the four skills with communicative activities. 49 students took part in the study. The study was conducted in two parts and comprised firstly of the analysis of existing ordinary grammar-based language lessons and secondly of a series of *focused lessons* targeting criticality development in special cultural and linguistic components inserted into the courses. This section describes the first part and the second part is presented in the next section.

Qualitative data, including teacher's diary records and researcher's field notes, were collected over one academic year. Data were also collected from students in group interviews and post-lesson questionnaires, which became the main sources of data. Data were analysed carefully using qualitative data analysis methods (LeCompte and Preissle 1993; Miles and Huberman 1994) and grounded theory (Strauss and Corbin 1998). In addition, observations of beginner-level language lessons in other universities were carried out to ensure that the aims and syllabus of the ordinary lessons of the target courses met the same standards. Analysis of the data gathered in ordinary grammar-based language lessons suggested that students were developing their own original theories (or hypotheses) related to Japanese language learning in the absence of instruction explicitly aimed at developing criticality. A pattern in student theory-building processes was identified through data analysis, which is presented in the form of a model in figure 8-1 below.

Three stages emerged in the theory-building process that started with inquiry and ended with conclusion, a sequence that could be repeated cyclically. Students' initial, original theories (or hypotheses) did not seem to represent an absolute terminal point of the theory-building process, as their initial theories could be challenged later by encounters with different points of view or opinions.

The *analysis* and *conclusion* stages in figure 8-1 were found in group interview data, and the *inquiry* stage was found later in post-lesson questionnaire data. In the extract from group interview data[3] presented below, it can be seen that Original Theory (Student's Hypothesis) 1 was drawn from the underlined part in the data, which took place in the third stage, the *conclusion* stage, of the student's theory-building process. The italicised part took part in the second stage, the *analysis* stage, of the theory-building process. This part suggests that students try to justify and explain their theories (or hypotheses) in the *conclusion* stage.

Original Theory 1: The existing common image of Japanese as a difficult language is not correct.

Student 1: *I think there is a perception that as soon as you tell [   ] you are studying Japanese-they just think that it's impossible thing to do*-but I think **we are learning that it's not that hard** and *I think that speaking and listening parts are a lot easier than reading and writing*

(Interview 4: 137-140)

In Original Theory 1, the student reasoned that the general assumption that Japanese is a difficult language to learn is attributable to people who have never studied Japanese. The generally accepted assumption was questioned and tested against the student's own experience of learning Japanese.

Three different patterns were found in the second stage, the *analysis* stage, of the theory-building process before reaching the *conclusion* stage:

- *analysis by investigating (observation, studying, reviewing)*
- *analysis by comparison (categorisation, contrasting):* **Original Theory 3** (presented in the next section)
- *analysis by linking (connecting, relating with other theories):* **Original Theories 1 and 2** (presented in the next section)

---

[3] Period, comma and the capital at the beginning of the sentence were not used in the transcript because they are not always suitable for spoken discourse. Omissions are expressed by (...), special terms and Japanese words, '   ', and inaudible syllables words, [ ].

Figure 8-1 Student theory-building model

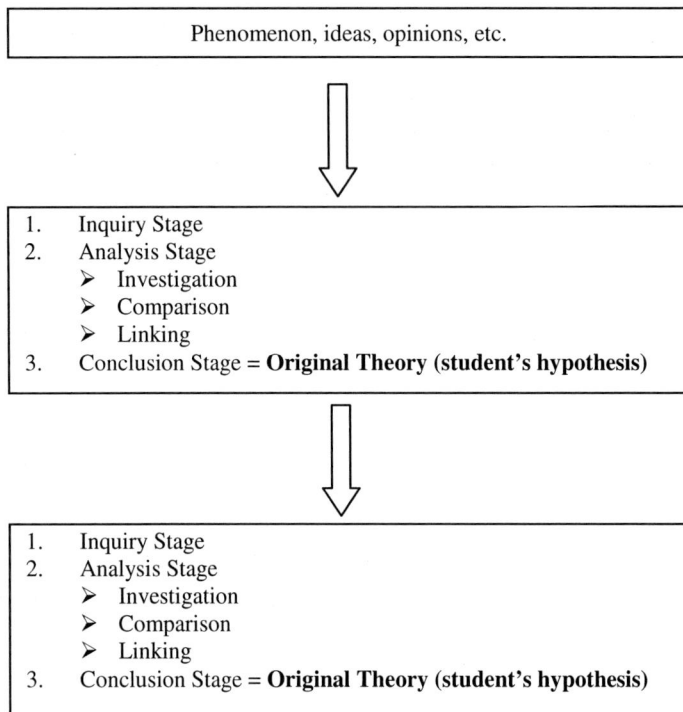

```
┌──────────────────────────────────────────────────────────┐
│              Phenomenon, ideas, opinions, etc.             │
└──────────────────────────────────────────────────────────┘
```

```
┌──────────────────────────────────────────────────────────┐
│  1.   Inquiry Stage                                        │
│  2.   Analysis Stage                                       │
│       ➤  Investigation                                     │
│       ➤  Comparison                                        │
│       ➤  Linking                                           │
│  3.   Conclusion Stage = Original Theory (student's hypothesis) │
└──────────────────────────────────────────────────────────┘
```

```
┌──────────────────────────────────────────────────────────┐
│  1.   Inquiry Stage                                        │
│  2.   Analysis Stage                                       │
│       ➤  Investigation                                     │
│       ➤  Comparison                                        │
│       ➤  Linking                                           │
│  3.   Conclusion Stage = Original Theory (student's hypothesis) │
└──────────────────────────────────────────────────────────┘
```

Analysis by investigating simply involves observing and investigating the details of phenomena, ideas and opinions students have identified as they seek answers to questions that have occurred to them. Such investigation sometimes develops into further analysis of two types. One is *analysis by comparison*, which gets students involved not only in categorising and contrasting between two or more languages or cultures, but also in reflecting on their own language and culture. *Analysis by comparison* is presented later in relation to Original Theory 3. The second one is *analysis by linking*, presented later in relation to Original Theories 1 and 2, in which the students are developing their thoughts by making links with their prior knowledge from sources, in addition to what they are learning in the Japanese language course and pre-existing ideas and opinions.

Secondly, post-lesson questionnaire data were examined in relation to the group interview data analysis presented above. Group interview data shed light on the *analysis* and *conclusion* stages of theory-building, but not on the initiation of the *analysis* stage. However, some elements of post-lesson questionnaire answers indicated that the students were in the process of inquiring, which was evident in expressions such as "I wonder..." and "why". Such data suggests that whilst the students had not yet moved into the *analysis* stage, they were not ignorant of certain phenomena, either. They had spotted something and started to wonder about it.

The two pieces of data presented below are answers to the open-ended question "please tell me about your thoughts on Japan during the lesson", which appeared in the post-lesson questionnaire. The first piece of data relates to a lesson about grammatical structure describing direction and location, in which the Japanese structure differed considerably from English. The second one shows another student beginning to wonder about the language itself.

> I wondered why Japanese language developed in this way, if that was for any particular cultural reason.
> (Post-lesson Questionnaire: 11-25-Fri-13-1A-N-4/5-Q3)

> Wondered why some modern words use katakana rather than hiragana and why they need to distinguish.
> (Post-lesson Questionnaire: 11-25-Fri-13-1A-N-5/5-Q3)

When the students are in the middle of the *inquiry* stage, they are not conscious of it. This is a possible reason why the *inquiry* stage emerged without being obviously related to either the *analysis* or *conclusion* stages. But when students first encounter new phenomena and ideas, and stop for inquiry, the process of *being critical* has already started. Even if they decide to agree with the ideas in the end, it is a different action from simply accepting the presented ideas without thinking. The original theories (or hypotheses) generated by students are the products of question-raising in response to new knowledge, and the consequent search for answers through three stages of analysis. Therefore, it is assumed that any theory-building process has the *inquiry* stage as a starting point, even if it is not visible in the data, and that it is a crucial point in the student theory-building flow, which can be visualised as the first stepping stone in the theory-building process, as illustrated in figure 8-1 above.

Scepticism involves stopping to question what is being presented, and according to Burbules and Berk (1999), scepticism towards commonly accepted truisms is what critical pedagogy and critical thinking have in common. Dewey defines it as suspended judgment and criticality also features in the definition of reflective learning presented below:

> The essence of critical thinking is suspended judgment; and the essence of this suspense is inquiry to determine the nature of the problem before proceeding to attempts at its solution.
>
> (Dewey 1997, 74)

> Non-reflective learning is just the process of accepting what is being presented and memorizing or repeating it, or accepting a situation within which an experience occurs and learning from it. In contrast, reflective learning is the process of being critical. This can mean thinking about the situation (and / or what is presented) and then deciding to accept or seek to change the situation. It can also involve accepting or seeking to change the information which has been presented.
>
> (Jarvis, Holford and Griffin 2003, 70)

The importance of "inquiry" for everyone concerned with teaching and learning is also highlighted by Barnett:

> Rather than imagine afresh a process that we call teaching and learning, the first requirement is that academics reveal themselves to their students as the hard-pressed inquirers that they are. In a genuine process of inquiry, they have to engage in a struggle to formulate their thoughts, to labour to develop their thoughts (whether in the laboratory, the clinical situation or in the library) to expose, their thoughts to others, to encounter critical evaluations of that thinking, to engage in risky undertakings and to move on in the light of those critical comments.
>
> (Barnett 1997, 109, emphasis added)

The *inquiry* stage that emerged in the study described in this chapter is consistent with the notion of scepticism as used in the critical theories referred to above. In this light, figure 8-1 is thus proposed as a model of criticality development, and scepticism is recognised as a fundamental concept of *being critical*.

Further, the Original Theories (or hypotheses) developed by students were grouped into three thematic categories: language, culture and learning process. In this study, Original Theory 1 presented above and Original Theory 3 presented in the next section were categorised under "learning process". And Original Theory 2 presented in the next section were categorised under both "language" and "culture". The development of these three categories suggest therefore that criticality development, as it appeared in this study, was related to *language awareness, cultural awareness* and *learning process*. It can be inferred that grammar-based lessons seemed to hold the potential for criticality development in these three areas. In other words, foreign language learning itself can contribute to the development of criticality.

In addition, this study shows that factors unrelated to the content element of the course contributed to the development of criticality in important ways. It can be inferred that language learning at the beginners' level itself, even if it takes place within the grammar-based framework, has of the potential to develop criticality. Furthermore, *language awareness* and *the learning process* are two dimensions unrelated to "content" that seem to play a special role in criticality development, which in turn sheds light on the "precise role of the language element itself (Brumfit et al. 2005, 160)" in the development of criticality in foreign language education.

An Approach to Criticality Development

In the previous section, it was established that criticality development can be expected in beginners' level language study, to some extent, in the following three dimensions: *language awareness, cultural awareness* and *learning process.* Drawing upon past teaching experience rooted in long-standing interest in the cultural and linguistic dimensions of language teaching, the author of this chapter had come to think that some kinds of classroom activities seemed to stimulate the *thinking* of the learners. These activities were experimented with to develop a teaching approach that would intensify criticality development in learners. The courses in which the activities were situated did not take the development of intercultural competence as their main aim, and the activities had to be slotted into existing grammar-based courses. Consequently, 13 lessons with activities targeting criticality development in cultural and linguistic dimensions were inserted into the existing grammar-based language course framework. They were named *focused lessons* to distinguish them from ordinary grammar-based lessons. In focused lessons, target activities were incorporated into lessons, although the whole contact period was not spent exclusively on them.

Data were gathered concurrently from the 13 focused lessons in the same beginners' Japanese language courses. Data analysis was conducted in the same way as in the study on ordinary grammar-based lessons. Data gathered from the focused lessons suggested that students were engaging in the same original theory-building processes as illustrated in figure 8-1 above. One of the focused lessons (see the Appendix) dealt with *haiku*.[4] After completing a reading comprehension of simple texts about haiku, a list of seasonal words often used in haiku was given to the students, and they were asked to guess the seasons represented in the words. The following interview data illustrate how students were developing their original theory (or hypothesis) in this focused lesson.

Original Theory 2: It is very difficult to translate poems into other languages to high standard.

Student 2:   I mean there are a few things that are sort of similar to English
Student 3:   the fact that *I don't think that there is something more difficult to translate than poems - from a language to another*-because [   ]
Student 2:   yeah
Author: do you think it's difficult or not difficult?
Student 3:   really difficult
Author: difficult
Student 3:   I think it's nearly impossible-*because you have a meaning which is given by the culture-culture of the people himself- which is inside for person -which is inside the people- which is inside the nation-which is inside the country- which is really different from the background of the even the [   ] you-it's so different-for example-French and English poems will be so different because we have so different background*-even if [   ] something like a stupid [   ] between the [two countries]
Student 2:   I mean–even-even just translating a book into another language-I'm sure that's maybe in Japan-there are some books-that in the UK we think really good and then get translated into Japanese-and people don't like it-it seems a rubbish-it's not because the translation is bad-*it's not because it's been written in the UK-it's just because it can't translate from another language–well-cultural context as well as [   ] supposed*
                                            (Interview 5: 388-407)

---

[4] This is a Japanese poem of seventeen syllables, in three lines of five, seven, and five, traditionally containing a reference to the seasons.

The discussion presented in the data above indicates that the participants were linking the theory with their experience of translation. They claimed that the difficulty of translation derived from the difficulty of developing a deep understanding of the background information of two languages and cultures, and were linking this with knowledge of books they knew had been translated from English into other languages. The discussion started with the focused lesson on *haiku*, and then expanded to translation issues more generally as connections were made with their existing knowledge and experience. The discussion presented above also related to their responses to the lesson, which highlighted the difference between the sense of the seasons and the use of seasonal words in Japanese and other languages. Let us focus on student 3, who came from France. He expressed his surprise, both during and after the lesson, at learning that "mikan (satsuma oranges, in Japanese)" was a word representing winter in *haiku*. He insisted that since oranges were harvested in the summer in southern France, any citrus fruit symbolised summer for him. The data presented below, gathered from the post-lesson questionnaire, illustrate this student's point:

To the question, "Have you gained any view which you have not had before? Or is there any new discovery?"

Hum, never forgetting again that there are some differences between European and Japanese seasons.
(Post-lesson Questionnaire: 3-2-Thr-11-2-F-5/5-Q2)

To the question, "In today's lesson, were there any points you had difficulty with? If so, what were they?"

Just thinking that if みかん[5] are harvested in summer in south of France doesn't mean it's the same in Japan (冬)
(Post-lesson Questionnaire: 3-2-Thr-11-2-F-5/5-Q5)

Similar responses were gathered from other students. Having this occasion to think about the sense of season had a certain impact on their way of thinking. Here is another answer to the question, "Have you developed any viewpoints you did not have before? Or did you make any new discoveries?"

---

[5] みかん (mikan) means satsuma orange in British English, and 冬 (fuyu) means winter.

About the significance of particular things to seasons/seasonal words.
(Post-lesson Questionnaire: 3-2-Thr-11-2-F-2/5-Q2)

To the question, "Please tell me about your thought on Japan during the lesson."

How strongly nature plays a part in Japanese life/culture.
(Post-lesson Questionnaire: 3-2-Thr-11-2-F-2/5-Q3)

It is evident from data presented above that the differences that emerged in the lesson between their own and Japanese culture stimulated the students to engage in inquiry, which led to further analysis. This suggests that focused lessons can lead to criticality development, which is directly related to the lessons. Further, analysis of the data gathered from post-lesson questionnaires showed that almost twice as many answers indicating criticality development were found in focused lessons than in ordinary grammar-based lessons. Thus, it can be concluded that the results of this action research study suggest that focused lessons contributed to criticality development more than ordinary grammar-based lessons, although ordinary lessons can also develop criticality to some extent. Therefore carefully designed teaching activities revolving around the three dimensions of *language awareness, cultural awareness* and *learning process* can help intensify criticality development.

Barnett's Model of Criticality in Higher Education

As noted at the start of this chapter, Barnett (1997) developed a theory of criticality to counter the current inclination to practical skills teaching in higher education, particularly in the humanities. Highlighting the importance of fostering "criticality" and setting clear educational aims, Barnett proposed the two axes of domain and level, as shown in table 8-1 below.

How does Barnett's (1997) conceptualisation of criticality compare with other critical theories such as critical pedagogy (e.g. Freire 1972; Giroux 1983) and critical thinking (e.g. McPeck 1981; Siegel 1988)? The ultimate goal of critical pedagogy is "action in the world", and education is seen as a way of fostering critical citizens who can actively engage in transformative action in democratic societies. Therefore, critical pedagogy has an explicitly political mission (Doyé 1996; Guilherme 2002). On the other hand, the goal of critical thinking is to foster criticality within the context of teaching and learning. It aims to foster critical thinking skills for the purposes of persuasion and the justification of one's claims. It does not necessarily have an ultimate goal beyond the school or university. Thus, critical pedagogy is a collective process based on institutions such as schools and universities and it extends to the outside world, while critical thinking is more focused on the individual and their development as thinking begins.

Barnett's (1997) concept of criticality can be distinguished from those that characterise critical pedagogy and critical thinking. He locates critical thinking as a prerequisite of the upper stages of criticality but as a skill operating in the domain of the "world", although critical thinking in other critical theories does not necessarily involve "action in the world". Barnett's (1997) concept of criticality has more in common with critical pedagogy with its focus on education in compulsory schooling, in that both see "action in the world" as being the final collective goal of education. Barnett's (1997) theory, however, is exclusively aimed at higher education. More specifically, he argues that "higher education needs to set up clear *educational aims*: the development of criticality" and emphasises the importance of clarifying the purpose of criticality. Instead of asking what critical thinking is, Barnett (1997, 65) suggests we should start by asking what it is for.

Table 8-1 Barnett's (1997, 103) levels, domains and forms of critical being

Levels of Criticality	Domains		
	Knowledge	Self	World
4. Transformatory critique	Knowledge critique	Reconstruction of self	Critique-in-action (collective reconstruction of world)
3. Refashioning of traditions	Critical thought (malleable traditions of thought)	Development of self within traditions	Mutual understanding and development of traditions
2. Reflexivity	Critical thinking (reflection on one's understanding)	Self-reflection (reflection on one's own projects)	Reflective practice ('metacompetence', 'adaptability', 'flexibility')
1. Critical skills	Discipline-specific critical thinking skills	Self-monitoring to given standards and norms	Problem-solving (means-end instrumentalism)
Forms of criticality	Critical reason	Critical self-reflection	Critical action

Now, let us connect the study described in this chapter with Barnett's concept of criticality. The study was found to support some parts of Barnett's (1997) criticality concept as presented in table 8-1 above, in the domains of knowledge and self at levels 1 to 3. But there was no evidence found of activity at level 4, nor in the domain of "world". In "Original Theory 1: The existing common image of Japanese as a difficult language is not correct", the students were questioning general beliefs by relating and critically testing them against their own experience, and produced their own theories as a result. For this reason, Original Theory 1 was categorised under "Level 3: Refashioning of traditions", which was the highest level of categorisation of any of the data gathered in the study.

Therefore, it can be inferred from the study described in this chapter that some parts of Barnett's (1997) model of criticality can be found in beginners' language courses, even within a grammar-based framework, and that some of the slots presented in table 8-1 above can be filled by beginners' language study only. However, the key point of Barnett's concept is *the integrated form of criticality,* which ultimately leads to social action in the world. Barnett claims that when all of the slots in table 8-1 are integrated for social action in the "world", including the three domains and four levels of criticality, the mission of higher education can be achieved. This highlights the limitation of one part of the degree programme, beginners' language study, which implies in turn that other components of a Modern Languages degree programme, such as the Year Abroad[6] programme and academic content subjects, can and should be used to fill the remaining slots of table 8-1.

The Model of Criticality Developed by the Criticality Project at the University of Southampton

The Criticality Project at the University of Southampton explored criticality in two disciplines: the Modern Languages degree and Social Work courses. Qualitative data gathered from observations and interviews were analysed by project members to explore the possibility of developing "criticality" in higher education in the U.K. They took as their theoretical base the concept of criticality elucidated by Barnett (1997). The project aimed to bridge the gap between theory and practice in higher education. The main outcome of the project was the addition of an empirical dimension to Barnett's (1997) theory, by developing the definition of criticality empirically. According to them, fully functioning criticality involves:

- the motivation to persuade, engage and act on the world
- through the operation of critical understanding of a body of relevant knowledge
- mediated by assimilated experience of how the social and physical environment is structured
- combined with a willingness to question and problematise our shared perceptions of relevance and experience.

(Brumfit et al. 2005, 149)

To what extent did those elements emerge in the study described in this paper? The first element was not found because the domain of "world' itself did not appear, as stated previously. "The operation of critical understanding", however, does correspond to action in *the analysis stage*

---

[6] The Year Abroad programme requires students to spend a year (or a half) in a country where their language is spoken.

in three patterns that emerged in this study. The third element is assumed to result from experience on the Year Abroad and Social Work programmes, both of which involve experience "outside the university community". Therefore, it could not be expected to emerge from data gathered in this study. The fourth element is particularly relevant to the *inquiry* stage, however, which emerged as a fundamental concept of "criticality".

Thus, it can be inferred from this comparison is that beginners' language courses have something to offer within the above definition, but there are limitations. Barnett's (1997) theoretical model of criticality conceptualised in terms of domains and levels is supported by both the study described in this paper and the Criticality Project. However, criticality development does not appear in as neat an order as suggested in table 8-1 above. As both Barnett (1997) and the researchers who took part in the Criticality Project at the University of Southampton admit, the borders of the domains are fuzzy, and it was evident from the data gathered in the study described in this paper that the data do not correspond precisely, one-to-one, to each of the slots in table 8-1.

Reflection on the Self through Encounters with Otherness

The study described in this paper showed that criticality development through the encounters with "otherness" can occur not only in the dimension of *cultural awareness* but also in the dimension of *language awareness*. This was illustrated in Original Theory 2, which highlighted the important role played by students' comparative analysis of cultures and languages in the development of criticality. Theorising about the learning process appeared in the student data related to the language learning process and strategies, as students engaged in critical reflection on their own language learning experience. "Original Theory 1: The existing common image of Japanese as a difficult language is not correct'" was developed by the students in response to their own language experience. This indicates that factors contributing to criticality development which are unrelated to the content element of the course are also important.

In his discussion of intercultural communicative competence (ICC), Byram (1997, 35) suggested that "relativisation of one's own and valuing of others' meanings, beliefs and behaviours does not happen without a reflective and analytical challenge to the ways in which they have been formed and the complex of social forces within which they are experienced". Considering data gathered from the study described in this paper, let us now focus on cases that showed students were "decentring from (their) own taken-for-granted world" (Byram and Fleming 1998, 7), and being led to enquire and reflect upon their own language and culture.

The focused lesson on *haiku* described above suggested that students perceived a clear difference in the sense of seasons between two cultures. The difference between their own (European) and Japanese language and culture stimulated them to engaged in analysis, especially by comparing and contrasting. Students recognised Japanese as being a non-European language and claimed they had started to develop a different view of the English language, their own mother-tongue, by learning it. They thought this was because Japanese was a non-European language that had developed differently from English.

Considering the data presented below, it seems that learning a foreign language itself, especially one that differs from the mother-tongue language group, can encourage students to reflect on their "taken-for-granted" notions. It can be considered as a kind of comparative analysis with reflection between before and after learning Japanese. As Humboldt (1907 (1836), 30) cited in Risager (2006, 60) noted, "the learning of a foreign language ought (…) to entail the gaining of a new standpoint in the previous world view", although the students are assumed not to be aware of the theory.

Original Theory 3: Learning Japanese language makes you reflect on your own language. The fact that it is a non-European language which was developed in a different way from English is an important factor.

Student 4:   it sounds pretentious but it's true that **you do actually see the world differently when you learn a new language-** *because you've only been stocking your language-and then you learn to see the world through somebody else's language-you do actually see the things differently-*that's may does happen-[   ]

Student 5:   **maybe your perspective changes-**so *you learn to be in your own culture from a different life than what you were before*

(Interview 3: 14-20)

Student 5:   **I think you develop your understanding of certain words better as a result of having learnt Japanese**
Student 4:   yeah-yeah
Author: you mean-English word
Student 5:   um

(Interview 3: 77-81)

In the following two stretches of data, one student describes changes in his attitudes towards the English language in more detail. The changes are described in the italicised sections of the data below.

Student 4:   because you like know [   ] we look at something and it means heart and [   ] the thing will be heart as well and the drawing will be heart-I start looking at English words and realise that all the conjugations of other words that exist in English-[   ] that's how you get that and I have never used to do that before-*I just speak it because I was English-but now I look it up and add it and from more my mechanical point of view–I've never did that before I start learning a language-*.

(Interview 3: 84-90)

Student 4:   *because of learning Japanese-it made me look at my language and see -aah–OK-I see I've done it-I see I've built that language up-because I am learning-*I think for Japanese person-you might not make that recognition-unless they themselves are learning another language–because it's natural to them-so [   ] even though the Japanese are fortunate because they speak it naturally-we can get something from it-because we are not speaking it naturally-something that they might not get-we will get a chance to look at it mechanically and build it up as an adult-so it gives you that-it does give you that

(Interview 3: 99-107)

Student 5:   S-5:   *I've done Latin and French before at school-***and I think maybe it's [   ] the 'kanji' as well-that it does definitely bring a whole new level of meaning for words-***thing you don't get in French*

(Interview 3: 111-113)

It can be inferred from the data presented above that even at beginners' level, foreign language education can provide learners with opportunities to encounter *otherness* in other cultures and languages with different systems, and also to reflect upon themselves. Critical reflection plays an important role in fostering sensitivity and awareness towards cultures in the learning of a language. It is, in a sense, about getting to know oneself better by developing relationships with *others* through the interaction of various components. "FLT should lead to cognitive and evaluative orientation towards learners' own society, a relativisation of the taken-for-granted, and consequently to an action orientation" (Byram 1997, 44).

Conclusion

To conclude, the study described in this chapter suggests that criticality can be defined in terms of inquiry and scepticism. Foreign language education itself can develop criticality to some extent even without targeted instruction, but it can be intensified through more conscious teaching design. Encountering "otherness" is a key element that can stimulate critical reflection. However, the study also highlights limitations in the development of the integrated form of criticality by Barnett (1997) at the beginner-level of language studies. Further, the study only investigated one aspect of the Modern Languages degree programme, but its findings carry implications for the larger framework, which needs to be organised by connecting individual components of the degree programme in ways that can jointly promote the development of the integrated form of criticality, which in turn can help to set the agenda for future curricula of the degree programme as a whole in higher education.

Bibliography

Barnett, R. 1997. *Higher education: A critical business.* Buckingham: Open University Press.

Brumfit, C., F. Myles, R. Mitchell, B. Johnston, and P. Ford. 2005. Language study in higher education and the development of criticality. *International Journal of Applied Linguistics* 15, no. 2: 145-168.

Burbules, N. C. and R. Berk. 1999. Critical thinking and critical pedagogy: Relations, differences, and limits. In *Critical theories in education: Changing terrains of knowledge and politics*, ed. T. S. Popkewitz and L. Fendler, 45-66. New York: Routledge.

Byram, M. 1997. *Teaching and assessing intercultural communicative competence*. Clevedon, England: Multilingual Matters.

Byram, M. and M. Fleming. 1998. Introduction to *Language learning in intercultural perspective. Approaches through drama and ethnography*, eds. M. Byram and M. Fleming, 1-10. Cambridge: Cambridge University Press.

Dewey, J. 1997. *How we think.* New York: Dover Publications. (Reprint of the original published in 1933.)

Doyé, P. 1996. Foreign language teaching and education for intercultural and international understanding. *Evaluation and Research in Education* 10, nos.2-3: 104-112.

Freire, P. 1972. *Pedagogy of the oppressed.* London: Sheed and Ward Ltd.

Giroux, H. A. 1983. *Theory and resistance in education. A pedagogy for the opposition.* London: Bergin and Garvey Publishers, Inc.

Greenwood, D. J. and M. Levin. 1998. *Introduction to action research. Social research for social change.* Thousand Oaks, CA: Sage Publications, Inc.

Guilherme, M. 2002. *Critical citizens for an intercultural world. Foreign language education as cultural politics.* Clevedon, England: Multilingual Matters.

Heron, J. and P. Reason. 2001. The practice of co-operative inquiry: Research 'with' rather than 'on' people.In *Handbook of action research. Participative inquiry and practice*, eds. P. Reason and H. Bradbury, 179-188. London: Sage Publications Ltd.

Jarvis, P., J. Holford, and C. Griffin. 2003. *The theory and practice of learning.* London: Kogan Page.

LeCompte, M. and J. Preissle. 1993. *Ethnography and qualitative design in educational research.* San Diego: Academic Press, Inc.

McNiff, J. and J. Whitehead. 2002. *Action research: Principles and practice.* London: Routledge Falmer.

McNiff, J. and J. Whitehead. 2005. *Action research for teachers. A practical guide.* London: David Fulton Publishers Ltd.

McPeck, J. 1981. *Critical thinking and education.* Oxford: Martin Robertson & Company Ltd.

Miles, M. B. and A. M. Huberman. 1994. *Qualitative data analysis. An expanded sourcebook.* Thousand Oaks, CA: Sage Publications, Inc.

Reason, P. and H. Bradbury. 2001. Introduction: Inquiry and participation in search of a world worthy of human aspiration. In *Handbook of action research. Participative inquiry and practice*, eds. P. Reason and H. Bradbury, 1-14. London: Sage Publications Ltd.

Risager, K. 2006. *Language and culture: Global flows and local complexity.* Clevedon, England: Multilingual Matters.

Siegel, H. 1988. *Educating reason: Rationality, critical thinking and education.* New York and London: Routledge.

Strauss, A. L. and J. Corbin. 1998. *Basics of qualitative research: Techniques and procedures for developing grounded theory.* Thousand Oaks, CA: Sage Publications, Inc.

Wadsworth, Y. 1998. What is participatory action research? *Action Research International,* Paper 2,
http://www.scu.edu.au/schools/gcm/ar/ari/p-ywadsworth98.html

Yamada, E. 2009. Discussion on the concept of criticality. *Literacies* 4: 33-50. Kuroshio Publishers. (Also available in *Literacies WEB Journal* 6, no.1: 11-20. http://literacies.9640.jp/)

APPENDIX 1

Focused lesson plan		
Lesson Title: Haiku (Japanese Poetry)	**Date: 2 Mar. 06**	**Upper beginners sem. 2-2**

Main Activities
- Reading comprehension of simple texts about haiku.
- To guess seasons represented by seasonal words in the list.

Can do (language competence)
- To make full use of kanji knowledge in guessing compound words.
- To recognise syllables and rhythms in Japanese language.

Know (knowledge of language and culture)
- To know basic syllables pattern of haiku.
- To recognise the seasons in Japan through the seasonal words.

Why (thinking): intercultural and linguistic dimensions
- To think about why haiku exists in Japan especially in relation to seasonal words.
- To compare the poetry in each country.

CHAPTER NINE

AUTOETHNOGRAPHY AND SELF-REFLECTION: TOOLS FOR SELF-ASSESSING INTERCULTURAL COMPETENCE

PRUE HOLMES AND GILLIAN O'NEILL

Current approaches in language teaching emphasise the need for language learners to acquire not just linguistic competence, but also intercultural competence. Yet, there is a compelling need for all students to develop intercultural competence, given the likelihood of their encountering people from other cultures—in the workplace, schools, universities, and elsewhere. However, answering fundamental questions about what intercultural competence is, how it is acquired, and how people know if they have got it continue to challenge researchers (Byram 2009; Deardorff 2009; Holmes 2005, Rathje 2007; Spitzberg and Changnon 2009). In this chapter, drawing on a study we designed for university students taking an advanced intercultural communication course in a management school, we focus primarily on the third of these questions: "How can people know if they are interculturally competent?"[1] First, we present the theory and methodology underpinning the study we designed for our students. Next, we outline the specific model—the PEER model—which the students were required to apply in their study and the processes involved in it. Finally, we show how our interpretations of the data gained from our students' study helped us to answer the research question.

---

[1] How students develop intercultural competence in intercultural encounters, and how they evaluate their competence as a result of their engagement with a cultural other in these encounters, is reported in another study (O'Neill & Holmes, 2007). Student researchers show how the PEER process enabled them to explore, and thus evaluate, their intercultural competence through the intercultural communication experience itself.

Developing and Assessing Intercultural Competence:
The State of the Art

Recent reviews of intercultural competence indicate the variety of conceptual and methodological approaches to the phenomenon, as well as a multiplicity of definitions of the term itself (Deardorff 2009; Fantini, 2009; Rathje 2007; Spitzberg and Changnon 2009). For example, Spitzberg and Changnon (2009) note that much of the research and conceptualising to date has focused on the individual. By contrast, Rathje (2007) draws the reader's attention to the role of culture: the place where intercultural individuals draw on their knowledge of their own and the other's culture and construct a third way of sense making and knowing in a third place. However, Deardorff (2009), in her synthesis of the extant literature on intercultural competence, notes the dearth of research, particularly in Western models, that investigates the relational aspect of intercultural competence—where relationship building and dialogue take place between the interactants in the intercultural encounter. Our study seeks to address that gap by focusing on the nature of communication in the intercultural encounter over a period of time, the relationship building that takes place, and how these processes impact an individual's ability to self-assess intercultural competence.

To make sense of these processes, we draw on Byram's (1997; 2008; 2009) notion of the intercultural speaker—the person who is "aware of both their own and others' culturally constructed selves" (quoted in Roberts et al. 2001, 30). This person is able to utilise the skills, tools, and attributes of intercultural competence (the five *savoirs*) to manage communication and interaction with people from other social/cultural groups in daily experience. In further developing the notion of the intercultural speaker, Byram (2008, 68) includes the idea of mediation, between oneself and others. He describes mediation as "being able to take an 'external' perspective on oneself as one interacts with others and to analyse and, where desirable, adapt one's behaviour and underlying values and beliefs." He also notes that mediating requires individuals to act interculturally, which requires a "willingness to suspend those deeper values, at least temporarily, in order to be able to understand and empathise with the values of others that are incompatible with one's own" (69).

Further, we acknowledge the emphasis Byram places on the role of language when individuals are required to act as intercultural mediators

(2008). Here he notes that the best mediators are those who have an understanding of the relationship between their own language and language varieties, and those of others. Yet, monoglots too must learn how to act interculturally and mediate between their own and another's language and culture. Therefore, our focus here is on the intercultural competence that individuals require to manage intercultural interactions—the attitudes, knowledge, critical cultural awareness, etc. (those behavioural, cognitive, and affective aspects of the five savoirs)—rather than on their linguistic competence.

Intercultural Encounters and Intercultural Dialogue

Knowing the self is an awareness that comes about through knowing others. The intercultural encounter, the place where individuals bring their own socially and culturally constructed world-views and ways of communicating (Kramsch 1998), is an appropriate place to begin assessing one's intercultural competence. Here, individuals experience others' ways of speaking, being, and doing, and may consequently see the relativity of their own culture. Byram (2003) describes this state as analytical awareness, an awareness that encourages further thought on what is worth retaining, and what might be (re)constructed and (re)negotiated in light of intercultural engagement. Individuals are also afforded the opportunity to reflect on their cultural identity, and their own intercultural competence in light of their lived experience and communication with a cultural other. As Clifford (quoted in Jordan 2002) notes, it is in the travelling between cultures, in the crossing of boundaries, where self-interrogation and self-reflection are enacted. Such encounters are where "experiential learning about self and other gets done, where meanings are tried out, [and] where experience slowly becomes understanding" (Jordan 2002, 96). These communicative processes with the cultural other also provide fertile ground for follow-up field notes, diary writing, and reflection.

Intercultural dialogue has been defined as "a process that comprises an open and respectful exchange or interaction between individuals, groups and organisations with different cultural backgrounds or world-views" ("What is Intercultural Dialogue?" 2008). It also includes tolerance and respect for others as new knowledge is related to one's own self-knowledge and values (Byram et al. 2009). But what happens to this emergent new knowledge as it is introduced, (re)considered, and (re)evaluated? Is this new knowledge absorbed, or left in limbo for later (re)consideration and (re)negotiation in light of further reflection and experience? More importantly, how do people make sense of the dialogue and interaction in intercultural encounters, and how do these experiences impact on their own knowledge of their intercultural competence?

In keeping with ethnographic tradition, developing this kind of critical intercultural awareness is predicated on what Jackson (2006, 80) terms "making the ordinary strange," that is, reflecting on behaviour, communication, and interaction that might go unquestioned in one's own community. Such reflection is usually the result of an experience with someone from another culture.

Therefore, an approach that foregrounds critical analysis of and reflection on the intercultural dialogue that takes place in intercultural encounters offers a rich context for individuals to explore the development and self-assessment of their own intercultural competence.

Autoethnography for Developing and Assessing Intercultural Competence

Engaging students in autoethnography fits within a tradition that offers insights and methods accessible to students doing fieldwork in their own communities (Angrosino 2002; Spradley and McCurdy 1972). More recently, Goodall (quoted in Jordan 2001, 54) speaks of the "new ethnography." Here, novice (or student) ethnographers, through lived experience, can "rediscover the world" through a process of self-reflexivity leading to fresh understandings of self in relation to the other.

New ethnography has been adapted to contexts where language learners can apply ethnographic methods to encounters (e.g., Jackson 2006; Jordan 2002; Roberts et al. 2001) which, it is claimed, will help to develop their intercultural competence (Byram and Zarate 1997). According to Roberts et al., the process of new ethnography "engages them [students] as people, requires them to reflect upon and analyze how they interact with others. The process is thus both cognitive and affective . . . an engagement with a new social identity which is integral with the acquisition of methods and concepts for reflection and analysis" (239). They further argue that an ethnographic approach assists in the development of intercultural competence. Specifically:

> [I]t involves learners in a type of interaction with people of another language and society which makes them conscious of and reflexive about

cross-cultural relationships by engaging them directly with the local and the specific. (242)

As we wanted students to capture experiences, reactions, emotions and reflections drawn from their intercultural encounters, we believe that the processes of autoethnography offer an appropriate approach.

Writing the Self: A Model for Self-Assessment of Intercultural Competence

There is no shortage of instruments for assessing intercultural competence (see for example Fantini's 2009, 466-474, list of 44 assessment tools). However, Fantini warns that, of these instruments, none is adequate for measuring all aspects of intercultural competence: assessment of intercultural competence should be "multidimensional as well as multiperspective [sic], ongoing, integrated, aligned, and intentional" (465), since the process of becoming interculturally competent is usually longitudinal, ongoing, and developmental (even over a life-time).

Given this proviso, recent developments in assessment have begun to focus more on including the learner in the evaluative process (through self-evaluation, reflection and feedback) and methods that include interviews, observation, and judgment by self and others (Deardorff 2009, Jordan 2001, 2002; Jackson 2006, Roberts et al. 2001). Fantini (2009, 464) notes that these processes result in "better and more varied indicators of progress and attainment of learning objectives," in this case, developing and self-assessing intercultural competence.

However, where self-assessment of intercultural competence is concerned, there is an absence of models that 1) describe and explain the *process(es)* by which people become interculturally competent, 2) enable individuals to understand how they are developing it, and 3) assess the extent to which they have acquired it. While models that incorporate portfolios, logs, observation, interviews, and performative tasks are generally considered valuable for assessing intercultural competence (Fantini 2009), no study to date has demonstrated how ethnography reveals the processes that underpin individuals' assessment of their intercultural competence.

It would seem then that written reflections of communication in action—of both self and other—offer a good starting point. However, such descriptive autoethnographic accounts are subject to a number of limitations, especially when enacted and written by novice/student ethnographers. Jordan (2001), for example, states that such accounts are neither objective, neutral, nor definitive. Yet, in the style of Van Maanen's (1988) confessional tales, they do offer insights into the lived and ordinary everyday experiences of individuals at the level of the intercultural encounter.

The writing up of intercultural and interpersonal experience may be messy, incomplete, partial, and even disconfirming, perhaps even leading to a sense of failure (Jordan 2001). Yet, such writings facilitate understanding of self, an understanding that results from detailed, in-depth analysis of prolonged engagement with a specific cultural other. Notwithstanding critiques of self-indulgence or narcissism, or shortcomings in student ethnographic writing abilities, these accounts are useful for investigating how individuals might develop and evaluate intercultural competence because they reflect the ways in which (cultural, religious, historical, personal) identities are "maintained, modified and transformed" (43).

Methodology: An Approach for Developing and Self-Assessing Intercultural Competence

In this section we first describe the study we designed for our student researchers, and then, the ways in which we drew upon it to answer our research question (How do people assess their intercultural competence?).

The Design of the Students' Study

Drawing on the theoretical and methodological approaches discussed above, we designed an assignment that required students to investigate how they went about developing and self-assessing their intercultural competence (see Appendix 1 for the full assignment details). The students, who were enrolled in an advanced undergraduate intercultural communication course within a management faculty, were required to undertake a research assignment involving ethnographic fieldwork as part of their coursework assessment. The assignment had two key objectives. The first objective was to enable students to gain a better understanding of someone from another culture, and therefore, benefit from the opportunity provided by the diversity on their university campus. The second objective was for them, through that engagement, to assess their intercultural competence.[2]

Altogether 64 students engaged with the research assignment over two iterations of the course. They included New Zealand students from a range of ethnic groups, and international students primarily from East and South-East Asia. Each of these 64 students was required to find an informant, or cultural other (a student from another culture who was not taking this same course). Each pair of students had to meet for an hour or more at least six times over a six-week period. The student researchers were asked to apply the PEER model (discussed below) to their meetings, and in the subsequent recording of data, as they tried to make sense of their own intercultural encounters. Finally, they wrote a research report which centred on analysis and interpretation of four or five encounters, followed by a reflection on the research experience. The objective here was for the students to assess their intercultural competence in these encounters. The research approach received ethical approval and included participants' consent, protection of anonymity, and respect for confidentiality. It is these reflections, disguised under pseudonyms, which we draw on in this chapter.

The PEER Model

As our research aim was to understand how our students might assess their intercultural competence, we provided them with a model that we believed would facilitate both their exploration of intercultural engagement with a cultural other and reflection on their own intercultural competence. For two reasons, we named this the PEER model. First, we wanted to capture the idea that the two participants in the intercultural encounters were equals. Secondly, we wanted to indicate the processes underpinning the model.

The PEER model consists of four interconnected and interrelated phases: 1) Prepare, 2) Engage, 3) Evaluate, and 4) Reflect. In preparation for the intercultural encounter, students were asked to *bracket* their experience, that is, to foreground any assumptions, prejudices, and

---

[2] As with many compulsory tasks in controlled environments—whether class-based research assignments as in this case, or intercultural training in a multicultural organisation—students' levels of engagement in and commitment to the task, as would be expected, varied. Their experiences, reported in this chapter, present just some of the students' written reflections.

stereotypes they might hold about their cultural other, as well as any social and communicative phenomena which might not immediately seem to connect and which might be unexpected (Holliday, Hyde and Kullman 2004). Through this piecing together, they were later able to make connections, or identify dissonances and disjunctures between their own interpretations of intercultural communication events, and those of their cultural other.

Next, students engaged—through experiential learning—with their cultural peer over a period of time and across a range of socio-cultural contexts. They had to arrange six meetings with their cultural other across a range of contexts to create intercultural experience, by which we mean experience which "takes place when people from different social groups with different cultures (values, beliefs and behaviours) meet" (Alred, Byram and Fleming 2002, 233-234). The student researchers were given a list of guiding topics (such as family, education, career aspirations, their home town/country, sporting/leisure interests, holiday/work experiences, etc. (See Appendix 2) which they could use as a basis for conversation during their meetings. They were, however, also encouraged to find their own ways of engaging with their cultural other, e.g., sharing a social activity such as a meal, going to the cinema, meeting in a café, partaking in a sporting activity, etc.

The evaluation phase enabled them to draw on the concepts of (intercultural) communication, culture, and intercultural competence that they had been introduced to in the course. Although students were not required to use these terms and concepts in their written accounts, we wanted to expose them to these concepts for two reasons: to sensitise them to the terms used in understanding and analysing intercultural competence, and to assist them in making more informed interpretations of their experiences and the intercultural competence they displayed in their encounters. Students also drew on their ethnographic data (observation, field notes, diary notes, and personal reflections).

The reflection phase required students to reflect on their encounters critically by drawing on their written notes and experiences. They were asked to note any challenges to their preconceptions about communicating with their cultural other, and any ways in which their communicative competence was somehow revealed, exposed, questioned, and/or challenged, and which thus prompted a (re)construction and/or (re)negotiation of previously taken-for-granted ways of communicating, thinking, and behaving. Utilising reflection upon and sense-making of communicative events, action, and conversations as their primary tools, each student captured a picture of his or her individual lived experience and interculturality.

To some extent, the PEER model embodies aspects of Kolb's (1984) four stages of experiential learning (concrete experience, reflective observation, abstract conceptualisation, active experimentation). Kolb noted that the learning cycle can begin at any of the four stages, and it may also be continuous, that is, learners may repeat the learning cycle as many times as they need to. Similarly, the PEER model accommodates this flexibility. The value of this approach (over others that test dimensions, or require Likert scale assessments of intercultural competence) is that it has the potential to be both empowering and emancipatory: it encourages students to critically self-reflect through questioning, emotional involvement and self-discovery. The resulting congruences and dissonances—between their own cultural identities and those of their intercultural other—that emerge in the intercultural encounter enable self-evaluation.

Autoethnographic Writing

The study engaged the student researchers in the following: the recording and analysis of field notes, the writing up of intercultural encounters, and the subsequent personal reflections that emerged. The process is akin to Ellis and Bochner's (2000) authoethnography, which they describe as an autobiographical genre of writing and research whereby the researcher focuses "outward on social and cultural aspects of [his/her] personal experiences" and "inward, exposing a vulnerable self" (739). Researchers create texts which feature "concrete action, dialogue, emotion, embodiment, spirituality, and self-consciousness," revealed through "action, feeling, thought, and language" (739). In writing their reports, students constructed unique understandings of how to assess their own intercultural competence.

Their reflections also embodied a phenomenological approach—one that encouraged self-conscious examination of "lived experience" through engagement with a cultural other. *Verstehen*—of moving into the mind of the other by way of empathy (Patton 1990)—was also an important resource for this examination. Students were required to use processes of self-reflection that, we hoped, would lead to critical self-awareness. We were also interested in those things that might limit students to make sense of their intercultural interactions; as a result of unshared culture, worldview, and communication codes and practices.

The Design of our Study

As stated in the introduction to this chapter, our research purpose was to answer the question: "How do people know if they are interculturally competent?" We centred on the data provided by the students' self-reflections on their intercultural encounters to help us answer this question, looking for examples that illustrated how the students themselves judged their competence in intercultural encounters. We sought "sensitising concepts" that "offer[ed] ways of seeing, organizing, and understanding experience" which might be used as "points of departure from which to study the data" (Charmaz 2003, 259). We then applied Braun and Clarke's (2006) thematic analysis approach, looking for themes that identified recurrent, important, significant, and unique episodes, as well as compelling extracts. Our interest lay not only in examples where students judged themselves as competent/successful intercultural communicators, but also in those self-evaluations that described partial, limited, or even failed competence.

Thus, the selected student researchers' experiences, reported in the findings that follow, demonstrate varieties of engagement, reflection and self-evaluation.

Findings

"We don't see things as they are, we see them as we are." Anias Nin (authors' emphasis)

When it comes to exploring and assessing intercultural competence, the intercultural encounter offers an opportunity to peel back the limiting layers of self and so see ourselves more fully. In this study, the intercultural encounter was also the place where the four elements of the PEER model were brought together to form an interconnected and interdependent process that would, it was hoped, facilitate self-evaluation of intercultural competence.

Reflecting on Self and the Other

The prepare stage is designed to encourage us to first see ourselves *as we are*. It is a crucial part of the self-assessment process. It requires a conscious foregrounding and acknowledgement of our tendency to stereotype, categorise, and judge others according to our own narrow, unquestioned criteria, and also to construct the other as someone totally different from ourselves—a stranger. Such negative perceptions can disincline us to engage with a cultural other, or even create a fear of engagement, as seen in the case of Joe, a Korean New Zealander: "When I was in high school I had a negative stereotype of Maori students who were extremely offensive to Asian students like me. Maoris always scared me with their terrible faces and by sticking out their tongues . . . thus I shunned contact with them. In order to be competent in the intercultural communication with my cultural other, who has [a] Maori background, I had to overcome the feelings of anxiety which had existed in my mind for a long time."

Scepticism about the value of seeing ourselves through the eyes of others also surfaced at the initial stage: "Before I met with my cultural other, I kept asking myself why I needed to do this research to understand myself better by interviewing [another]. Is there anyone else more clear about if I am interculturally competent than myself?" However, having engaged, evaluated, and critically reflected on her intercultural encounters, Wei Wei concluded: "And now I think I got the answer. I did need my cultural other to refer to and reflect myself from him as a mirror. And through this mirror, I saw a different me."

Once engagement begins, the PEER process takes on an iterative nature as each fresh encounter calls for evaluation, reflection, and self-reflection, and then further preparation for the next encounter. From then on, it also becomes much less easy for individuals to disentangle the threads of the recurrent phases as the interactions between self and the cultural other develop. Nonetheless, a number of key elements emerged from the data.

Reflecting on Challenge and Discomfort

First, gaining self-knowledge through intercultural interaction is not always straightforward or positive. Mary, a New Zealander reflected:

At times the learning I received and my interaction with my cultural other have been very challenging and uncomfortable. I have found that change is not comfortable. What happened then? Did I want to shut my mind to otherness and different ways of thinking? Yes. The shift in thinking created strain against what was nestled comfortably in the crevices of my mind. But then there came a mixture of wonder with the reluctance towards my "new view." The mixture of feelings created a softening towards change, and a gradual acceptance of my new world-view has occurred.

As a result of working through challenge and discomfort, Mary was able to begin the process of loosening the cultural typifications that constrain individuals and restrict their ability to see the relativity of their own cultures. Reflecting finally on her series of intercultural encounters, Mary concluded:

It took me to a new level of awareness of how to relate to others from the place of my own culture. . . . The meetings' purpose gave us "permission" to enter into a deeper level of conversation, one that I believe was mutually beneficial and enjoyable. We both got to interact and learn from a cultural other. I asked Laila (my cultural other) how she found the meetings, and she said, "This has been like meeting with a friend". We have become friends.

Reflecting on Difference

As the students moved back and forth through the phases of the PEER process, their fear of difference lessened and they became more accepting of it: "For competence to exist within my interactions with cultural others," reflected Michaela, a New Zealander, "I must first recognise there will be differences. These differences help form the unique relationships between people of different cultures." The ability to accept difference was also a source of pleasure, as illustrated by Joe's reflection: "Once I opened my mind, I felt much easier to accept cultural differences, and also unconsciously established a sentiment of enjoyment . . . I felt like I had become re-socialised and became closer to New Zealand culture." A newfound ability to tolerate dissonance was often welcomed as a sign of increasing intercultural competence:

This shift [away from a neat categorisation process] created room for a new idea which has been very thought-provoking: one view is not the right view, but only one view. This thought creates a space to stand and look around; a place where I can listen and start to enter into dialogue from. I'm thinking I will grow to enjoy this new space. (Michaela)

Engaging with a cultural other also creates an opportunity to (re)construct and (re)negotiate one's own views and identity. Ashleigh, a New Zealander, found that her intercultural encounters brought a revelation about her thinking and attitudes to others:

> Before I interviewed my cultural other, I did not realise I had many negative views of groups that are different from me. I am beginning to understand that when people have different views to me, it does not mean I have to believe these views as well, I just have to accept that we view things differently. Before . . . I was viewing people who did not share my views as wrong, which is a highly ignorant perspective. I am very glad that I have reflected on this communication and realised where I have poor intercultural competence. I judged people too quickly and stereotyped people's cultures before taking the time to get to know them. I think I still hold some stereotypical views but I am conscious that I need to change these.

Reflecting on Cultural and Religious Relativity

Religious difference emerged as a particularly challenging aspect of culture. Faith is central to many people's identity and accepting or accommodating religious differences can prove difficult as evidenced by Elena: "I still find it hard to accept people's religion but understand that I do not need to believe what they believe for us to communicate."

Elena's critical insight into the fact that we do not need to agree with people in order to communicate with them was also echoed by Rahima, a Muslim participant in our study. Rahima is an Afghani with New Zealand permanent resident status. She describes herself as well travelled, multilingual, confident in her Muslim identity and dress and interested in others and their cultures. She asserted, however, after much critical reflection that her religion and culture would always influence the degree of comfort and competence she felt when interacting with cultural others:

> I believe it is easier for [people in] some cultures and more difficult for [those] in other cultures to become culturally competent . . . Because I hold strong religious beliefs, it often becomes a challenge for me to communicate and interact or perhaps get to a closer relationship with people from other cultures. I do understand that it is interesting for a lot of people to see us with head scarves. And I do appreciate it when somebody asks why we wear it. However, I do get sad when someone intentionally and deliberately tries to insult my religion. The most interesting, or funny thing is when I'm asked if I have hair on my head. I used to laugh and say, of course I do. But one thing that amuses me is how one can think like that.

I mean we're all human, chemically, physiologically, biologically the same, but culture provides the different views of the world we have.

Rahima goes on to clarify her position: "Perhaps I could never be competent in this context [social interaction with secularised New Zealand females about clubbing and boyfriends] because that would mean that I have to cross my values, change my behaviour and attitude to be competent." Rahima's reflections here challenge the extent to which people may have to (re)construct or (re)negotiate their (religious, cultural, historical, regional, personal, etc.) identities in order to consider themselves competent. As a result of her self-reflection, Rahima displayed self-enlightenment, acknowledging that she did not need to compromise or abandon the values and beliefs in which she had been educated and socialised. This position implies that there are limits to adaptability and open-mindedness, and the extent to which people do/do not judge cultural others. Rahima's experience also raises questions regarding the extent to which reconstruction and renegotiation of identity is necessary for intercultural competence, questions to which there are as yet no satisfactory answers.

Exposing a Vulnerable Self

The extent, if any, to which individuals are required to adjust or adapt in order to achieve intercultural competence in their own eyes, or in those of others, is poignantly illustrated in Shanshan's story. As it also reveals how powerfully the intercultural interaction can act upon the individual's sense of self, it is recounted in detail. As Shanshan explores her reactions to her cultural other, Jim, she begins to question his motivation in being so nice to her:

He was honest but not rude and he always worried about my feeling when he quoted his friends' opinion on Chinese students. And he also respected and showed lots of interest to my culture. He always asked my opinion when he suggested something by saying, "What do you think, Shanshan?" And all these things kind of made me feel unreal. Then I began to think, "Is this his true colour or is he trying to give me the right answer to make him look competent?"

In response to her self-questioning she writes:

And I began to ask myself "Why am I having this feeling?" – "Because you are not confident of your own culture, you don't even have the belief of your own culture." I heard this voice and I was so afraid of this reason, as it is the truth that I didn't realise until now and still want to deny. And I continued to ask myself "How does it come that I lost the confidence in my own culture?" I tried so hard to find out where is the beginning of this "culturally lost" and finally I thought there is no reason but my own experiences and my own judgements. I guess the second night of my arriving in New Zealand played an important role on my first impression of how the society feels about our Chinese students. I was walking and tried to familiar[ise myself] with the way back home to my home-stay family. Then a car drove by with the yelling of "You ugly yellow Chinese, go back home!" And somebody threw an egg towards me and it broke on my shoulder. I guess it broke my heart as well at that time. It was something I was really not prepared for or expected.

In her personal reflections, Shanshan confided: "I have never told anybody about this, not even my home-stay family." This unpleasant encounter clearly coloured her subsequent attitudes to intercultural interaction and negatively impacted her sense of her Chinese self. She goes on to say:

I remember that night. I went back home and washed my clothes by myself with sobbing. And I guess this experience made me want to be different from other Chinese as I thought there must be some really bad Chinese here . . . that people would yell that at me.

Thoughts that her Chinese self might be unacceptable in New Zealand were confirmed by her first experience of university life.

When I started my campus life I found that all the Kiwi students were sitting together and Chinese students have their own group. I did not want to sit with Chinese at that time as I assumed that is not good and I didn't dare sit with the Kiwi students as I thought they might dislike me . . . so I always sit at some free place.

Reflecting on her intercultural competence prior to engaging with Jim, Shanshan writes: "I thought I was more competent than others as I was willing to make Kiwi friends and try to connect with the local society. However, after taking this course and meeting Jim and writing this report, I realise that I was not competent at all." She arrives at this conclusion because she now sees her true motivation for wanting to interact with Kiwis: "I did all this to recover the shadow of the breaking egg. I'm sorry to say that – as the song says 'The first cut is the deepest'". The egg incident had so clouded Shanshan's world that it dictated much of her subsequent intercultural behaviour and thinking about her own culture.

In the case of Shanshan, ethnography, coupled with the PEER model for intercultural interaction, did indeed reveal the vulnerable self which we all take into our intercultural encounters. However, Shanshan ultimately judged herself "lucky that she had the opportunity to revalue and re-evaluate" herself: "I found the problem when I engaged with my cultural other, and I know that I need to find myself and have belief in my own culture from now on."

The quest to determine and assess one's intercultural competence is, as shown by the stories of Rahima and Shanshan in particular, a complex yet highly individual one. It begins with an attempt to understand one's own limitations, ethnocentrism, stereotypes and preconceptions and develops in line with a willingness to test and question them through lived experience and critical self-reflection.

Conclusion

As stated at the outset, the aim of this chapter is to show the value of ethnography as a tool for developing and self-assessing intercultural competence. First, at a methodological level, the students' reflections that emerged as a result of this study show that understanding one's own intercultural competence necessitates a process of ongoing critical reflection and self-reflection. Setting up a process that involves preparation, engagement, evaluation, and reflection—by way of the PEER model—provides a methodology for achieving this goal.

Second, the writing process itself constituted much more than "writing up" the field notes and "writing down" the narrative of personal/cultural experience. The student researchers' examples illustrated that writing became a process of discovery as they drew on texts, notes, presentations, and possibilities. As Shanshan's story illustrates, writing about intercultural competence encouraged "a conscious experiencing of the self as both inquirer and respondent, as teacher and learner, as the one coming to know the self within the processes of research itself" (Lincoln and Guba 2000, 183). This self-reflexive process entails not only interrogation and discovery of the cultural other through intercultural encounters, but also discovery of the self. While open to the criticisms of being produced by novice ethnographers, the resultant student texts did expose their vulnerable, and at times, incompetent selves. As such they are "hybrid," embodying all the limitations of "anglicised student ethnography code" (Roberts, quoted in Jordan 2001, 53).

Third, at a theoretical level, several outcomes emerge. The student texts offer important insights into the processes of developing and assessing intercultural competence. Students gained a deeper self-knowledge, often leading to a greater understanding of their own critical cultural awareness by 1) moving from a position of complacency to seeing the complexity of communication in the intercultural encounter; 2) noting their emotions as they experienced intercultural communication as pleasure, satisfaction, but also as pain, and communicative inadequacy; 3) experiencing failure through inadequate self-knowledge, but celebrating the success that came of enlightenment and growth as a result of their intercultural communication experiences; and 4) acknowledging that competence does not predicate compromise where values and beliefs must be reconstructed or abandoned.

The intercultural encounter, and the relationships individuals experience within its context, is critical to understanding where intercultural competence resides. Within the intercultural encounter, and by way of the PEER process, individuals monitor and self-assess their competence in interaction with cultural others. Kramsch (1998, 26) argues that the intercultural encounter is about "the way each culture views the other in the mirror of itself". However, while we may be helped by seeing ourselves in the mirror of the other, the ultimate challenge is to see ourselves as we are. As Celia wrote in her reflection:

> I've always assessed my intercultural competence based on the faults I've seen in other people's intercultural communication instead of on my interactions with a cultural other. . . . It caused me to more honestly ask myself the hard questions about my interactions.

Although this study presents a framework that others could use to assess their intercultural competence, some aspects of intercultural competence itself remain unresolved. For example, Rahima's questioning of her own degree of competence echoes Deardorff's (2009) point that there remains much to discuss and explore about adaptability, what specifically is meant by adaptation, and who adapts to whom and to what degree.

In conclusion, these student autoethnographic self-reflections—imperfect, incomplete, and idiosyncratic as they are—provide a tool or process for developing and self-assessing intercultural competence. Their self-reflections reveal the process as messy, open-ended, and ongoing. There is no one-size-fits-all definition of what constitutes intercultural competence. Further, as our students' reflections demonstrate, there is no single threshold by which individuals may measure the extent of their intercultural competence. If anything, intercultural competence might be described as an openness to self and others, a readiness to tolerate difference, and an ability to maintain an acceptably intact sense of self while also exposing oneself to the risks and challenges resulting from intercultural encounters. Self-reflection, by way of the PEER model, provides the tool for this self-assessment.

Acknowledgements

We would like to thank the students in the Intercultural Communication course for engaging with the assignment and contributing their written reflections to our analysis.

Bibliography

Alred, G., M. Byram, and M. Fleming. 2003. *Intercultural experience and education*. Clevedon, England: Multilingual Matters.

Angrosino, M. ed. 2002. *Doing cultural anthropology: Projects for ethnographic data collection*. Prospect Heights, IL: Waveland Press.

Braun, V. and V. Clarke. 2006. Using thematic analysis in psychology. *Qualitative Research in Psychology* 3: 77-101.

Byram, M., M. Barrett, J. Ipgrave, R. Jackson and M. Mendez Garcia. 2009. *Autobiography of intercultural encounters*. Strasbourg: Council of Europe. http://www.coe.int/t/dg4/autobiography/default_EN.asp?

Byram, M. 1997. *Teaching and assessing intercultural communicative competence*. Clevedon, England: Multilingual Matters.

—. 2003. "On being 'bicultural' and 'intercultural'". In *Intercultural Experience and Education*, eds. Geof Alred, Michael Byram and Michael Fleming, 50-66. Clevedon, England: Multilingual Matters.

—. 2008. *From foreign language education to education for intercultural citizenship: Essays and reflections*. Clevedon, England: Multilingual Matters.

—. 2009. "Intercultural competence in foreign language education". In *The Sage handbook of intercultural competence*, ed. Darla Deardorff, 321-332. Thousand Oaks, CA: Sage.

Byram, M. and G. Zarate. 1997. Defining and assessing intercultural competence: Some principles and proposals for the European context. *Language Teaching, 29,* 14-18.

Charmaz, K. 2003. "Grounded theory: Objectivist and constructivist methods". In *Strategies for qualitative inquiry,* eds. Norman Denzin and Yvonna Lincoln, 249-291. Thousand Oaks, CA: Sage.

Deardorff, D. (2009). "Synthesizing conceptualizations of intercultural competence: A summary and emerging themes". In *The Sage handbook of intercultural competence,* ed. Darla Deardorff, 264-270. Thousand Oaks, CA: Sage.

Ellis, C. and A. Bochner. 2000. "Autoethnography, personal narrative, reflexivity: Researcher as subject". In *Handbook of qualitative research,* eds. Norman Denzin and Yvonna Lincoln, 733-768. Thousand Oaks, CA: Sage.

Fantini, A. 2009. "Assessing intercultural competence". In *The Sage handbook of intercultural competence,* ed. D. Deardorff, ed. 456-476. Thousand Oaks, CA: Sage.

Holliday, A., M. Hyde and J. Kullman. 2004. *Intercultural communication: An advanced reader.* London: Routledge.

Holmes, P. 2006. Problematising intercultural communication competence in the pluricultural classroom: Chinese students in a New Zealand university. *Language and Intercultural Communication* 6, no. 1: 18-34.

Jackson, J. 2006. Ethnographic preparation for short-term study and residence in the target culture. *International Journal of Intercultural Relations* 30: 77-98.

Jordan, S. 2001. Writing the other, writing the self: Transforming consciousness through ethnographic writing. *Language and Intercultural Communication* 1: 40-56.

—. 2002. Ethnographic encounters: The processes of cultural translation. *Language and Intercultural Communication* 2: 96-110.

Kolb, D. 1984. *Experiential learning: Experience as the source of learning and development.* Englewood Cliffs, NJ: Prentice-Hall.

Kramsch, C. 1998. *Language and culture.* Oxford, England: Oxford University Press.

Lincoln, Y. and E. Guba. 2000. "Paradigmatic controversies, contradictions, and emerging confluences". In *Handbook of qualitative research,* eds. Norman Denzin and Yvonna Lincoln, 163-188. Thousand Oaks, CA: Sage.

Nin, A. 2009. Diaries. http://www.inet.ba/~admahmut/quotes/anais-nin-quotes/html.

O'Neill, G. and P. Holmes. 2007. Managing intercultural interactions in multicultural contexts: A framework for intercultural communication competence self assessment. Paper presented at Assessing Language and (Inter-)Cultural Competences in Higher Education, International

Bilingual Conference (English and French), August 30–September 1. University of Turku, Finland.

Patton, M. 1990. *Qualitative evaluation and research methods.* Newbury Park, CA: Sage.

Rathje, S. 2007. Intercultural competence: The status and future of a controversial concept. *Language and Intercultural Communication* 7: 254-266.

Roberts, C., M. Byram, A. Barro, S. Jordan, and B. Street. 2001. *Language learners as ethnographers.* Multilingual Matters: Clevedon, England.

Spitzberg, B. and G. Changnon. 2009. Conceptualizing intercultural competence. In *The Sage handbook of intercultural competence,* ed. Darla Deardorff, 2-52. Thousand Oaks, CA: Sage.

Spradley, J. and D. McCurdy. 1972. *The cultural experience: Ethnography in complex societies.* Chicago: Science Research Associates.

Van Maanen, J. 1988. *Tales of the field: On writing ethnography.* Chicago: Chicago University Press.

What is intercultural dialogue? 2008. European Institute for Comparative Cultural Research.
http://www.interculturaldialogue.eu/web/intercultural-dialogue.php

APPENDIX 1

Intercultural Competence Research Report

Purpose

The purpose of this assignment is to learn about and assess your own intercultural competence. You will carry out ethnographic research with a student at (name of campus) who is from another culture. You will identify an appropriate participant, a cultural other, and meet at least five times. The purpose of the meetings is to explore your own intercultural competence as you communicate with this person and come to understand his/her intercultural communication experiences. You will present your findings, analysis and assessment of **your own** intercultural competence (as a result of your encounters with your chosen cultural other) in a self-reflective research report of about 2000 words.

Specifically, the objectives are to:

1. Get a better understanding about someone from another culture, and therefore, benefit from the opportunity provided by the diversity at (name of campus);
2. Develop an understanding of your own intercultural competence (in light of your intercultural communication experiences with your cultural other), and learn how to assess it.

In the course of your meetings with your cultural other you will explore the first and second objectives. In writing the report (about 2000 words), you will address the second objective.

Process

As a researcher, you will engage in the following processes and steps:

Reading

First, you should familiarise yourself with the readings on intercultural competence in your text book and those in the course reader. We will discuss this topic in class as well. You may also need to draw on other concepts and materials discussed throughout the course, e.g., culture, world-view (religion), identity, language, nonverbal communication, etc.

Participant selection

You will choose the cultural other you would like to work with for this research project. Your cultural other must also be a student at (name of campus). If you are a New Zealand student you will need to find an international student from another culture to work with. If you are an international student, you will need to partner with a student who is from New Zealand. You must choose someone you do not already know (i.e., do not choose a friend). Seek my help if you need any assistance in finding a cultural other, or you might ask your classmates to identify one of their friends for this assignment.

Ethics requirements

The research involves collecting information from human subjects. You are, therefore, required to follow the guidelines set out by the (name of university) the right to withdraw from the research at any time, and is not required to answer questions if s/he so desires. Your cultural other must sign the consent form provided to indicate agreement to participate in the research. Please ensure that you submit your signed consent form to me at the time when you web-submit your assignment.

Guiding research questions

a) To what extent am I interculturally competent in my communication?
b) How do I assess my intercultural competence (i.e., how do I know I am interculturally competent)?

Collecting data: Keeping a journal

Since the purpose of this research is to assess your own intercultural competence, during the research process you will need to be focusing on your own intercultural competence. Therefore, you will be thinking about and conscious of your own responses and reactions to the topics and experiences you discuss with your cultural other. Record these ideas in a journal (use an exercise book) as you progress through the data collection.

After you have identified your cultural other and introduced him/her to the study, write a brief pen-portrait of this person. Write down any cultural expectations or preconceptions you have or had beforehand about someone from that culture.

You are required to meet with your participant for a minimum of five times. During or immediately after each of your meetings, you must record your encounters and conversations in your journal.

- Describe briefly what you and your cultural other discussed. Include examples of the dialogue between you, reactions, nonverbal communication, etc.
- Highlight areas of agreement and difference in communication and culture.
- Include any insights gained and reflections noted about your responses and thoughts.
- Record any challenges to your own, or to your cultural other's preconceptions about what is appropriate or effective communication and/or behaviour in the contexts you discuss. Describe what these are. To help you write about these self-reflections, you should draw on understandings of intercultural competence (your own, those discussed in class, and models and examples in the readings).

Interpreting/making sense of the emerging data (analysis)

In talking with your cultural other and in making sense of your own intercultural competence you will be engaging in a process of *thick description* (Geertz 1973), the recording of detail of human life in layers of contextual significance. This process requires you to derive meaning from a broad view of social phenomena and piece together different, interconnected perspectives. It also requires you to explore and make sense of the ongoing emergence of social phenomena, which may not immediately seem to connect and which may be unexpected (Holliday, Hyde & Kullman, 2004, p. 8). Thus, you are making connections between your own interpretations of communication events, as well as the interpretations of your cultural other, and other people's interpretations as well. We will look at this term and how we, as researchers, develop thick description as we progress through the course each week

Self-reflection

During and at the end of each meeting/interview, and also at the end of the data collection period, you should engage in personal reflection. Think about how you have changed as a result of each meeting and this research project. Reflect upon what you learned about your cultural other, and what you learned about yourself. Continue to ask yourself the following questions:

a) Am I continuing to hold any preconceptions (stereotypes, ethnocentric views, prejudices) I had about this person? Why/why not?
b) Am I beginning to modify/adjust/challenge any of these preconceptions?
c) In what ways are these preconceptions being confirmed or challenged? How? Why?
d) To what extent are my assumptions and my own values and beliefs about my own culture being challenged, tested, (re)constructed, and/or (re)negotiated?
e) In what ways and in what contexts am I/am I not more interculturally competent?

During your encounters with your cultural other, consider how your observations, experiences, and insights might link with the learning you have been engaging with in class and in your reading about intercultural competence and intercultural communication. Do these theories/concepts in any way help to inform your understanding of how you might assess your own intercultural competence? Conversely, does your understanding of your encounters with your cultural other challenge the theories?

Conclusions

Using this research data, develop a set of criteria for self-assessment of intercultural competence. Use the two guiding research questions and the outcomes from your data collection and analysis to develop these criteria. Consider also the discussion in class in week 5 when we examined what intercultural competence is.

Personal reflection: (about 500 words and additional to the 2000 word count)

- Generally, what did you learn from doing this research assignment, including the parts you enjoyed, and/or the parts you found challenging?
- More specifically, what did you learn about your own intercultural competence? Do you believe you are now more interculturally competent or aware as a result of this research assignment? Whether yes or no, provide reasons and examples to support your answer.

Additional requirements

At the end of this course (around the time of web-submission of your assignment), please hand-submit your exercise book of journal entries and notes about the research assignment, and the signed consent form from your cultural other.

APPENDIX 2

Guidelines for Discussion at Meetings/Interviews and Recording of Journal Entries

Below is a list of possible topics intended for collaborative discussion. These are intended as a guide to get you started. You may also develop your own topics. You should be finding out about your cultural other as well as enabling him/her to find out about you. Thus, the conversation is two-way. However, your report will be mainly about your own intercultural competence when you engage with your cultural other.

The topics are intended for in-depth discussion, so you should spend your five meetings talking about one or two each time, although you do not need to cover all the topics. In-depth discussion around some of these topics should also provide interesting episodes of intercultural communication from which you can make judgments/assessments about your own intercultural competence.

You and your cultural other will need to be open and candid in your responses, especially if you want to challenge your own cultural values, beliefs, attitudes, etc. This engagement will require you to develop trust, but also to be honest. Therefore, it may be helpful to start by sharing the need to develop trust and honesty. You may, at some stage, have a discussion about what trust and honesty mean in your respective cultures.

During the discussion you will need to take notes in your journal of the ideas and dialogue that emerge. Explain to your partner why you are doing this. Note any concerns for reflection later. Immediately after the meeting write extensive notes, recalling important points, dialogue, and supporting details and examples as much as possible. Don't rely on your memory. Share field notes each week so as to check understandings and clear up uncertainties, and to gain further insights. Each time, record some of the positive/interest/challenging/unanswered points during your conversations and re-address them next time. This way, you are developing a picture of your own intercultural competence in relation to conversations with your cultural other.

Finally, remember to behave ethically at all times, to treat your cultural other as you yourself would want to be treated, and to respect confidences.

Possible Topics for Discussion with your Cultural Other

- Who are you? Discuss family, home town, reasons for coming here, aspirations, being here (differences, challenges, adjustments), living arrangements, changes you've experienced
- Family – importance to your life, influences on you/your values/ choices you made/your relationships with others
- Friends – best friends/influences/values/friendships with other students (from other cultures, including New Zealand students/friends on campus and in the community/issues around friendship
- Entertainment and social life - hobbies/interests/sports/leisure/holidays /leisure time
- University study – How did you choose? Why? For what purpose? What knowledge do you hope to gain? Where will your qualification take you?
- Being a student in the WMS/university/community – what do you like/find challenging/dislike about the experience? In what ways has it been different from your expectations? What is it like to enter a new culture or co-culture/meet new people? What guides your behaviour?
- Work – career aspirations/influences on these?
- Part-time work – experiences – describe interpersonal relationships at work/talking to colleagues and clients (communication/adjustment challenges)
- Future aspirations – work, family, friends, travel, work/study abroad
- A political problem (in your country) that concerns you – discuss using when/what/where/why/how. (You could download an article from the Internet or take one from the newspaper to bring along to discuss.)
- A social problem (in your country)…..(as above)
- Dating/socialising/marrying – expectations/constraints
- Problems of communication with people you encounter here from other cultures.
- How have you changed in coming to the University of Waikato? What differences do you notice about yourself? About others' reactions to you? How do these changes influence your relationships with family and friends?
- A possibility for a final session – evaluation
- What have each of you learned/gained (etc.)? Which parts of the process were challenging/unsatisfactory (etc.)?

CHAPTER TEN

SAVOIR SE TRANSFORMER: KNOWING HOW TO BECOME

STEPHANIE HOUGHTON

Introduction

Yamada (this volume) described a series of two studies that investigated the development of critical cultural awareness (Byram 1997, 63) in Japanese language classes at a British university that were inspired by the University of Southampton Criticality Project. Yamada suggested that whilst critical cultural awareness can develop on its own without targeted instruction, even in foreign language classes at the beginner level as students develop original theories related to foreign language learning through inquiry and analysis, the development of critical cultural awareness can be intensified through targeted instruction in focused lessons. This chapter will present an empirical view of the development of critical cultural awareness through experiential learning in English language classes at a Japanese university, focusing specifically upon evaluation as the core element of Byram's (1997, 63) definition.

Critical Cultural Awareness: An Historical Overview

In the early 1990's, Michael Byram and Geneviève Zarate were commissioned by the Council of Europe to provide input to the Common European Framework of Reference for languages which would allow the assessment of *sociocultural competence*. Together they developed a model that conceptualised *intercultural* competence – changing the term used to be more precise in meaning - in terms of having the declarative knowledge of a culture, the ability to learn cultures, the ability to apply intercultural skills, and a general disposition of respect and tolerance toward cultural difference. Their model was first presented in a Council of Europe publication (Byram and Zarate 1994) and its influence upon the Common European Framework of Reference for Languages is somewhat apparent (Council of Europe 2001, 101-106) in the sections listed below.

- Section 5.1.1: Declarative knowledge: *Savoir*
- Section 5.1.2: Skills and know-how: *Savoir-faire*
- Section 5.1.3: Existential competence: *Savoir être*
- Section 5.1.4: Ability to learn: *Savoir apprendre*

Byram (1997) went on to develop the model independently of Zarate in part by adding *savoir s'engager*, or critical cultural awareness/political education, as a fifth component. An outline of the resulting model (Byram 1997, 34) is presented below, where it can be seen that only the first three components found some expression in the Common European Framework. It has since been developed but his 1997 model is the main reference point for this paper.

- *Savoir être* : Attitudes
  o Curiosity and openness, readiness to suspend disbelief about other cultures and belief about one's own.

- *Savoir*: Knowledge
  o Of social groups and their products and practices in one's own and in one's interlocutor's country, and of the general processes of societal and individual interaction.

- *Savoir apprendre/faire*: Skills of discovery and interaction
  o Ability to acquire new knowledge of a culture and cultural practices and the ability to operate knowledge, attitudes and skills under the constraints of real-time communication and interaction.

- *Savoir comprendre*: Skills of interpreting and relating
  o Ability to interpret a document or event from another culture, to explain it and relate it to documents from one's own.

- *Savoir s'engager*: Critical cultural awareness/political education
  o Ability to evaluate critically and on the basis of explicit criteria perspectives, practices and products in one's own and other cultures and countries.

Byram's "list model" (Byram 2009, 325) suggests a range of teaching objectives that can be used by foreign language teachers when planning teaching and assessment without specifying "links of dependency or interdependency among the competences" (Byram 2009, 325). The aim of the model, then, is to "help foreign language teachers to plan more deliberately than they often do, to include intercultural competence in their pedagogical aims" (Byram 2009, 324). *Savoir s'engager*, or critical cultural awareness/political education is in Byram's view "the most educationally significant of the savoirs" because it fundamentally re-characterises language teaching and learning as education for citizenship and democracy (Byram 2008, 233-236), and this brings into question the relationship between teacher and learner values. Whilst Byram recognises that teachers may not want to guide learner evaluations in a particular direction, he recommends teachers to at least encourage learners to make their evaluations explicit and to be consistent.

> Although the teacher may not wish to interfere in the views of their learners, for ethical reasons, they can encourage them to make the basis of their judgments explicit and expect them to be consistent in their judgments of their own society as well as others (Byram 2008, 233)

To develop critical cultural awareness in students, Byram (1997, 53) recommends the following learning objectives to teachers:

- Identify and interpret explicit or implicit **values** (emphasis mine) in documents and events in one's own and other cultures.

- Make an **evaluative** (emphasis mine) analysis of the documents and events, which refer to an explicit perspective and **criteria** (emphasis mine).

- Interact and mediate in intercultural exchanges in accordance with explicit **criteria** (emphasis mine), negotiating where necessary a degree of acceptance of them by drawing upon one's knowledge, skills and attitudes.

At the heart of each of these learning objectives, and indeed at the heart of critical cultural awareness itself, lies the issue of judgment which involves applying values as specific standards or criteria for evaluation. Sensitivity to values can help us to identify and interpret values in documents or events. And once we have analysed them, we can make judgments by applying our values as standards or criteria during evaluation.

Having critical cultural awareness is basically about knowing how to bring to different kinds of cultural experience "a rational and explicit standpoint from which to evaluate" (Byram 2008, 233-236).

In sum, critical cultural awareness did not feature in the original version of Byram and Zarate's (1994) model or in the Common European Framework, but was added later by Byram (1997). And it is taking time to establish itself as a concept in the political arena. It can, however, be seen impacting upon recent European policy contained in the Council of Europe's White Paper on Intercultural Dialogue through the vehicle of the Autobiography of Intercultural Encounters (Byram et al. 2009, 25), which is a set of theoretically-driven self-assessment materials developed to support the implementation of the White Paper through language education. It can be seen in that critical cultural awareness is starting to gain some political recognition as a concept.

> The Autobiography of Intercultural Encounters has been developed as a follow up to the Council of Europe's White Paper on Intercultural Dialogue "Living together as equals in dignity" (www.coe.int/dialogue), and in particular in application of Section 5.3 Learning and teaching intercultural competences (page 25, paragraph 152):

> Complementary tools should be developed to encourage students to exercise independent **critical faculties** (emphasis mine) including to reflect **critically** (emphasis mine) on their own responses and attitudes to experiences of other cultures. (Byram et al. 2009, 25).

It was noted above that critical cultural awareness is basically about knowing how to bring to different kinds of cultural experience "a rational and explicit standpoint from which to evaluate" (Byram 2008, 233-236). However, reflecting upon the concept in the light of Wringe's (2007, 105-106) work on moral education, Byram (2009, 324) has suggested more recently that his past emphasis upon the development of an explicit rational standpoint may have been too narrow, in recognition of the fact that making critical evaluations may lead to evaluations being made that are "not according to criteria of rationality but of "maximising happiness", "communitarianism" or "caring".

It was also noted above that Byram's list model of teaching objectives does not suggest "links of dependency or interdependency among the competences" (Byram 2009, 325). This is perhaps because the model was generated by theory and has not been reconsidered and revised in the light of empirical studies based on teaching practice that were inspired by or built upon the original concepts presented in the model. Since the model does not suggest "a didactic ordering of which aspects of which competences should be taught prior to others" (Byram 2009, 325) and "because the model is a schematization and does not specify in every detail an intercultural speaker, the prescription of how learners should develop is limited" (Byram 2009, 325), so foreign language teachers who attempt "to include intercultural competence in their pedagogical aims" (Byram 2009, 324) are left without a clear vision of the different ways in which they could organise teaching activities and of how their students could or should develop although much advice is given on objective-setting. The purpose of this chapter is to address those concerns.

The Study

An empirical study based on action research (Houghton 2007, 2009a) was conducted to explore and reflect upon the kinds of learning objectives that can and should be set when foreign language teachers attempt to manage the issue of evaluation, or judgment, in foreign language education, in recognition of the complex relationship between values, prejudice (pre-judgment) and evaluative processes more generally. Whilst the development of critical cultural awareness as defined by Byram in 1997 was recognised as one possible approach, it was not accepted at face-value because alternative and conflicting approaches were identified in the academic literature.

At the time the study was conceptualised, Byram was taking the position that teachers should train learners to adopt a judgmental stance focusing their attention squarely back on themselves to develop critical awareness of their own evaluative processes to control them, but teachers should not try to change learner values (Byram 1997; Byram, Gribkova and Starkey 2002). This approach, however, seemed too weak for Guilherme (2002), who suggested that teachers should also aim to bring student values into line with democratic principles and human rights promoting social justice and changing learner values if necessary. This view gradually came to be supported by Byram (Byram and Guilherme 2000) as work on intercultural competence started to fuse with that being done on citizenship education (Osler and Starkey 1996).

Despite subtle differences between the positions of these European researchers at different times, what they all shared was a rejection of neutrality in intercultural communication, which was precisely what was being advocated by many researchers of intercultural communication in North America, and by de Bono (1990) and indeed by Byram and Zarate (1994) in their early work. Bennett (1993), Gudykunst (1998) and Paul and Elder (2002) amongst others, all seemed to agree upon the importance of learning to adopt a non-judgmental stance when communicating with different others, to engage in intellectual empathy and appreciate different perspectives upon social phenomena.

From a theoretical standpoint alone, it was impossible to reconcile the differing approaches to evaluation outlined above and action research was brought to bear upon them with a view to illuminating gaps, weaknesses or inconsistencies within the theoretical standpoints from practical points of view. From the outset, then, the study described in this chapter was never solely aimed at transforming the state of the researcher's own knowledge and improving her own and other teachers' practice, although it would attempt to do both. It was to ultimately refer theory-driven practice back to the theory itself to provide concrete examples from practice that may either validate or invalidate various conflicting claims that had been identified in the literature analysis (Houghton 2009a, 121). This research priority corresponds closely to Hopkins' view of action research:

> Action research might be defined as "the study of a social situation with a view to improving the quality of action within it". It aims to feed practical judgment in concrete situations, and the validity of the "theories" or hypotheses it generates depends not so much on "scientific" tests of truth, as on their usefulness in helping people to act more intelligently and skilfully. In action research, "theories" are not validated independently and then applied to practice. They are validated through practice (Hopkins 2002, 43).

Before proceeding, let us summarise the three different teaching approaches, which will be referred to as courses 1, 2 and 3 hereafter.

- Course 1: Teachers should train learners to adopt non-judgmental stance towards differences and engage in intellectual empathy to take the perspective of others.

- Course 2: Teachers should train learners to focus their attention squarely back on themselves to develop critical awareness of their own evaluative processes and biases to control them, but teachers should not try to change learner values.

- Course 3: Teachers should basically follow the course 2 approach but should also aim to bring student values into line with democratic principles and human rights promoting social justice, changing learner values if necessary.

To explore the three different teaching approaches outlined above in practice, three separate courses of study were designed without reference to existing textbooks (Houghton 2009a) and implemented over one academic year over a nine-month period in three different upper-intermediate English language classes at a university in southern Japan, where the author was teaching English as a foreign language (EFL).Thirty-six students took part in the study, and students were split randomly into three groups. Each class consisted of a group of twelve female Japanese students in their second year of study in the Faculty of Humanities, and the author as teacher-researcher.

Qualitative data were gathered mainly in English over one academic year and data collection techniques included the audio recording of lessons, the gathering of student work as a form of documentary data, and post-class student and teacher diaries. Data collection techniques were combined in this way to gather different perspectives on the phenomena under investigation from different people (Hopkins 2002). In this study, the different perspectives of research participants were taken as separate data sources and triangulation was taken to mean the gathering of valid data from these different sources. In terms of the people involved, the main data sources were the students (through interactive student diaries) and the teacher-researcher (through the teacher diary). Whilst there was no separate observer in lessons, the audio-recordings allowed the teacher-researcher to listen to the lessons during the data analysis period, from the standpoint of a researcher, to provide a third perspective on the phenomena in line with action research theory to overcome the limitation imposed upon this kind of research by the fact that the teacher and researcher are one and the same person. Ethical issues were duly considered (Cohen, Manion and Morrison 2000; Creswell 2003; McDonough and McDonough 1997).

Syllabus Design

In this section, teaching approaches and syllabus design will be reviewed before student reactions (Houghton 2010) are presented. The three different teaching approaches drawn from the theoretical background set the parameters for the design of three different courses of English language study. They were each, however, rooted in a common "core course" that aimed to bring learner cultural values and perspectives to the surface as potential sources of perspective difference in a mono-lingual, mono-cultural classroom where the only non-Japanese research participant was the teacher-researcher.

The three courses were spread over two terms of study, containing a total of twenty-seven classes. All three courses ran through five interlocking stages, each of which contained core course and course-specific components that sometimes overlapped. Stage 1 fed into stages 2 and 3 which ran parallel to Stage 4 (sub-stage 1). Stage 3 and Stage 4 (sub-stage 1) both finished at the end of the first term in July. Sub-Stage 4 (sub-stage 2) took the form of a summer assignment that fed into Stage 4 (sub-stage 2) in the middle of the second term between Stage 5 (sub-stages 1 and 2) around November.

In stage 1 (weeks 1-8), a conceptual framework was provided within which to raise learners' cultural presuppositions (Lantolf 1999; Endicott, Bock and Narvaez 2003; Byram 1989; Fantini 1995; de Bono 1991) to the surface in working configurations to reveal perspective difference to work with later. Themes selected reflected teacher perceptions of underlying teacher and learner cultural and conceptual differences between the Japanese and English languages based on personal experience. Having distinguished values from beliefs and norms (Lustig and Koester 1999), the concept of values was broken down into more detail to set up enough conceptual categories to reveal value difference between students.

A taxonomy of ten universal value types (Schwartz and Sagiv 1995; Schwartz et al 1997) was introduced to learners and various tasks were designed to promote learners' self-reflection with reference to the same overarching conceptual framework during stage 1. Having identified the values built into short dialogues, students were then asked to reflect on their own values and discuss them with reference to new topics that further expanded the conceptual framework. This would increasingly activate schemata prior to homework activities in which students had to write a series of four paragraphs reflectively describing their values with a view to presenting them to other students in the form of a speech in weeks 6-8. Students also made a value chart ranking the relative strength of their values on a scale from minus 5 to plus 5.

With regard to course-specific components, course 1 tasks involved empathising with using specific communication skills that would help learners construct accurate mental maps of speaker perspectives but courses 2 and 3 instead involved learning the basic steps of critical evaluation in terms of comparing, contrasting, judging and justifying judgments with reasons. In weeks 6-8, students had to deploy these course-specific skills in various activities but in course 3, I also aimed to change their values. I selected values from the taxonomy that I considered more desirable for the purposes of intercultural communication and sought their agreement to a list of teacher-recommended target values for intercultural communication.

In stage 2 (weeks 8-12), attempts were made to expose all learners to value difference before asking them to respond in course-specific ways. Having identified areas of value difference between learners by juxtaposing their value charts, I paired them up focusing their attention on particular differences asking them to imagine a potential problem that might be caused by the value difference and writing a short dialogue to illustrate it. When learners presented their dialogues to the class, other learners were asked to respond in course specific ways. A third student was then placed into some pairs to mediate conflict in course-specific ways prior to reflecting upon the activities in follow-up essays.

In stage 3, (weeks 11-14), learner attention was focused on conceptual differences that can cause misunderstandings considering (a) words or concepts that exist in Japanese or English but not both languages, and (b) words that exist in each language but have different meaning. Drawing upon personal experience, I wrote conflict dialogues rooted in both conceptual and value differences learners had to respond to and mediate in course-specific ways.

Stage 4 (weeks 2-25) was divided into three sub-stages. In sub-stage 1 (weeks 2-14), students had to write three questions for each of the 10 values in the taxonomy (Schwartz and Sagiv 1995; Schwartz et al 1997) developing a questionnaire with which to interview a foreigner about their values in the summer assignment before responding in course-specific ways. This central task was enveloped by sub-stage 2 (week 14, summer assignment and week 15) when the stage 3 discussion on the concept was extended to include stereotypes as a particular kind of concept used to categorise people. Whilst week 14 activities focused on defining and examining the nature of stereotypes, week 15 focused on whether or not student stereotypes had been broken by their foreign interviewees. Students were asked to write reflective essays on group interviews held at the end of term 1 in week 15 homework tasks.

In sub-stage 3 (weeks 23-25), students had to present their course-specific summer assignments to other students in speeches responding in course-specific ways. Students were also set a number of other tasks during Stage 4 within which previous work was recycled back into the course to promote for further reflection and discussion of student-generated themes. In some cases, students' views expressed in homework or the interactive student dairy were presented to other students for comments. An end-of-course assignment was also set towards the end of Stage 4 in which students were given recordings of their pre-course interviews to transcribe before writing a reflective essay on how their ideas had developed or changed during the course. Students were also asked to submit discussion points for the end-of-course group interviews.

Stage 5 (week 16-week 27) was structured around Hofstede's (1980) four dimensions of value difference, power distance, individualism/collectivism, masculinity/femininity and uncertainty avoidance. Having learned to identify the values in dialogues and video clips, learners were asked to respond in course-specific ways before mediating conflict dialogues rooted in value and concept differences between Japanese and English. In week 18, course 3 students branched off further to focus on democracy as a political system comparing and contrasting their definition with other students before considering possible incompatibilities between aspects of Japanese culture and democratic society suggested by the teacher. Course 3 students were asked to evaluate not with reference to their own values as in course 2 but with reference to universal values contained in international human rights treaties prior to conducting a democratic citizenship project by taking social action to help a minority group following the example set by the teacher as a role-model.

Data Interpretation

Once decisions had been made as to the extent learning objectives had been met and their viability and desirability, the relationship between the bodies of data generated by the three courses were examined and brought into relation, treating them as a single complex case study. First, let us consider empathy. Some students seemed to consider it to be a viable skill but students sometimes showed they had failed to empathise effectively with interviewees by injecting themselves into written accounts of interviewee values, comparing and contrasting interviewee values and ideas with their own and sometimes judging. When students empathised with their partners verbally in class, teachers' guidance was sometimes needed as students judged, or allowed their own ideas intrude, although satisfactory descriptions were achievable in the end. Whether or not students found it easy to empathise seemed to depend partly on the degree of similarity and difference between self and other.

Whilst some students claimed it was easy to empathise with similar others because it was easy to imagine what they were thinking, this may have indicated their perspectives were in play during empathy, and students may have later come to suspect they may have been mistaking the opinions of similar others for their own. Also, prior knowledge appeared to facilitate empathy, although this may indicate that students' concepts were being utilised rather than suspended. Whilst empathy was generally recognised to be an important communication skill helping people get to know each other better, clarify ideas and improve self-expression by facilitating the development of detail and accuracy, some students also felt that they were sinking under the influence of others.

Student B1: Week 15 Homework 2
Somehow, easy or difficult it is, empathy is useful especially to improve our communication skills. If we consider other's side and try to understand their opinion or position, we can remove the cultural gap or some kind of misunderstanding. On the other hand, to empathy too much is sometimes dangerous a little bit I think. How is it so? Because I think sometimes people who give priority empathy tend to change their opinion and sink in a strong people who have a big influence. So before we use empathy, we have to treasure our culture, mind, value, nationality and belief.

The problem seemed to lie in some students confusing their opinions with those of others during empathy, perhaps feeling shocked at the ideas of others and changing their minds in response, especially if they lacked confidence in their own opinions. Other students, however, thought it was not possible to be influenced if they had empathised properly, claiming that effective empathy was precisely what held their own ideas intact as they were suspended. They took influence as evidence of failure to empathise properly. Some students suggested that judging follows empathy and involves influence. In course 1, some students claimed they did not want to judge because people generally have trouble understanding themselves hold changeable opinions, or cannot be categorised as good or bad. Some students claimed that judging can undermine accurate understanding of the perspectives of others, prioritising information-gathering over judging.

In course 2, an important link between information-gathering and judging surfaced when students were critically evaluating each other's speeches on values in weeks 6-8. Information-gathering was found to be necessarily partial insofar as the identification of key points through information-gathering involved selection of some points and rejection of others. Whether or not students managed to complete the task depended upon whether or not they had written enough information in the form of key points on the critical evaluation worksheet. If not, they could not complete the task because they could not remember the content of the speeches after class. Thinking head, if information-gathering takes place during empathy and is also a pre-requisite for judging, empathy must precede judging, which places empathy before critical evaluation in the ideal process.

> Student A8 Week 15 Homework
> When I missed to hear and note other's presentation, to recall them was so difficult and more, it was serious, because I had to compare and judge them later. I thought I could not say anything when I don't grasp it, because my statement may make someone uncomfortable and give misunderstandings.

However, course 1 students exhibited many reactions to the empathy-oriented activities and the researcher was taken by surprise by student introduction of discussion points after summer assignment speeches. Student B8, for example, shifted her reactions into a post-speech discussion point, indicating that she wanted to change in response to her interviewee. In course 1, the discussion points absorbed time that had been set aside for listeners to empathise with speakers and analysis seemed to take over. The identification of discrepancy within the self was also common, as students identified discrepancies between their stated value and behaviour, stated value and ideal/hope, perhaps feeling bothered by the gap. Also, within a given value, students sometimes evaluated some aspects of it positively but others aspects of it negatively. This seemed to place students in a position to select between their own conflicting values.

Student B5: Winter Assignment
I found the reason in a gap between my ideal values and my actual values.
In my mind, I want to shift to my ideal one, so gradually I have been
shifting to it. For example, in my ideal value chart, self-direction was plus
4, but in a reality, I couldn't decide something by myself, and I completely
depended on others when I decide something. But now, I strongly think I
want to decide my life by myself. Actually, I decided to go Britain alone
and stay there about for 4 weeks in this spring vacation and I made
reservation for it before saying to my parents.

In course 3, the identification of discrepancy following analysis forms
a common thread. Students were supposed to critically evaluate their own
values with reference to target values. Through consciousness-raising, and
having got used to the approach over time, students sometimes identified
discrepancies between (a) their own current and target values, or (b) their
stated values and their actual behaviour. They sometimes accepted the
discrepancy or felt disturbed by the gap. Sometimes, they resolved to
develop themselves and expressed the inclination to change later, perhaps
starting to evaluate with reference not to their own values but to the target
values instead.

Student C6: Week 10 Homework 1
I'm not weak to go around with strange people, but I don't like to do and I
don't care about them. But this attitude is disadvantage for intercultural
communication, I think... I hope to challenge new things on the other hand
I'm afraid to meet new things. I don't think my opinion is bad, but I should
have a bigger view. I think it helps me to communicate with strange
people.

Even requests for clarification of certain speech part sometimes
seemed to cause conceptual reclassification in the speaker. Classification
seemed to underpin judging insofar as concepts could be split into
component parts and evaluated separately, such that students who claimed
they could not judge the concept because they can see both good and bad
points later found they could judge quite clearly if they broke the concept
down into component parts. Confusion seemed to be a common product
not only of the clash of classification systems, but also of the clash of
teacher and student logics as the teacher drew student attention to
inconsistencies in their lines of reasoning. In course 3, the teacher actively
and consciously tried to change student values sometimes apparently
succeeding.

However, if such students were simply accepting the view of the teacher in contrast with students who finally disagree in the face of authority pressure, the course 3 teacher wondered which should be considered more pedagogically desirable. Student C3 from course 3 noticed the intentional application of pressure by the teacher and claimed that being handicapped by having to communicate in a foreign language prompted student value change as the teacher not only supported student self-expression in English but also pressured students to say things they didn't really mean. Further, she claimed that course 3 students gradually came to accept the teacher's opinion unconsciously.

> Student C3: End-of-Course Interview (Japanese Interviewer)
> We are handicapped to speak English because English is not our mother tongue. (The teacher) led us to what we want to say under real consideration of our situation. But I thought she sometimes led us to what she wanted to listen under expectation. I really appreciate her to cover our language disadvantage. I could learn the phrase and how to construct the sentence. But when I was urged to say something by her under expectation, the opinion strayed a little from what I really wanted to say. And unconsciously I came to admit the other opinion.

Let us now consider what seemed to be the by-products of analysis. Meta-cognitive and meta-affective awareness seemed to surface as students consciously compared and contrasted self and other noting their own tendencies in response to others. Students noticed that (a) they tended to seek differences instead of similarities (b) they felt at ease when they identified similarities, or (c) identifying differences highlighted particular aspects of their own distinct character. However, there were many negative reactions to critical evaluation and to judging in particular, although some concerns about judging were alleviated when the definition of critical evaluation and reasons for doing it was discussed in more detail.

But later in the course, critical evaluations were sometimes left incomplete as students seemed to avoid judging, perhaps even hiding, as they critically evaluated others. However, some students also seemed to get used to analysing their own judging tendencies, noting the emotional underpinnings of their evaluative processes. As they gradually identified their standards, they later developed strategies for judging better perhaps taking ideals as guiding principles, which involved refining the definition and purpose of critical evaluation in terms of clarifying thought, situations, ideal society and self with mediation being identified as one part of the process.

Student A1: Week 15 Homework
Second, about judge, at the beginning, I don't like judging, because I felt that I was a rude person by deciding others good or bad. However after I analyzed my judging tendency, I could be getting used to it little by little. In first semester, I hadn't found my standard for judging yet, so my judging depended on my feeling, whether I felt good or bad. It was so simple. However I think the hint to get the standard for judging was hiding, because I wrote in my diary" I judged differences positively if I can agree with them." It means if the differences are reasonable or good, I can accept them. In 2nd semester, thanks to (the teacher), I could get the word of "ideal" as my key word for judging.

Student A8 from course 2, who had initially rejected the idea of judging, gradually came to see critical evaluation as an unpleasant but necessary step towards mutual understanding between people from different cultures. She emphasised the need to explore why people react in certain ways to prevent barriers forming. When critically evaluating others in public, however, she felt terribly shocked afterwards. Ultimately, student A8 seemed to want to hide her honest opinions out of concern at the prospect of being shocked by the negative evaluations of other people but finally concluded that whilst she recognised the importance of expressing judgment, she thought it needed to be done with care.

The division of opinion on judging and critical evaluation may have been so divided through to the end of the course because of possible underlying Japanese tendencies. Some students may have dropped out of course 3 because it was too painful to judge. Some students identified harmony (*wa*: 和) as an important aspect of communication in Japan noting that students were asked to express themselves without regard to harmony.

Student C3: End-of-Course Interview (Japanese Interviewer)
I am not going to judge eternally, even though I learned the way to judge through this course. I'm not good at judging anything anyway. Especially I'd not like to judge whether it is good or bad toward culture, people, and historical things in my life although I sometimes need to judge. In fact, those who felt painful dropped out of this course. The Japanese conception, *wa*, in other word, 'harmony' is indeed beautiful. We don't have to be westernized by denying such a beautiful conception. The point is that even though we try to become cosmopolitans, it is wrong to deny the way with agony, which Japanese have cultivated so far. I am not going to introduce the way to judge everything into my life. All of things have both good and bad elements. We can argue a lot against Westerns who judge such Japanese as indecisive people.

Despite this possible cultural resistance to judging, an important by-product of this controversial discussion about judging seemed to be an increase in meta-cognitive awareness, as students started to notice and describe their various judgmental tendencies to others. As students became familiar with the judgmental tendencies of others through ongoing discussion, personal approaches towards critical evaluation gradually surfaced, although discussion of this kind seemed to require greater English language ability. Identifying their own tendencies, and a range of possible other tendencies generated by others, seemed to place students in a position to make conscious selection between them. Positivity emerged as a selected tendency in some students whilst others chose to make both positive and negative judgments in recognition of the fact that they were not always right, associating negative self-evaluation with self-enhancement or attempting to increase honesty, fairness, self-knowledge or bias-reduction by considering both positive and negative aspects before reconsidering their position rejecting emotional judgment. Yet others students seemed to prioritise flexibility over the taking of a clear position required in critical evaluation.

The Intercultural Dialogue (ID) Model

Following data interpretation, the Intercultural Dialogue Model was devised to structure the course of learning for the promotion of intercultural dialogue, primarily through foreign language education. It will hereafter be referred to as the ID model (Houghton, 2007). It is hoped that teachers will find the ID Model easy to apply to future and similar teaching contexts in whole or in part (Cohen, Manion and Morrison 2000, 182), which naturally carries implications for course design (Houghton 2009c). The course of learning can be broken down into the five steps listed in table 10-1 below, which all involve student attention to task, student change and student development of awareness at a meta-level, the latter of which comprises self-awareness, meta-cognitive awareness and meta-affective awareness.

The course of learning is conceptualised as revolving primarily around the analysis of value systems (VS). The ID model is also conceptualised as moving forward in time as students progress from one step to the next, reflecting back on the past, considering the present and looking towards the future. Students may return to previous steps for reconsideration, which gives it a spiral quality. It can be considered an orientation to otherness within which the conscious and considered selection of values and evaluative tendency are encouraged, and it prioritises real-time communication between real people.

Teachers can provide students with conceptual systems to analyse their value systems which can be conceptualised as complex, hierarchically organised and possibly internally inconsistent, rather unstable systems. They are partly held unconsciously and contain various interconnected parts including stated values, real, ideal and target values which may underpin yet contradict behaviour. Reflectively analysing their values using given conceptual systems, students can come to see themselves in terms of discrete, valenced (Rogers 1951, 501) categories they can use to interpret their present, reinterpret their past and orient themselves to the future. Through consciousness-raising activities, students may notice new parts of themselves or identify discrepancies within their analytical self-accounts between various combinations of their stated values, actual behaviour, real, ideal or target values. Whilst concepts may seem reasonable when focused on separately, focusing on the relations between them may reveal contradictions. Whilst some students may accept discrepancy, others may feel disturbed by the gap, resolving to improve, expressing the inclination to change actually changing now or perhaps later. In any case, analytical consciousness-raising can empower students to consciously reprioritise or select between their own conflicting values.

Empathy-oriented communication should be taught to enhance the communication process and development of meta-cognitive awareness and decentring in students as they identify and describe their own tendencies and reactions. Teachers should be aware of what makes empathy difficult and recognise that information-gathering and judging are integrally linked. Gathering information about the perspectives of others seems necessarily to be partial insofar as the identification of key points involves the selection of some points and rejection of others. Initial failure to gather enough information may render later critical evaluation difficult, if not impossible, if students cannot remember all the content.

Detailed information-gathering in the early stages and appropriate worksheet design are vital. If information-gathering takes place during empathy and is also a pre-requisite for evaluation, then empathy-oriented information-gathering tasks should precede those involving evaluation. Concern about the unconscious influence of empathy is a strong argument in favour of not stopping the process here, but continuing on to conscious evaluation to help students understand the processes by which they come to accept or reject the ideas of others. This can empower students to take responsibility for their decisions hopefully minimising student insecurities.

Table 10-1 The ID model (Houghton 2007): Steps in the course of learning and meta-levels

	Steps in the course of learning	Meta-levels
1	Student analysis of own value system (VS1)	Development of Awareness Self-awareness Meta-cognitive awareness Meta-affective awareness
2	Student analysis of the value system of another person (VS2) having gathered information through empathy-oriented communication	
3	Juxtaposition, comparison and contrast of the two value systems (VS1 and VS2) to identify similarities and differences	
4	Student evaluation of the value systems of self and other (VS1 and VS2) with reference to a standard	
5	Student orientation of self to others by selecting standards and evaluative tendencies	

When analysing the values of others, teachers should remember that student value system variance may be rooted partly in alternative underlying classification systems. Whilst conceptual parts can be labelled with words, the same words may mean different things to different people but can be unmasked through communication. Conceptual parts may exist in one system but not the other, but gaps can be identified through communication. Analysis partly seems to involve connecting pieces of information about different aspects of different values, identifying links between particular values, their sources or functions and relative prioritisation. Students may identify discrepancies between the interlocutor's stated values, behaviour, real, ideal and target values.

Analysis also seems to be supported by prior knowledge of the interlocutor, with some students able to identify discrepancies between interlocutor stated values and their normal behaviour. Other people including teachers and students may unintentionally generate change in others by focusing on discrepancy or introducing concepts or ideas that conflict with the existing system. Teachers need to be prepared to respond to sometimes high levels of student confusion and should at least recognise the various elements and dynamics that can come into play.

Next, the descriptions of the value systems of self and other are juxtaposed, compared and contrasted to identify similarities and differences in preparation for evaluation. A positive effect is the development of meta-cognitive and meta-affective awareness, as students monitor their own tendencies and reactions. Students may simply consider both similarities and differences to be natural or find them interesting. Others may feel at ease when finding similarities perhaps tending to seek or expect similarities, but students working in pairs may disagree about the degree of similarity between them and students may be surprised at the amount of difference they find between self and other or between members of the group. Seeking difference may cause discomfort, self-doubt or confidence loss. Some students may initially feel uneasy about revealing their opinion to others, but later enjoy finding differences and recognising their importance. The identification of difference may also help some students identify special aspects of their own character developing their viewpoint as they notice new points reinforcing both personal identity and opinion.

The identification of evaluative standards is the key concern when students evaluate self and other. A positive effect is the development of meta-cognitive awareness in students as they notice and describe their reactions and tendencies. Teachers should be aware that a wide range of tendencies may come to light. When evaluating others, some students may tend to evaluate either positively or negatively, perhaps evaluating everything positively hiding negative evaluations. Students may recognise not only their own bias but also see connections between their evaluations of self and other, possibly tracking change in their evaluative tendency over time. Possible links between the evaluation of others and self-evaluation may emerge and evaluation may be accompanied by the desire to change.

Negative reaction to making evaluations of others seems to be another important factor if it makes students feel rude, guilty or uncomfortable. So unnecessary negative reaction should be minimised by clearly defining critical evaluation and justifying its practice carefully to students in language they can understand. Students may react negatively to the very words *criticism* and *judging*, believing them to mean the identification of negative points only or speaking ill of others without good reason (i.e. the expression of *prejudice*). The terms themselves should be clearly defined and distinguished in the first place to avoid misunderstanding. Evaluation is perhaps best defined as consciously evaluating similarities and differences between self and other positively or negatively with conscious reference to a clear standard. The need for consciousness-raising, self-monitoring and meta-cognitive control in evaluation can be explained in terms of discouraging focus on negative points only or speaking ill of others without good reason (i.e. the expression of prejudice).

But even students who accept the process in principle, and perform it well, may feel quite shocked after evaluating another person publicly. Student resistance to evaluation may run deep with some reservations persisting until the end of the course, especially among Japanese students, but others may come to recognise the importance of the evaluation process as they get used to analysing their own evaluative tendencies, identifying their standards, perhaps developing strategies to evaluate in a better way by taking ideals as guiding principles, for example.

Perhaps the most important factor regarding evaluation is the selection of standards for evaluating, which is the key concern in this final stage as students decide how to orient themselves to others in the future. Cultural preferences notwithstanding, an important positive effect of asking students to make evaluations of self and other is the emergence of a range of possible reactions and tendencies that may then be consciously selected by students Attaining discussion of this kind, however, may require higher levels of English language ability. Students need to identify their own evaluative standards before considering other options, but a range of options is likely to already reside within them.

Recalling that value systems contain both positive and negative, possibly discrepant parts, students can move from a position of not knowing their own standards to identifying them, before being able to choose from among their own alternatives. Teachers may recommend or enforce external evaluative standards for particular pedagogical purposes in the hope of influencing student orientation to others and the future. Prescriptive ideals and standards may be lifted from international human rights law, for example, which may or may not conflict with existing student value systems, preferences and selections. Inducing discrepancy between internal and external evaluative standards may be the most effective way of generating student change but change may be happening anyway as a natural part of the analytical consciousness-raising process regardless of teacher approach. The ID Model (Houghton 2007) also carries implications for intercultural mediation (Houghton 2009b).

Discussion

In this study, two taxonomies of values were used as conceptual frameworks to scaffold student self-reflection and self-analysis (Hofstede 1980; Schwartz and Sagiv 1995; Schwartz et al 1997). Grappling with and bringing abstract conceptual frameworks into relation may be considered legitimate goals of higher education that aims to promote critical forms of mental life (Barnett 1997, 22). Barnett (1997, 22) posits a framework of rules, values or theories as a condition for developing critical mentality in tertiary education, suggesting they be used as mounts for critical commentary that themselves can be criticised in relation to competing frameworks not favoured or selected by teachers. Barnett (1997, 21) relates this to the development of understanding, autonomy and contemplation, claiming that working with multiple intellectual frames develops understanding of any one frame, increasing the possibility for autonomous thought as critical space opens up between students and the world. In this way, intellectual frames can be considered resources that can be imaginatively deployed to illuminate the world.

Barnett (1997) suggests that domains lie in knowledge, the self and the world, and that three separate objects of critical thinking can be focused on in the same purposeful act, although their individual purposes may differ. Knowledge in the forms of propositions, ideas and theories (including value taxonomies, for example) can be taken as objects of analysis and opened up to criticism. The self can be taken as object for analysis and opened up to criticism through what Barnett calls, "critical self-reflection", which I prioritise. On this, Barnett (1997, 69) recognises that higher states of mind in academic life reside as much in intra-student dialogue as they do in consenting inter-student dialogue. The external world can be taken as object for analysis and opened up to criticism.

Further, Barnett (1997) splits each of these three domains into the six clearly-defined levels listed in table 10-2 below. An important distinction can be made between Barnett's and Houghton's (2007) models regarding domain. Whereas Barnett places the three domains of knowledge, self and world at equal standing, The ID Model (Houghton 2007) prioritises the internal domain of self over the two external domains of knowledge and the world, with the four domains broadly sequenced in that order. Analysis of the self precedes analysis of the other which can be conducted in any class of two or more students, and even in what might be considered a mono-lingual, mono-cultural class. Production of the written documents containing the separate analyses of self and other can be considered the production of new forms of knowledge in two concrete documents, which can then be compared, contrasted and analysed prior to evaluation of self and other, ultimately leading to personal reorientation to others and the world more generally.

Through Barnett's domains, we can carry the discussion on reconstruction of the self from the level of the student to the level of society (i.e. the world). Barnett (1997) emphasises the role of higher education in offering society alternative conceptual resources, injecting into it new forms of action and knowing, enabling society to see itself anew. To this end, Barnett (1997, 46) suggests that education should promote not only intra-student critical self-reflection but also inter-student critical discourse. Personal dispositions and inter-subjective relations should be addressed through discussion that extends beyond the mere cognitive to the essence of being itself.

Thus, Barnett approaches the world, at least in part, by passing through the domains of self and other, as envisaged in the earlier stages of the ID Model (Houghton 2007), within which both intra-student critical self-reflection and inter-student critical discourse are prioritised. In the initial description of the ID Model (Houghton 2007), I suggested that the interface between self and world might be addressed at higher levels by taking the world, or selected aspects of it, as alternative objects of analysis to those of self and other. But adopting Barnett's standpoint helps us appreciate that both intra-student critical self-reflection and inter-student critical discourse can themselves impact upon society by stimulating the generation of alternative conceptual resources, injecting into society new forms of action and knowing enabling society to see itself anew.

Table 10-2 Domains and levels of critical thought (Barnett 1997)

		Domains		
	Levels	Knowledge	Self	World
1	Critical thinking skills			
2	Meta-critical capacities			
3	Critical thinking			
4	Critical thought			
5	Philosophical meta-critique			
6	Sociological meta-critique			

Further, Barnett (1997) also emphasises the role of reflection in stabilising the educational, personal and cognitive disturbances students face within the self, as they are pulled in new ways through a range of knowing activities. The ID Model (Houghton 2007) frames this not only in terms of the development of self-awareness, meta-cognitive and meta-awareness within individual students but also in terms of the ensuing group discussion generating new alternatives for being that present themselves for conscious selection by students. In the ID Model (Houghton 2007), these aspects are conceptualised within the domains of self and other, but from Barnett's standpoint, they also impact upon the domain of the world. Barnett (1997, 94) recognises the role of reflection in the three domains of self, knowledge and the world noting that in the latter two, critical thinking not only involves reflection but also evaluation, analysis, the production of alternatives and ultimately better constructions, including the reconstruction of the self.

The conceptual consistency between Barnett's ideas and those shaping the ID Model (Houghton 2007) is obvious, so let us bring it into sharper focus. Barnett (1997) concept of critical self-reflection is framed in terms of autonomy, personhood and self-actualisation. He emphasises that reflection is accompanied by a range of alternatives and self-criticism, and suggests there are eight forms of private reflection pertinent to higher education.

Table 10-3 Forms of private reflection pertinent to higher education (Barnett 1997)

1	Disciplinary	Reflection on own disciplinary competence	Conversation within the academic discipline becomes inner dialogue within students as they interrogate their own understandings	
2	Educational	Cross-disciplinary reflection oriented towards education, communication and human development	1. Self-control 2. Breadth 3. Tolerance of perspectives 4. Mutual understanding 5. Appreciating the limitations of own perspective	Dispositions/ stance: 1. Determination to search deeper and seek breadth not resting on current understandings 2. Willingness to step outside own perspective to appreciate others 3. Concern for truth and precision in communication and analysis
3	Critical	Emancipation, transformation, liberation, freedom from ideological illusion	New way of perceiving oneself by addressing self-concept, divesting old conceptions of the self, of the world and of the self in relation to the world	
4	Meta-competence	Self-monitoring, adaptability, flexibility	Read situations selectively deploying specific competences	
5	Action	Choice and implementation of action putting into practice decisions that have already been made reflectively	Aspects of decision-making: 1. evaluation of multiple options 2. selection of some and rejection of others 3. general attempt to bring order to chaos	
6	Self-realisation	Realising individual projects by integrating self-reflection, understanding and action	Reflect upon personal experience defining the self through personal projects seeing attempts to understand the world as projects of self discovery using education as a vehicle for realising one's own projects.	

| 7 | Social formation | Drawing on others for self-realisation | Reflection anchors in dialogue as students go openly into the language and perspectives of others and springs out of the inner disturbance caused by unfamiliar social interaction |
| 8 | Societal | Problem- solving in the world | The world presents situation-specific problems, which are susceptible to purposive intervention through skill-deployment |

Barnett conceives of disciplinary reflection in terms of students reflecting on their own disciplinary competence as conversation within the academic discipline becomes inner dialogue within students as they interrogate their own understandings. This relates to the ID Model (Houghton 2007) insofar as students had to grapple with, and refer themselves to, the abstract value taxonomies generated within the field of intercultural communication as related to English language learning in this study. Focusing on self-referencing, Barnett's (1997, 95-96) use of the term "inner dialogue" suggests not only that ideas interplay within a single individual but that the individual comes to be reshaped by this dialogue "forming a disciplinary person who comes to see the world through a particular set of cognitive spectacles".

Thus inner dialogue capable of transforming the self can be generated as students refer themselves or relate their ideas to disciplinary dialogue. But in my view, addressing self-concept is what initially leads students to perceive themselves in new ways, which characterises Barnett's third level of critical reflection. I would thus link levels 1 and 3 of Barnett's critical reflection directly. Also, since student accounts of their own value system generated at this early stage constitute the generation of new knowledge about the self with reference to the abstract conceptual framework provided, I would also link this stage with Barnett's domain of knowledge, and with Byram's two dimensions of *savoir* and *savoir être*. Regarding the latter, however, I would emphasise the description of one's own value and concept system, rather than of one's cognitive and affective tendencies, which are addressed in later stages of the ID Model (Houghton 2007).

Table 10-4 Conceptual links between stage 1 of the ID Model (Houghton 2007), Byram's (1997) model of intercultural communicative competence and Barnett's (1997) levels of critical reflection

	The ID Model (Houghton 2007): Stage 1	Byram's (1997) model of intercultural communicative competence	Barnett's (1997) levels of critical reflection
1	Analysis of Self	*Savoir être* Partial description of own value and concept system with reference to overarching conceptual disciplinary frameworks	Disciplinary Conversation within the academic discipline becomes inner dialogue within students as they interrogate their own understandings
	Contradiction within the self can be expected to emerge	*Savoir* Generation of new knowledge about the self	Critical New way of perceiving oneself by addressing self-concept, divesting old conceptions of the self, of the world and of the self in relation to the world
			Societal The world presents situation-specific problems, which are susceptible to purposive intervention through skill-deployment

Barnett relates the second level of critical reflection to education, emphasising cross-disciplinary reflection. More specifically, Barnett identifies the development of self-control, breadth, tolerance of perspectives and mutual understanding, and the appreciation of the limitations of own perspective as key features of this level. This involves moving beyond current understandings, stepping outside one's own perspective to appreciate those of others and prioritising truth and precision in communication and analysis as matters of disposition and stance. Here, parallels exist with the *analysis of other* stage of the ID Model (Houghton 2007) since it requires students to explore the perspectives of another person. This, in turn, implies that students need to function within the domains of self and other with a view to consciously selecting their dispositions in later stages.

In stage 2 of the ID Model (Houghton 2007), however, I envisage students exploring each other's perspectives in practice, deploying empathy-oriented communicative skills that facilitate the production of accurate accounts of the perspectives of other. This can be considered a process involving the generation of new knowledge that carries the potential to impact upon the world by injecting new meanings into it, as we have seen. Thus, we can link this stage with Byram's dimensions of *savoir* and *savoir apprendre/faire*. Within the latter, students are required to elicit information from their interlocutor by deploying empathy-oriented communication skills clarifying information and developing detail in practical ways, which involves the adoption of a non-judgmental stance. This leads us to draw a further link with the fourth level of Barnett's critical reflection, within which students are expected to read situations selectively and deploy specific competences. But we can also relate this to level 8 of Barnett's concept of self-reflection, within which the world presents situation-specific problems susceptible to purposive intervention through skill-deployment.

Table 10-5 Conceptual links between stage 2 of the ID Model (Houghton 2007), Byram's (1997) model of intercultural communicative competence and Barnett's (1997) levels of critical reflection

	Houghton's (2007) model: Stage 2	Byram's (1997) model of intercultural communicative competence	Barnett's (1997) levels of critical reflection
2	Analysis of Other This relies upon the successful deployment of empathy-oriented communication skills Contradiction within the self can be expected to emerge	*Savoir apprendre/faire* Eliciting information about interlocutor perspective real-time clarifying points and developing detail. *Savoir* Generation of new knowledge about the other	Educational 1. Determination to search deeper and seek breadth not resting on current understandings 2. Willingness to step outside own perspective to appreciate others 3. Concern for truth and precision in communication and analysis Social Formation Reflection anchors in dialogue as students go openly into the language and perspectives of others and springs out of the inner disturbance caused by unfamiliar social interaction Societal The world presents situation-specific problems, which are susceptible to purposive intervention through skill-deployment

A link arises here in relation to the emergence, through analysis, of contradiction. This could constitute internal contradiction within one's own value and conceptual systems or between self and situations in the world. I link this with the seventh level of Barnett's concept of critical reflection, within which reflection anchors in dialogue as students go openly into the language and perspectives of others. As contradiction springs out of the inner disturbance caused by unfamiliar social interaction, social development is stimulated. This is consistent with the view taken in stage 2 of the ID Model (Houghton 2007) that interaction between self and other generates inner disturbance which is then explored systematically. Students gradually draw on others for self-realisation, as suggested by Barnett.

The third stage of the ID Model (Houghton 2007) involves juxtaposing, and systematically analysing, the perspectives of self and other to identify similarities and differences between them. This relates to level 2 of Barnett's critical reflection in that careful analysis is required to understand perspectives of others as they are considered separately from one's own. It also relates to the part of Byram's dimension of *savoir s'engager* that emphasises comparison and contrast.

Table 10-6 Conceptual links between stage 3 of the ID Model (Houghton 2007), Byram's (1997) model of intercultural communicative competence and Barnett's (1997) levels of critical reflection

	The ID Model (Houghton 2007): Stage 3	Byram's (1997) model of intercultural communicative competence	Barnett's (1997) levels of critical reflection
3	Compare and Contrast the Perspectives of Self and Other	*Savoir s'engager* Compare and Contrast the Perspectives of Self and Other	Educational Dispositions/stance: 1. Determination to search deeper and seek breadth not resting on current understandings 2. Willingness to step outside own perspective to appreciate others 3. Concern for truth and precision in communication and analysis

The evaluative dimension of Byram's *savoir s'engager* characterises stage 4 of the ID Model (Houghton 2007). Links can be drawn with level 5 of Barnett's critical reflection, which involves the evaluation of multiple options, the selection of some and rejection of others, and general attempts to bring order to chaos as key aspects of decision-making. Barnett frames this in terms of action insofar as choice and implementation of action puts into practice decisions that have already been made reflectively. Evaluation leads towards selection between alternatives and within the ID Model (Houghton 2007), this includes selecting from among the many cognitive and affective tendencies identified through self-reflection over time, and through discussion of those tendencies with others who have, in turn, been reflecting upon their own tendencies during the same course of study.

In this way, orientation to otherness can be selected by students as a process of self-definition, or "self-authoring" as suggested by Kramsch (1993, 27). This factor characterises level 6 of Barnett's concept of critical reflection. And as stated earlier, a clear link exists here with the part of Byram's dimension of savoir être that focuses student attention on their own tendencies as opposed to the internal structures of their self concept. This, in turn, refers us back to the overarching theme of reconstruction of the self as students start to exert selective control over their own identity development orienting themselves to otherness in the process.

Table 10-7 Conceptual links between stages 4-6 of the ID Model (Houghton 2007), Byram's (1997) model of intercultural communicative competence and Barnett's (1997) levels of critical reflection

	The ID Model (Houghton 2007): Stages 4-6	Byram's (1997) model of intercultural communicative competence	Barnett's (1997) levels of critical reflection
4	Evaluate the Perspectives of Self and Other	*Savoir s'engager* Evaluate the Perspectives of Self and Other	Action Aspects of decision making:
5	Selection between Alternatives	*Savoir être* Selective tendencies and future orientations to otherness from a possible range	1. evaluation of multiple options 2. selection of some and rejection of others 3. general attempt to bring order to chaos
6	Orient Self to Other	*Savoir se transformer* Knowing how to become: Knowing how to develop oneself selectively through interaction with others	Self-realisation Reflect upon personal experience defining the self through personal projects seeing attempts to understand the world as projects of self-discovery using education as a vehicle for realising one's own projects

It can be seen in table 10-7 above that clear conceptual links exist between stages 4-6 of the ID Model (Houghton 2007), Byram's notions of *savoir s'engager* and *savoir être,* and with Barnett's levels of critical reflection. At this stage, it is envisaged that having interacted with and gathered detailed information about different others, students are now evaluating both self and other with reference to clear standards and selecting between alternatives having considered a range of new potential options generated by interaction and the discovery of difference, which carries profound implications for self-development and students make decisions about how they want to become, as people, in the future, which may involve some students attempting to bring order to internal chaos. As students evaluate self and other in this way, they are deploying critical cultural awareness as defined by Byram (1997, 63) insofar as they evaluate the perspectives of self and other but table 10-7 highlights the fact that more explicit recognition is needed in Byram's (1997) model that the deployment of critical cultural awareness through structured self-reflection causes students to start to defining and redefining the self as they attempt to understand themselves in the world. The process of critical evaluation carries profound implications for identity and self-development in ways that connect Byram's (1997) concepts of *savoir s'engager* and *savoir être* in the later stages of the critical evaluation process.

Conclusion

It is thus recommended, as the main conclusion of this chapter, that the concept of *savoir se transformer* be added to Byram's (1997, 2008) models to supplement attitudes (*savoir être*), knowledge (*savoir*), skills of interpreting and relating (*savoir comprendre*), skills of discovery and interaction (*savoir apprendre/faire*), critical cultural awareness/political education (*savoir s'engager*) to focus the attention of teachers upon the fact that students can learn to develop themselves selectively through interaction with different others. By the same logic, *savoir se transformer* should also be recognised in the Common European Framework of Reference for Languages (Council of Europe 2001) to supplement declarative knowledge (*savoir*), skills and know-how (*savoir-faire*), existential competence (*savoir être*) and the ability to learn (*savoir apprendre*). Also, "links of dependency or interdependency among the competences" (Byram 2009, 325) should be made more explicit to render the models more useful to teachers.

Acknowledgements

I would like to thank research participants for their enthusiastic cooperation, Alison Phipps for suggesting the term *savoir se transformer* to capture the concept of *knowing how to become*, and Mike Byram for reading an earlier version of this chapter.

Bibliography

Barnett, R. 1997. *Higher education: A critical business.* Buckingham: Society for Research into Higher Education: Open University Press

Bennett, M. J. 1993. Towards ethno-relativism: A developmental model of intercultural sensitivity. In *Education for the intercultural experience,* ed. M. Paige, 21-73. Yarmouth, Me.: Intercultural Press.

Byram, M. 1989. *Cultural studies in foreign language education.* Clevedon, England: Multilingual Matters.

—. 1997. *Teaching and assessing intercultural communicative Competence.* Clevedon, England: Multilingual Matters.

—. 2008. *From foreign language education to education for intercultural citizenship: Essays and Reflections.* Clevedon, England: Multilingual Matters.

—. 2009. Intercultural competence in foreign languages: the intercultural speaker and the pedagogy of foreign language education. In *The Sage handbook of intercultural competence,* ed. D. Deardoff, 321-332. Thousand Oaks, California: Sage publications.

Byram, M., M. Barrett, J. Ipgrave, R. Jackson and M. Mendez Garcia. 2009. *Autobiography of intercultural encounters.* Strasbourg: Council of Europe. http://www.coe.int/t/dg4/autobiography/default_EN.asp?

Byram, M., B. Gribkova, and H. Starkey. 2002. *Developing the intercultural dimension in language teaching: A practical introduction for teachers.* Council of Europe.

Byram, M. and M. Guilherme 2000. Human rights culture and language teaching. In *Citizenship and democracy in schools: Diversity, identity, equality,* ed. A. Osler, 63-79. Stoke on Trent, England: Trentham Books.

Byram, M. and G. Zarate. 1994. *Definitions, objectives and evaluation of cultural competence.* Strasbourg: Council of Europe.

Cohen, L, L. Manion. and K. Morrison. 2000. *Research methods in education.* London: Routledge Falmer.

Council of Europe. 2001. *Common European framework of reference for languages.* Strasbourg: Council of Europe. http://www.coe.int/T/DG4/Linguistic/Source/Framework_EN.pdf

—. 2008. *White paper on intercultural dialogue: Living together as equals in dignity.* http://www.coe.int/T/dg4/intercultural/Source/White%20 Paper_final_revised_EN.pdf.

Creswell, J. W. 2003. *Research design: Qualitative, quantitative and mixed method approaches.* Beverly Hills, California: Sage Publications

de Bono, E. 1990. *Lateral thinking.* Harmondsworth: Penguin Books.

—. 1991. *I am right: You are wrong.* Harmondsworth: Penguin Books.

Endicott, L., Bock, T. and Narvaez, D. 2003. Moral reasoning, intercultural development and multicultural experiences: Relations and cognitive underpinnings. *International Journal of Intercultural Relations* 27, no. 4: 403-419.

Fantini, A. 1995. Introduction – Language, culture and worldview: Exploring the nexus. *International Journal of Intercultural Relations* 19, 143- 153.

Gudykunst, W. 1998. *Bridging differences: Effective intergroup communication.* Thousand Oaks: Sage Publications.

Guilherme, M. 2002. *Critical citizens for an intercultural world: Foreign language education as cultural politics.* Clevedon, England: Multilingual Matters.

Hofstede, G. 1980. *Culture's consequences: International differences in work-related values.* Beverly Hills, California: Sage Publications.

Hopkins, D. 2002. *A teacher's guide to classroom research.* Oxford: Oxford University Press.

Houghton, S. 2007. *Managing the evaluation of difference in foreign language education: A complex case study in a tertiary level context in Japan.* PhD diss., Durham University.

—. 2008. Harmony versus critical cultural awareness: A case study of intercultural language education in Japan. *Intercultural Communication Studies* XVII 2: 222-235. http://www.uri.edu/iaics/content/2008v17n2/ 19%20Stephanie%20Houghton.pdf

—. 2009a. *Managing the evaluation of difference in foreign language education: A complex case study in a tertiary level context in Japan.* Ph.D. diss., Durham University. http://proquest.umi.com/pqdweb?did=1771527591&Fmt=6&clientId= 79356&RQT=309&VName=PQD

—. 2009b. Intercultural mediation in the mono-lingual, mono-cultural foreign language classroom; A case study in Japan. *Cultus 2: Mediation and Competence* 2, 117-132.

—. 2009c. Within-self diversity: Implications for ELT materials design. *SoLLs.INTEC.09 Conference Proceedings: Language and Culture: Creating and Fostering Global Communities 2009:* 469-492. http://pkukmweb.ukm.my/~solls09/Proceeding/PDF/StephanieHought on.pdf

—. 2010. Evaluating difference in the foreign language classroom: Teaching approaches, syllabus design and student reactions. *SPIL PLUS* 39, 29-45.

Kramsch, C. 1993. *Context and culture in language teaching.* Oxford: Oxford University Press.

Lantolf, J. 1999. Second culture acquisition: Cognitive considerations. In *Culture in second language teaching and learning*, ed. E. Hinkel, 28-47. Cambridge: Cambridge University Press.

Lustig, M. and J. Koester. 1999. *Intercultural competence: Interpersonal communication across cultures.* New York: Longman.

McDonough, J. and S. McDonough. 1997. *Research methods for English language teachers.* London: Arnold.

Osler, A. and H. Starkey. 1996. *Teacher education and human rights.* London. David Fulton.

Paul, R. and L. Elder. 2002. *Critical thinking: Tools for taking charge of your professional and personal Life.* Upper Saddle River, N.J.; Tokyo: Financial Times/Prentice Hall.

Rogers, C. 1951. *Client-centred the*rapy. Boston: Houghton Mifflin.

Schwartz, S. and L. Sagiv. 1995. Identifying culture-specifics in the content and structure of values. *Journal of Cross-Cultural Psychology* 26, no. (1: 92-116.

Schwartz, S., M. Verkasalo, A. Antonovsky and L. Sagiv. 1997. Value priorities and social desirability: Much substance, some style. *British Journal of Social Psychology* 36: 3-18.

Wringe, C. 2007. *Moral education: Beyond the teaching of right and wrong.* Dordrecht. The Netherlands: Springer.

CONTRIBUTORS

Mari Ayano holds a doctorate in education from Durham University, England. She is currently working at Seijyo University in Japan.

Michael Byram is Professor Emeritus in the School of Education at Durham University, England. He studied French, German and Danish at King's College Cambridge, and wrote a PhD on Danish literature. He then taught French and German at secondary school level and in adult education in an English comprehensive community school. Since being appointed to a post in teacher education at Durham in 1980, he has carried out research into the education of linguistic minorities, foreign language education and student residence abroad. His books and articles include *Teaching and Assessing Intercultural Communicative Competence; Language Teachers, Politics and Cultures* (with Karen Risager); *Education for Intercultural Citizenship: Concepts and Comparisons* (edited with G. Alred and M. Fleming). He is the editor of the *Routledge Encyclopedia of Language Teaching and Learning*. His latest book is *From Foreign Language Education to Education for Intercultural Citizenship*. He is an Adviser to the Council of Europe Language Policy Division, and is currently interested in language education policy and the politics of language teaching.

Josep M. Cots earned his Ph.D. in English Philology at the University of Barcelona in 1991. He is a senior lecturer in the Department of English and Linguistics of the University of Lleida, where he teaches English language and applied linguistics. He has carried out most of his research in the field of applied linguistics, focusing on applied discourse analysis, foreign language teaching and learning, multilingualism, and intercultural competence. He is the director of a research group on internationalisation and multilingualism in higher education, including researchers from three different universities and supervises several Ph.D. dissertation projects. He is the author of the book *Teaching by chatting* (1998), co-author of *Competencia comunicativa* (1995), *La parla com a espectacle* (1997), *La conciencia lingüística en la enseñanza de lenguas* (2007), *Plurilingüismo e interculturalidad en la escuela* (2010), and co-editor of *Pensar lo dicho* (2002). He is also the author or co-author of more than 50 articles

published in edited volumes or specialised journals like *ELT Journal,
Language Awareness, Innovation in Language Learning and Teaching,
Journal of Multilingualism, Acquisition et Interaction en Langue Étrangère,
Cuadernos de Pedagogía* or *Estudios de Sociolingüística.*

Yumiko Furumura is an Assistant Professor at Kyushu University in
Fukuoka, Japan, where she teaches the English language to both Korean
and Japanese students, and supports an optional foreign-language-course
for undergraduates, graduate students, and university staff. She was
awarded a doctorate in social and cultural studies from Kyushu University
in 2007. She is interested in intercultural communication, especially
conflict management in intercultural situations, pragmatics, and second
language acquisition.

Manuela Guilherme is a researcher in Intercultural Education and
Communication for the Centro de Estudos Sociais, Universidade de
Coimbra where she coordinated two European projects, namely (a)
INTERACT – Intercultural Active Citizenship Education (funded by Sixth
European Framework Programme and Fundação Calouste Gulbenkian
[2004-2007]) and (b) ICOPROMO – Intercultural Competence for
Professional Mobility (Leonardo da Vinci Programme [2003-2006]). She
is the author of *Critical Citizens for an Intercultural World: Foreign
Language Education as Cultural Politics*, Multilingual Matters, 2002 and
co-editor of *Critical Pedagogy: Political Approaches to Language and
Intercultural Communication*, Multilingual Matters, 2004. She is the first
co-editor of *The Intercultural Dynamics of Multicultural Working*, also with
Multilingual Matters, 2010, in which she is the author of the Introduction
and co-author of two chapters entitled "Intercultural responsibility: Power
and ethics in intercultural dialogue and interaction" and "Diversity
Management: Negotiating representations in multicultural contexts". In
2001, she was granted the Birkmaier Award for doctoral research by the
ACTFL and *The Modern Language Journal*, Washington D. C. She is a
member of the *Language and Intercultural Communication Journal* and
Revista Roteiro, Brasil, Editorial Boards and is the European Book
Review Coordinator for the *Arts and Humanities Journal in Higher
Education* (Sage).

Yannan Guo obtained her PhD from the Durham University, England on language and cultural education in 2007 and her MA previously from the same university on the same field. Her PhD study focused on intercultural competence development through sojourning experience. Yannan Guo is currently teaching translation at the University of Nottingham.

Prue Holmes has recently moved to the School of Education, Durham University to take up a position as Senior Lecturer in International and Intercultural Education. The research in this chapter derives from her teaching in intercultural communication in the Department of Management Communication, University of Waikato, Hamilton, New Zealand. Prue has taught English and English language teaching in Italy, China, and Hong Kong. Her research has focused on the communication and learning experiences of international students, in particular, ethnic Chinese in tertiary education and in the wider community. She has also been commissioned by the Ministry of Education and Education New Zealand to investigate the social, learning and communication experiences of international students in New Zealand secondary and higher institutions. More recently, her research activities have explored intercultural communication competence. She has also researched immigrant communication experiences with ICTs and intercultural communication and conflict in the workplace.

Stephanie Houghton is an Associate Professor at the University of Kitakyushu in southern Japan. Having taught English as a Foreign Language in Japan for 15 years and in the Czech Republic for 1 year since 1993, she graduated with a doctorate in Education from Durham University, England in June 2008. Her main research interest lies in the development of intercultural communicative competence through English language education with a specific focus upon values. She was an intern in the Division of Cultural Policies and Intercultural Dialogue at UNESCO in Paris in spring 2004, and is now on the editorial boards of the Asian EFL Journal and Intercultural Communication Studies. She is the author of *Intercultural dialogue: Managing value judgment in foreign language education,* Multilingual Matters, co-editor of *The native speaker English language teacher: From exclusion to inclusion*, also with Multilingual Matters, and co-author of *Criticality in foreign language education*, Peter Lang Publishing (all forthcoming).

Enric Llurda is a lecturer at Universitat de Lleida (Catalonia, Spain), where he coordinates the undergraduate degree in English Studies. He teaches the English language as well as courses on second language acquisition and multilingual intercultural education. He has done research on bilingualism, language attitudes, language awareness and language teaching, with a strong emphasis on non-native teachers' identity and contributions in teaching English as a Lingua Franca. He is the editor of the book *Non-native language teachers: Perceptions, challenges and contributions to the profession* (2005) and has co-authored two books in Spanish: *La conciencia lingüística en la enseñanza de lenguas* (2007) on the promotion of language awareness in language education; and *Plurilingüismo e interculturalidad en la escuela: Reflexiones y propuestas didácticas* (2010) on the development of multilingual and intercultural competence in secondary education. He is currently involved in a research project on internationalisation and multilingualism in higher education.

Gillian O'Neill is the Language and Learning Development Consultant in the Waikato Management School, Hamilton, New Zealand. She has extensive experience teaching international students in the U.K. and New Zealand. Her present research interests focus on ways in which to facilitate and develop effective intercultural communication between domestic and international students.

Lynne Parmenter is a professor in the School of Culture, Media and Society at Waseda University, Tokyo, Japan. She has lived and taught in Japan for the past 17 years, at junior high school and university levels. Her research interests are in global citizenship education and intercultural education, and she is particularly interested in the ways in which young people negotiate their sense of self in the global sphere.

Yau Tsai is a faculty member of the Department of Applied Foreign Languages at Fooyin University in Taiwan and also a fellow of the Higher Education Academy in the United Kingdom. She holds a doctorate in education from Durham University in England. So far she has been on the reviewer list of the International Journal of Educational Management. Her research interests include intercultural studies, second/foreign language acquisition, teaching English as a foreign language and higher education.

Etsuko Yamada is a Lecturer at Kanda University of International Studies, near Tokyo, where she teaches Japanese as a foreign language (JFL) to international students on the exchange programme with partner institutions abroad. Previously, she taught JFL in Germany and in the UK for eight years in total, which include International School of Düsseldorf, University of Sheffield and University of Newcastle upon Tyne. She also worked as language advisor at the Japan Foundation London Language Centre to support JFL in the UK for six years. She was awarded a PhD from Durham University, England in June 2008 and has continued conducting research mainly in the areas of Criticality and Critical Thinking within foreign language education, with a particular focus on the beginner level. She is co-author of *Criticality in Foreign Language Education*, Peter Lang Publishing (forthcoming).

INDEX